International Education Programs and Political Influence

International Education Programs and Political Influence

Manufacturing Sympathy?

Iain Wilson

INTERNATIONAL EDUCATION PROGRAMS AND POLITICAL INFLUENCE
Copyright © Iain Wilson, 2014.

All rights reserved.

First published in 2014 by PALGRAVE MACMILLAN® in the United States—a division of St. Martin's Press LLC, 175 Fifth Avenue, New York, NY 10010.

Where this book is distributed in the UK, Europe, and the rest of the world, this is by Palgrave Macmillan, a division of Macmillan Publishers Limited, registered in England, company number 785998, of Houndmills, Basingstoke, Hampshire RG21 6XS.

Palgrave Macmillan is the global academic imprint of the above companies and has companies and representatives throughout the world.

Palgrave® and Macmillan® are registered trademarks in the United States, the United Kingdom, Europe and other countries.

ISBN: 978-1-137-36628-3

Library of Congress Cataloging-in-Publication Data

Wilson, Iain (Research fellow)
    International education programs and political influence: manufacturing sympathy? / Iain Wilson.
      pages cm
    Includes bibliographical references.
    ISBN 978-1-137-36628-3 (hardcover)
 1. Student exchange programs—Political aspects. 2. Student exchange programs—Finance—Government policy. 3. College student mobility—Political aspects. 4.—ERASMUS (Organization) I. Title.
LB2375.W55 2014
370.116'2—dc23

                                                                                      2013041966

A catalogue record of the book is available from the British Library.

Design by Amnet.

First edition: April 2014

10 9 8 7 6 5 4 3 2 1

Contents

List of Tables	vii
List of Figures	ix
Acknowledgments	xi
Introduction	1
1 Political Expectations	9
2 Can We Infer That Mobility Has Political Impact? Some Historical Case Studies	19
3 How Strong Is the Evidence of Political Impact?	47
4 How Can We Detect Short-Term Impact (and What Does That Mean)?	59
5 Short-Term Impacts of Erasmus Mobility	87
6 Varieties of Experience	139
7 Individual Perspectives	151
8 Impact over Decades	175
Conclusion	193
Appendices	203
Notes	205
References	215
Index	227

List of Tables

4.1	Overall attrition, Erasmus panel	81
5.1	Attrition diagnostics on cognitive mobilization	89
5.2	Attrition diagnostics on Moreno question	91
5.3	Attrition diagnostics on World Values	95
5.4	Attrition diagnostics on party politics	101
5.5	Erasmus/Non-Erasmus status and change in voting intentions	103
5.6	Differential attrition on party placement	104
5.7	French students' support for right-wing parties	106
5.8	Attrition diagnostics on foreign affairs	109
5.9	Attrition diagnostics on demographics	111
5.10	Attrition diagnostics on policy transfer from host	117
5.11	Change in approval of copying host country policies	118
5.12	Change between yes/no responses, policy transfer from host	119
5.13	Changes from "don't know" to all other responses, policy transfer	119
5.14	Approval of transferring specific policies to home, after the Erasmus year, not significantly associated with Erasmus status	120
5.15	Changes on policy transfer, home to host	122
5.16	Yes/No movement on policy transfer from home	123
5.17	Know/Don't know movement on policy transfer from home	123

5.18	Attrition diagnostics for host country attitudes	124
5.19	Differential attrition in attitude to host	131
5.20	Summary of changes	134 and 135
6.1	Logistic regression model, probability of making host-national friends	149
6.2	Logistic Regression Standard Errors	150
7.1	Consent to interview and change in view of host country, no significant correlation	152

List of Figures

5.1	Group means on the Moreno question do not diverge	92
5.2	Group means for tolerance converge	97
5.3	Views on redistribution did not diverge significantly	98
5.4	A chart summarizing the differential attrition in party placement	105
5.5	Divergence in left-right placement appears to be insignificant	107
5.6	Erasmus students' knowledge of the host language increased	113
5.7	Divergence in understanding of the host's foreign policy	126
5.8	Perceived understanding of host nationals diverged	127
5.9	Interest in learning more converged	129
5.10	Apparent lack of divergence in attitudes to the host	130
5.11	Differential attrition on attitude to the host country	132

Acknowledgments

One of the best parts of writing this book was discovering how many people were willing to help out for no benefit to them. In particular, I would like to thank my academic supervisors at various stages in the project's gestation: James Vaughan and Roger Scully at Aberystwyth, Elizabeth Bomberg at Edinburgh, and Brian Hogwood at Strathclyde. Rob Johns, David Sanders, and Mick Cox also offered some very helpful academic guidance.

The largest group of contributors—the hundreds of students who took the time to reply to the various surveys—is too often neglected, but they really did make this work possible. I should also offer thanks to the "gatekeepers" who helped me to reach the survey participants. Lottie Bulman at the German Academic Exchange Service, Chris Armstrong at Leeds University, Mary Denyer and Natasha Bevan at the Marshall Fund, Chad Galts at Brown University, and Patricia Rea at the University of Pennsylvania helped with the pilot. Dozens of universities' international officers and departmental secretaries in Reading and Leeds, as well as Anders Ahlstrand of the Swedish Programkontoret, helped to distribute the main survey. While most of the interviewees must remain anonymous, they know who they are. Sir Christopher Mallaby offered particularly helpful advice, and kindly allowed me to name him in the text.

The nature of this project made language skills greatly desirable, and unfortunately mine are a little limited. Ute Barrett at Glasgow, Wolfgang Mühlbauer (then a PhD student at the Technical University of Munich), and Ludwig Gelot converted my translations into something native speakers might recognize. I would also like to thank Emmanuel Sigalas and Paul Marion for passing on copies of their unpublished theses.

The team at Palgrave and the anonymous reviewers have helped to convert my turgid writing into something which I hope is at least a little more palatable. I am especially grateful to Sarah Nathan, Mara Berkoff, and Scarlet Neath.

This research could not have been completed without the financial support of the UK Economic and Social Research Council.

Finally, thanks to Gemma and my family for everything else.

All interpretations and of course all errors are my own.

Introduction

On campuses all over the world, autumn brings cool breezes, falling leaves, and the arrival of babbling groups of new students. For most of them, their new surroundings follow a well-worn path through their countries' national education system. Teenagers from rural Michigan arrive in Ann Arbor, the best and brightest from Swedish suburbs stroll into Uppsala, a few fortunate Parisians queue to enroll at the Sorbonne. Mixed in among them will be classmates who grew up in an eclectic assortment of foreign lands. For all of them, education will be expensive, and most will need some kind of public subsidy in order to afford the cost.

Almost all industrialized countries have some mechanism for supporting domestic students, either by ensuring they have access to credit or simply by depositing money in their bank accounts. There is a clear rationale for the government to do so. Students and their parents are taxpayers, who have contributed to the pool of resources used to educate others; they are voters, who can sanction a government that lets them down; and in all likelihood the students' increased future earnings will contribute to their home country's economy. This reasoning does not usually apply to the foreign students, most of whom are excluded from these conventional funding streams.

Many foreign students will be funded by private wealth, and a few by their own governments as if they were studying at home. A significant proportion, however, will be underwritten, directly or indirectly, by a foreign government to which they and their families have never contributed a penny of tax.

Why should governments treat foreign nationals so generously? A range of different reasons have been offered. International students may contribute to the educational quality of their host institution, introducing diversity and insights to which a monocultural student body would not otherwise be exposed. They may bring economic benefits which outweigh the cost of supporting their studies, either by staying on after graduation or by becoming major customers of their former hosts after they return home (Mitchell 1987). In some cases funded education may be seen as development aid in kind (although this does not explain why much funding is allocated to select students from wealthy countries). High-achieving students may advertise an institution's quality to their less stellar schoolmates, who will then pay for the privilege of attending.

This book focuses on another instrumental reason for governments to fund foreign students—an expectation that hosting them will bring political and diplomatic benefits.

Although it is not widely advertised to the general public, the political rationale for supporting impressionable young foreign visitors is widespread within foreign ministries (FCO 2005: 16). Many individual diplomats subscribe to this idea, and I will be referring to interviews with several of them throughout. Shaping the attitudes of foreign students is a central objective of such famed scholarship programs as the US Fulbright Awards, managed by the State Department (Arndt and Rubin 1993, Fulbright 2012, US-UK Fulbright 2008), and the British Chevening Awards, managed by the Foreign Office (Chevening 2006). An internal report on British Government scholarships funded by the Foreign and Commonwealth Office (FCO) makes this clear:

> [Several of our scholarships] are intended to help Britain win friends and influence people abroad. Most of these schemes aim to attract people taking a leading part in the future in their field of study and in their own countries generally, or who seem likely to do so. (FCO 1985 section 3.1)

Offering subsidized education to foreign nationals has a very long history. Richard Arndt (2005) traces it back thousands of years, all the way to the Ancient Egyptians educating subordinate powers' young aristocrats. In the twentieth century a proliferation of government programs offering support to talented foreign students became linked to worries about the tone of international relations (McMurry 1972 [1945]: 243). Exchanging (the right sort of) private citizens has come to be seen not only as a symptom of a healthy relationship, but also as a causal factor. The recent popularity of this idea within foreign ministries is reflected by a burgeoning body of conceptual work, with academic analysts keen to embed programs underwriting student mobility within the much broader concept of public diplomacy—or, in previous generations, cultural diplomacy or cultural relations[1] (Arndt 2005, Fisher and Bröckerhoff 2008: 3–8, Fiske de Gouveia 2005: 28, Henrikson 2006, Leonard, Stead and Smewing 2006, Melissen 2005, Mitchell 1986, Ninkovich 1996, Potter 2002, 2009, Riordan 2002, Scott-Smith 2008, Snow 2009, Yun 2005). Put simply, these analyses champion, or occasionally question, the potential for student mobility to help the governments which sponsor it shape foreign public opinion to their advantage. This is not necessarily sinister and, in fact, sponsoring foreign students is often presented as a sign of transparency and interest in correcting misunderstandings. In contrast with one-sided propaganda, encouraging social contact between citizens tends to be viewed as a benign activity.

This relatively innocuous image should not obscure the links between mobility programs and diplomatic strategy. Nye (1990, 2004) uses support for international students as a key example of how countries can exercise "soft power," shaping the behavior of other countries without resorting to coercion. This concept builds on a much larger tradition of thinking about how seemingly innocuous social interactions shape international relations. It has considerable influence—even ubiquity—as a slogan, and its popularity helps to propagate these ideas (Hayden 2011). The belief that academic mobility affects the relationship between countries is intertwined with them. But how could mobile students and academics, typically with few material resources or political connections, help shape the development of international relations?

The most obvious possibility is that the act of creating a program sends a signal about how the sponsor country views its relations with others; exchanging people suggests an expectation of future friendship. Unsurprisingly, diplomats do take some trouble to enhance the symbolic value of creating scholarships and inaugurating exchange programs, seeking favorable media coverage and tying them to state visits, benign anniversaries, international summits, and so on. But expectations about the political influence generated by academic mobility often go further, and draw on further assumptions about how these scholarships affect their recipients.[2]

International mobility, it is claimed, influences the beliefs and political behavior of the mobile. People who have spent time in a foreign country are expected to become "sympathetic" to that country.[3] They might go on to positions of power where they can directly influence the relationship between the two countries, but more commonly they are expected to become socially influential. That enables changes in their views to become infectious, as returnees help shape their compatriots' views of the countries they have visited. Those compatriots in turn can exert pressure on their governments. Giles Scott-Smith, in his analysis of a US State Department program bringing non-academic foreign elites to the United States (2003, 2006, 2008: e.g. 117), calls this the "opinion-leader" model. It is clearly being stretched to holders of academic scholarships, to such an extent that the officials who allocate them are regularly exhorted to choose more candidates who will go on to be influential (e.g. House of Commons Foreign Affairs Committee 2006, Miliband 2008, State Department 2006). Throughout the first section of this book I will be discussing how diplomats I interviewed, who are charged with managing scholarship programs, understood the political impact of their activities.

The "opinion-leader" model often seems to rest on the premise that studying in a foreign country affects scholars' attitudes to that country for the better. It would be tempting to assume that mobility changes attitudes, and changes them to the advantage of the sponsor. If this is true, international relations theorists and practitioners should be fixated on scholarships. A simple method of exerting power over countries without bombing or bribing them would be enormously useful. However, the evidence that the programs have any impact on international relations is curiously weak. In the words of Stephen Bochner et al

> the sponsors of international education have repeatedly justified the huge cost of the enterprise by claiming that exchange programmes self-evidently contribute to mutual understanding and international peace... the evidence all too often reveals a gap between promise and reality. (1977: 278)

Given the claims for political impact building up around student mobility programs, this is troubling. Perhaps the resources which are devoted to promoting mobility could be better allocated elsewhere. But more importantly, when advocates for mobility frame their cases for continued funding in terms of expected political influence, they are not talking about other benefits scholarly mobility may bring. Before the idea that offering scholarships was a political strategy became so widespread, advocates for international education claimed that their activities brought a range of other benefits, not least actually educating people about other cultures and polities (see e.g. Mitchell 1986). There is a risk that instrumentalizing support for foreign visitors as a diplomatic tool might lead to a neglect of other benefits that personal mobility should bring.

My Argument in Outline

I begin by exploring in more depth what the officials funding scholarships for foreign visitors expect to gain. To do this, I collect some of the most blatant examples of scholarships and publicly funded exchange programs being presented as means to political ends.

What governments say publicly is not always a good guide to their actual intention, so I also spent some time looking at how scholarships are discussed within the corridors of power. I searched civil service archives to find out how officials who set up scholarship programs go about building coalitions in support of the programs, and I also spent some time talking to administrators who are responsible for scholarship programs portrayed as having a political objective. Given that they are currently being presented as tools for securing influence, a casual observer could be forgiven for thinking that the programs were *created* in order to improve international relations. Surprisingly, when I delved into the histories of some well-known scholarship programs, I found that this was not the case at all. Scholarships were funded for a range of other (often more amusing) reasons, and the idea that they brought political influence was added retrospectively after they had been running for many years.

This finding should give us some pause for thought. Even when current government officials and academics are convinced that a program serves foreign policy objectives, it may not have been set up with this objective in mind. Hence, it may not have been deliberately designed to bring diplomatic benefits, it may not be well adapted to do so and it may, in fact, be much better suited to doing something else.

Even though scholarship programs may be set up for other reasons, many officials tasked with managing them seem to have accepted that they were set up to nurture sympathetic opinion leaders. This is a mythical account of why they do what they do, but it is still quite possible that scholarships do influence foreign public opinion. A thorough examination of the evidence that scholarships shape international relations, however, highlights many. They may not political outcomes in the way officials think they do. The mismatch between rhetoric about why scholarships are funded and how they actually came into being may be part of the explanation.

The subsequent chapters actually set out to test whether scholarly mobility can be expected to shape international relations in the way the opinion-leader model suggests. The third chapter deals with political change on the 'microscopic' level of individual participants. I developed a battery of questions to gauge scholars' political behavior and attitudes, as well as their understanding of the host country. I then persuaded a sample of students to complete the questionnaire before and after they went abroad. Crucially, a control group who studied in the home country was asked the same questions simultaneously, before and after the visitors' time abroad. If I detected significant differences in how the two groups' responses changed over time, this could be interpreted as evidence that going abroad had an impact on the individuals involved. These are far from the first surveys of foreign scholars (see e.g. Bochner et al. 1977, Golay 2006, Lazenby-Taylor 2004, Selltiz and Cook 1962), but they differ from existing studies in important respects. First, unlike many existing surveys of this population this study is large and systematic enough for statistical analysis of the results to be convincing. Second, it is unusual because it focuses on political behavior rather than patterns of social activity, contentment with the experience or participants' perceptions of their own identities. Most importantly, it is unusual because it has both a control group and a time-series design, allowing us to be confident that the impact of the studying abroad has been isolated from other possible influences.

Visiting scholars are not homogenous. An important lesson from the existing literature is that people's experiences while they are abroad—rather than the simple fact of being in a foreign country—are likely to shape their attitudes (Sell 1983). Treating them as a homogenous group may mask systematic changes in some subgroups' attitudes which are not shared by others. The fourth chapter breaks down the results of the larger panel study and considers students' individual experiences in more detail. I divide the exchange students into subgroups who reported having different experiences while abroad; for example, those who befriended host nationals and those who had more insular social lives. I also interviewed some of the panelists, allowing them to describe their experiences unconstrained by the necessarily rigid structure of a survey. These interviews reveal the visitors' very human experiences of a new, foreign culture and institution.

A common criticism of the academic literature on this subject is that it fixates on short-term changes in attitudes. Examining changes in attitudes over a few months cannot, in itself, provide a fair test. Only quite a small proportion of the population actually gets a chance to live and study in a foreign country. In order for microscopic changes in those individuals to influence the macroscopic world of international relations, they must be "multiplied" (a common piece of jargon found in, for example, Council of the EU, 2004: L30/12) or have a "trickle-down effect" (Mitchell 1986: 160). The world of international relations is dominated by large, complex corporate bodies like states and international organizations. Scholarships tend to go to young and capable people of the type who may well go on to occupy influential positions. The "multiplier" model alleges that when they get there they are influenced by their youthful adventures, more than paying back the investment made in them by their host governments. Scholars are selected because they are expected to become unusually influential in the future. As one interviewee put it,

> [the] ultimate aim is not to work with individuals, it's to use those individuals as [...] multipliers into a wider community. (British Council Interview Two)

Is it realistic to expect experiences twenty or thirty years earlier to shape how experienced professionals behave?

We cannot detect multiplication only by studying students who have gone abroad in the past year. Instead, in Chapter Eight I ask whether it is realistic to expect multiplication. To do this, I arranged interviews with individuals who received scholarships to go abroad many years ago and who have since moved into influential positions—the star alumni lionized by sponsors. Have they interacted with their former host country since the sojourn, and is there any evidence that their behavior was influenced by experiences twenty or thirty years earlier? Are their reports consistent with those of exchangees who returned a few months ago?

I argue that, while none of the research strategies employed here can support generalizable conclusions about the broader impact of international mobility without the others, combining them provides a stronger foundation. Does the evidence show that exchange programs bring the political benefits their advocates claim? The answer that emerges is much more nuanced than most of the literature on this question suggests: mobility has consequences, many of them very desirable, but if there is a link to international relations, it must be a rather indirect one. Studying abroad for a few months certainly does not make individuals into agents for their sponsors. I can also offer some partial answers to small mysteries uncovered by the research process. Why has the rhetoric surrounding these programs become so tied up with political influence? What kinds of things do sojourners learn that they could not pick up at home? Can mobility contribute to more effective governance? The answers suggest some new theory about how governments formulate policy and reveal perhaps underappreciated ways in which allowing humble students to spend a little time abroad might really help shape the future.

1

Political Expectations

"If you spend a year in a country then you probably fall in love with it and you will never forget it"

—Entente Cordiale Interview One

Governments support a range of international mobility programs, many of which are presented as means to political ends. I am supporting this claim with a small selection of the evidence I have come across showing that governments expect international mobility programs to generate political benefits.

By an "international mobility program," I mean a formal arrangement by a government or transnational organization to facilitate the physical movement of people from one country to another on a temporary basis. There have been various attempts to substitute long-distance correspondence for physical mobility through "are backwards pen pal" schemes (Paige 2002), online dialogue sessions such as those organized by Qantara. de (a German-government-funded website aimed at "the Islamic World") and so on. But physical mobility is the most intense form of intercultural contact. We might speculate that physically traveling to another country will have a significant effect on someone's attitudes while writing a few letters would not; it is hard to imagine that writing letters would have an effect if travel did not. The best-known programs tend to rely on this most old-fashioned technique: physically bringing people into close proximity to allow face-to-face contact. Participants may have different objectives, like students who travel to study under renowned experts or military officers who seek advanced training in tactics perfected by foreign soldiers, but the mobility remains. Even programs which are notionally about teaching specific skills, such as language teaching programs, bring foreigners into direct contact and encourage human nature to take its course. Examples include the activities of the Goethe Institute and Alliance Francaise.

Perhaps the most familiar type of mobility program is the exchange program, where a citizen of one country literally replaces a citizen of another country. For example, an American high school student might take the place of a Slovak, living with the Slovak's parents, sitting at the Slovak's desk in school and eating the food the Slovak would have eaten had she been at home. At the same time, the Slovak student whom the American replaced would be living with the American's parents, sitting at his desk and eating his food. This might be the cheapest way to facilitate cross-border mobility, since the two teenagers are using facilities which someone else would have been used anyway (although the students will obviously still need transport and there will, inevitably, be some administration involved). But it is important to realize that governments, and transnational organizations, fund a wide range of mobility programs which are designed very differently. Most mobility programs are actually pseudo-exchanges or, in effect, services which are reserved for foreign citizens. These can greatly increase the costs involved in sponsoring mobility.

The classic exchange program has some fairly significant limitations. There need to be two potential participants who wish to travel to each others' countries at the same time: if the American student wished to visit Slovakia, but there was no Slovak who wanted to visit America, the scheme would fall apart and no-one would go anywhere. An obvious solution would be for Slovakia to take an American one year on the understanding that the American school would accept a Slovak next time there was someone who wanted to go. But this would not solve the underlying problem if there were consistently more Americans wanting to go to Slovakia than Slovaks wanting to go to America. And if we consider more than two countries, the optimal solution becomes even more complicated: perhaps there would usually be more Americans who wanted to go to Slovakia than vice versa, but more Slovaks who wanted to go to Nigeria and more Nigerians who wanted to go to America. A pseudo-exchange might evolve in which administrators tried to maximize the number of exchangees who could travel, while also trying to ensure that no country ended up importing more than it exported, but then a fluctuation in the numbers of Nigerians wanting to travel would start to affect the flows between America and Slovakia as well. The limitations of this barter-like arrangement become ever clearer.

An alternative approach would be to simply create some dedicated services for foreign citizens—extra places in schools, for example, beyond those needed by the country's citizens. The host country could monetize these services by offering awards to select foreign nationals, for example, scholarships which pay for a year's tuition. They may even provide cash payments to meet living costs during the visit. In this scenario, some governments are likely to end up consistently receiving more visitors than they send out. Hence, the justification for spending money on hosting foreigners cannot be simply that foreign governments will reciprocate, creating equal opportunities for both countries' nationals. Mobility is rarely balanced, and in fact it is often very imbalanced, with some countries "importing" many more people in this way than they "export." This could be seen as either a problem, because they are spending more money on hosting foreign citizens than foreign countries are spending on their own citizens, or as an opportunity. If it is a big enough opportunity, governments could even be persuaded to pay very desirable foreigners to live in their countries, for example, by offering special scholarships to foreign nationals.

One way to see hosting foreigners as an opportunity is to think of it as the cause of a political effect. This implies some kind of mental model that links cause with effect. There are several possibilities. We might expect that mobility programs signal benign intent by the government that funds them, that they maintain informal lines of communication between countries which can be exploited during periods of strain, or that a well-informed populace abroad is helpful (I will come back to these ideas later). But perhaps the most common model applied to international mobility programs—including in the claims I am about to present and challenge—is what Scott-Smith calls the opinion-leader model.

The opinion-leader model links international mobility with the formation of attitudes to foreign countries (Scott-Smith 2008). It rests on a series of assumptions that suggest living in a country in the present will affect how a foreigner relates to it in the future. According to the model, this may in turn bring diplomatic benefits to the country which sponsored the mobility. If that is true, it suggests that countries that attract foreign visitors can turn this economic cost into a diplomatic advantage. It may even be worth paying certain kinds of foreign citizens, who will bring a big political benefit, to spend some time in the country.

Everyday experiences and increased interpersonal contacts with the country's citizens *might* change attitudes and beliefs about the host country. But only relatively small proportions of most populations will actually participate in mobility programs, so any microscopic impact on participants must be "multiplied" if it is to influence the macroscopic world of international relations. In an opinion-leader model, multiplication would be largely a matter of returning visitors spreading their changed attitudes to the host country to co-nationals. When the visitor returns home, he or she *might* gain an influential position which would "multiply" the impact. A common assumption underlying international education programs and academic scholarships is that participants, who tend to be young and very capable, are likely to go on to positions of influence long after they have passed through the program. In many cases, they are selected on the basis of their potential to do so. Alumni *might* become well-connected and transmit opinions to their social circles, or gain positions of power in opinion-leading industries, such as the media, giving them the potential to influence what many of their compatriots think about other countries. Alternatively, alumni *might* acquire direct power themselves, and then be influenced in their use of that power by their formative experience (we could also call this a "direct-influence" model, but it rests on essentially the same assumptions).

It is worth bearing in mind that opinion leadership is only one model of how countries might benefit from hosting foreign nationals. For example, overseas visitors might acquire consumption habits which lead them to purchase goods from the host country (Mitchell 1986). They might enhance institutions' prestige and improve the quality of education for others by attracting talented students, exchange useful knowledge with host nationals (see e.g. Adia 1998: Ch5; Mitchell 1986: 12–21, Schoch and Baumgartner 2005, Vickers and Bekhradnia 2007: 19–21; IIE 2007, Lincoln Commission 2007: 8–10 c.f. Messer and Wolter 2007). Alumni might act as interculturally competent mediators between countries (Bochner 1973, 1981). An ongoing theme of this book is that belief in the opinion-leader model is not necessary to believe that mobility programs bring benefits. Nonetheless, the opinion-leader model is very popular among officials who seek to justify government spending on international mobility (Mitchell 1986: 226–7).

The officials responsible for these programs are surprisingly willing to publicly tie their activities to the pursuit of political influence. When program administrators say that they have political objectives, this should be seen partly as a bid for resources to the custodians of public finances. However, their behavior also reflects political agendas.

Rhetoric

Mobility programs are frequently justified to governments in terms of "soft power," the ability to manipulate others, in this case other countries, through the attractiveness of culture and values rather than economic incentives or threats of force. International mobility is central to many of Nye's examples of how soft power can be generated (Nye 2005), and many former exchange administrators have made clear links in post-retirement publications. Arndt (2005: 394, 537) is one obvious example.

Programs frequently present themselves to policy makers as serving political ends. This is often obliquely mentioned in their public mission statements. The German Academic Exchange Service, for example, describes its mission as enabling

> young academic elites from around the world to become leaders in the fields of science, culture, economics and politics—*as well as friends and partners of Germany.* (DAAD 2005, my emphasis)

Such allusions to encouraging international cooperation in public materials are fairly common, but typically vague on why "winning friends" is an activity which deserves government funding. More explicit statements tend to be made in communications between the program organizers and their governments, which are less likely to be read by the general public. For example, reviews of mobility programs by the British House of Commons Foreign Affairs Committee (e.g. 2006) indicate that securing political influence is a primary aim, and frequently express concern that the programs may not be doing so efficiently enough. Announcing a significant reorganization of academic mobility programs, which provide scholarships to foreign nationals interested in studying at British universities, the Foreign Secretary of the day explained his decision on the basis that the existing schemes were not devoting enough resource to "potential future leaders."

Following on from such discourse within government, small industries have been developing, particularly in London and Washington, which provide consultancy on how mobility programmes can be used to gain political leverage in dealings with foreign countries. Their publications (e.g. Fisher and Bröckerhoff 2008, Leonard and Alakeson 2000, Leonard, Stead and Smewing 2002), clearly targeting policy makers, again envisage exchanges as nurturing positive views of the sponsoring country among influential foreign citizens.

One program which is explicit about its pursuit of political objectives is Fulbright. Describing a mobility program that targets young people from Post-Soviet states, the Polish[i] Fulbright Commission states that its

> main aim is to become part of the process of creating in these countries a new intellectual, political and economic elite—*open to Western values, and willing and able to work for democracy, market economy and civil society.* (Fulbright Poland 2007)

The main Fulbright administration is barely more circumspect about the political nature of its aims. It does not require a dramatic leap of imagination to link the classic mission statement, that the program is designed to "increase mutual understanding between the people of the United States and the people of other countries . . ." to the opinion-leader model.

A small elite identified as future leaders will receive Fulbright awards, in the expectation that they will go on to have influence disproportionate to their numbers.

While US programs are perhaps the most overt, similar claims are made in a wide range of countries. The British government reserves a large number of scholarships for foreign students in the hope of establishing bonds with future elites. As one very senior administrator put it "the object [is at least partly] to establish, if you like, crudely, ambassadors for Britain" (British Council Interview One). In bemoaning the limited resources Canada devotes to mobility programs, Potter (2002) establishes that government-funded visits are widely seen as a means of shaping foreign nationals' views of Canada. McConnell (2000) demonstrates convincingly that the Japan English Teaching (JET) program, which pays English-speaking graduates to teach in Japanese schools, is not simply intended to improve Japanese children's language skills. A coalition of support for importing English-speakers formed within the Japanese government in large part because this was seen as a means of improving Japan's diplomatic relations in the long term through those graduates' future influence.

The opinion-leader model is based on alumni contributing to political change. All the diplomats I contacted expressed a belief that mobility programs impact on international relations through their alumni. But interviewees did differ in what kinds of changes they expect to see in grantees. In particular, we need to be aware of the distinction between making visitors understand a country better, even if they come away disapproving of it, and hoping that visitors will "fall in love with" the host country (Entente Cordiale Interview One)—or at least that more of them will develop positive attitudes than negative ones.

There are managers of mobility program who see their objectives in terms of increasing understanding, and not necessarily making foreigners fans of their countries. This position was reflected in a particularly intriguing use of the word "sympathy" which recurred during my conversations with policy makers.

> The essential touchstone of the thinking of any cultural relations organization, whether it's the British Council, the Goethe Institute or the Japan Foundation . . . is that exposure to a country and its culture—the good, the bad, and the ugly of that culture—will, by definition, produce a better understanding— also for better or for worse—of that country, and therefore in the broadest sense of the word a greater sympathy toward that country. *Sympathy* can be negative too, to some extent. (British Council Interview One, my italics)

"Sympathy" here is an ambiguous term, which can connote affection but could also mean a more balanced awareness of why a country is as it is. This seems to leave open the curious possibility that a visitor who returned home with a more nuanced, but ultimately skeptical, attitude could count as a success story. In this case, sympathy reflects more a sense of understanding than necessarily approval or endorsement. This perhaps counter-intuitive understanding raises some questions, not least of which is how generating this kind of change in one individual would go on to improve international relations. And it is by no means a universal, perhaps not even a majority, view. Other interviewees had a greater expectation that the positive impact on visitors' attitudes would outweigh the negatives. For example, another administrator described his objective in terms that can be easily linked to support for foreign policy:

> to try and attract the future leaders of other countries for a period of study in the UK, to get a *good impression* of the UK, to become a *friend* of the UK and perhaps a partner of the UK in future years. (Chevening Interview One, my emphasis)

Unsurprisingly, there are diverse outlooks among practitioners. While they may agree that influencing alumni is an important part of the function of a mobility program, there are differences in how far mobility should be expected to inform or to enthuse.

Tying political objectives to mobility programs certainly raises the possibility that trying to generate mutual understanding elides into the pursuit of positive approval. Particularly when there is a demand to demonstrate success, it is easier to imagine a clear link between generating enthusiasm and future cooperation. The increasingly influential (Hayden 2011) "soft power" agenda strongly emphasizes attraction to a country, not just a deeper understanding of it. The possibilities for tension between supporting foreign policy by nurturing friendly audiences abroad and educating potential critics are clear, and will become significant to my argument. But some influential observers do expect mobility to encourage positive attitudes. Certainly, many academic evaluators before me have seen the development of positive attitudes and the adoption of cultural values as something we should expect if mobility programs are to fulfill their political aspirations (e.g. Atkinson 2010, Selltiz and Cook 1962, Sigalas 2010a, 2010b).

Administrative Behavior

The opinion-leader model is not simply a rhetorical device used by officials aiming to secure funding: behavior often conforms to the model. There are almost always more potential beneficiaries from subsidized mobility schemes than there are places, particularly where the programs support participants' pursuit of valuable goods such as educational qualifications. As a result, resources are targeted at particular groups, whose members are seen as more useful visitors to host. Selections also need to be made among individual applicants. Formal selection criteria need to be set, and these often favor applicants who seem likely to prove influential in the future.

Claims about what mobility programs achieve can shift with the foreign policy priorities of governments. As literature on how mobility might be used to fight terrorism blossomed after 2001 (Lennon 2003), Ross (2003: 259) provided a particularly open statement of this link when he wrote that "cultural programs [including sponsored mobility] are … a frank mobilization in the service of national security of what Joseph Nye referred to as "soft power." Accordingly, resources are targeted at the nationals of countries which can be linked to security issues.

Many mobility programs—for example, the British government's Chevening Scholarships (FCO 2005: 8)—are very open about their focus on strategically important countries. The need to respond to the Foreign Office's "short to medium term" strategy for international relations was behind the creation of Chevening Fellowships, to supplement the Scholarship allocation, in 2006 (House of Commons Foreign Affairs Committee 2006: 41): these Fellowships are more closely tied to diplomatic agendas than traditional academic awards. After 2001, attention shifted quite suddenly toward the "Islamic World" (Dolan 2002); the British Council, for example, was encouraged to redistribute large swathes of its resources from Europe to Muslim-majority countries (BBC 2007).

Selection Criteria for Participants

The selection criteria applied when selecting participants are generally consistent with an opinion-leader model. Some mobility programs aim to recruit large numbers of students, and the officials responsible for program administration often delegate selection simply because interviewing large numbers of applicants themselves would be impractical. The European Union's vast Erasmus Program, which is funded by the Union but organized as a network of pseudo-exchanges among hundreds of educational institutions, is one example—with tens of thousands of places available every year selection is delegated to universities. Erasmus aims for large numbers of mobile students, with the grants to each individual relatively modest. But with more capital-intensive programs, including the lucrative scholarships offered by the Fulbright and Chevening schemes, the officials responsible are able to scrutinize the selection process closely. Where they themselves select participants, the selection criteria are often driven by diplomatic considerations.

Again, the Fulbright Program provides a particularly clear illustration of how this works. Fulbright is divided into several divisions, of which the Fulbright Scholarships are probably the best-known. Although these do require a strong undergraduate academic record, the selection criteria also include "evidence of leadership and initiative" (US-UK Fulbright Commission 2003), characteristics likely to identify those who will go on to be influential in the future. The desire to see ex-Fulbrighters take on leadership positions in their home countries might partly explain why the Commission insists they spend two years in their home countries before they are eligible to return to the United States for a significant period. The Fulbright scheme is also notable for its offshoot, the International Visitor Leadership Program. This is one of the most overtly politicized programs, with the recruitment of future elites the core selection criterion. The Program has no application process as such: instead American diplomats track down individuals they expect to reach high office and invite them on prestigious, all-expenses-paid visits to the United States. Their judgments of potential have proved astonishingly accurate: the State Department boasts that over 330 past and present heads of states or governments are alumni (State 2013). British Prime Ministers Gordon Brown, Tony Blair, and Margaret Thatcher took part early in their careers (1984, 1986, and 1967 respectively), long before they were considered future party leaders (NCIV 2006, Scott-Smith 2003).

These criteria seem to be designed to include as many future leaders as possible in the programs' pool of alumni. *If* the exchange experience leads to improved attitudes toward a host country, then this should maximize the numbers of influential foreigners with positive views of the sponsoring country.

It is interesting to note, however, that even if recruiting students likely to go on to positions of power proves not to be in the objective interests of the sponsoring country or its government it can prove very helpful for the programs themselves – and thus might be a sustainable strategy even if it does not improve international relations. The alumni of these programs naturally tend to be supportive of their continuation, and can be a powerful constituency for exchanges. Fulbright alumni have lobbied successfully against threats to the program's budget on more than one occasion (Ninkovich 1996: 32–3); their alumni network maintains a system of alerts on its website which inform alumni of opportunities to lobby Congress for increased funding of academic mobility (Fulbright Association 2007).

Many mobility programs are sustained partly by an expectation that they will bring political influence. This is not simply a rhetorical move by their advocates, but it is reflected in how they operate. The expectation that mobility contributes to political influence affects how the programs are organized and who gets to take part when demand outstrips the available resources. That expectation deserves to be tested.

2

Can We Infer That Mobility Has Political Impact? Some Historical Case Studies

This book questions whether scholarly mobility affects international relations in the way many of its champions claim. In the subsequent chapter, I will discuss the published evidence to back this claim, showing that, in fact, that evidence is weaker than we might assume. But first I want to address a more fundamental point: why should we doubt it at all? The officials tasked with facilitating international mobility, organizing exchanges and awarding scholarships link their work to impact on the people they enable to travel. They are usually, in my experience, intelligent, honest, and often very curious about the impact of their work. Could so many of them have come to converge on expectations which were not backed by convincing evidence? Is the fact that so many people appear to sincerely believe that mobility improves how students and scholars relate to foreigners not a clue that this is probably true?

I argue that we do need empirical evidence to back a claim like this, even if the conventional wisdom does not seem to be seriously challenged within government. In fact, I will show that it is quite possible that the belief could be misleading, even when so many incisive people accept it. The explanation tells us something very interesting about how policy processes can work. Policy is rationalized in different ways, and these rationalizations can gradually change even as governments' actions remain relatively consistent. By delving into the histories of some specific scholarship programs, I can show that their objectives have shifted over time.

Publicly funded programs operate within the constraints of that funding: governments have limited resources, and there is almost always an array of other uses to which resources could be put. Demands on governments' resources are essentially infinite, but the supply is finite.

Given unlimited resources, governments could provide every citizen with ideal security by having a police officer standing guard over every house, ideal healthcare by having a team of medical experts waiting around the clock to provide instant treatment if a citizen became ill, or provide all citizens with free one-to-one tuition by experts in any subject they desired. In reality, however, governments will always fall short of such ideals because their resources are limited. Governments, therefore, need to prioritize some commitments over others, trading off security against healthcare and education to reach a tolerable compromise (Hogwood and Gunn 1984). If governments were simply to adhere rigidly to the "rational" model of policy making set out (and critiqued) by Herbert Simon (1957), then we would expect them to gather as much evidence as possible on the costs and benefits of spending on particular activities, then assign resources to those activities with the most favorable ratio of benefits to costs. If this were the case, then we could assume that spending on mobility programs is supported by a compelling body of evidence that they bring political benefits. Unfortunately, such a model quickly breaks down once we consider the perspectives of the vast numbers of groups and individual officials who actually make up a government (e.g. Kingdon 1984).

For officials responsible for given policy areas, limited resources lead to a situation where they need to compete against other policy areas, both to support programs for which they are responsible and to create new ones. For example, an official in a security department who is responsible for ensuring crime prevention needs to ensure police are paid, and in order to do so the official needs to ensure that the government does not devote all its resources to hiring new doctors or teachers. If the official believes that it would be desirable to obtain new resources for security protection, for example by providing police with motor vehicles, that official will need to make a case that money should be spent on those vehicles rather than, say, more teachers. To do so, officials must claim that spending on their area brings benefits (in this example, reduced crime). Identifying benefits from spending is important because it leads to a claim on spending.

It seems reasonable to assume that officials, as a general rule, want more resources to be devoted to programs in their policy area. There are many reasons to expect this. Expansion of activity in their area may bring them personal career benefits. They probably believe their area to be particularly important if they have chosen to work in it. Even if they do not believe this at the beginning, but end up in the post due to a quirk of circumstances, their priorities may change out of a psychological need to feel their work is important and worthwhile. The important consequence is that we can believe officials are more likely than not to want more resources for their area, and therefore to want to come up with the best arguments possible that what they do has benefits. Identifying benefits is important to the bureaucratic success of public programs, in the sense of those programs obtaining sufficient resources to survive. Therefore, officials should be expected to advertise the benefits of their activities, especially if they know these benefits are in high demand at the center. They may even be incentivized to claim benefits for their program which they know are sought by the disbursers of funds when their programs are not optimally designed to generate such benefits (Hogwood and Peters 1983: 142–8).

International mobility programs are no exception: in order to continue to exist, their organizers need to successfully claim resources. There are various justifications which could be offered for devoting limited resources to sponsorship of foreign visitors. The opinion-leader model offers a foundation for one of these justifications, which is being used to justify public support for a wide range of international mobility programs in countries around the world. Put simply, the claim is that spending money on international mobility provides benefits in the long run, in the form of more cooperative relations with other countries, and these benefits justify the immediate costs to the sponsor country.

There are many plausible goods that governments might aim to secure by funding foreign nationals to study. They might seek educational, economic, cultural or diplomatic benefits. They might seek to secure them through many different mechanisms. The opinion-leader model offers one possible mechanism by which sponsoring mobility might serve a national interest. It is becoming ubiquitous. Given the ample evidence that mobility is being "sold" as a solution to international relations problems, it might be tempting to assume that its ubiquity indicates its accuracy. The programs are currently presented as means of shaping public opinion in foreign countries. Therefore, we might naively reason, there must be good reason to believe that they are effective means to the end. After all, the officials responsible for mobility programs could focus on other benefits their activities bring to their country. Presumably they should choose to focus on a goal that they could clearly demonstrate they achieved, not least as a pre-emptive defense against anyone who questioned their budget allocation. Hence, we might expect that a model would be more likely to become widespread if it accurately depicted reality.

But it does not necessarily follow that mobility programs were set up to influence foreign public opinion, or that they actually do so. We certainly cannot infer that they were created based on evidence and reflection as to how this aim could best be achieved. Evidence that mobility programs are justified as means to a political end today does not mean the programs were created to do so in the past. Knowing how governments rationalize their activities now, in the present, does not necessarily tell the whole story about how this rationalization became so popular. Thinking about how governments operate in Kingdonian terms suggests that coalitions of support can shift over time, and so can rationalizations as to why things are being done.

The creation stories, as opposed to creation myths, of real mobility programs show why we need to question the opinion-leader model. I will examine the histories of some British government scholarship programs which are now presented as diplomatic missions. These historical vignettes include example programs whose objectives were initially seen rather differently but which have drifted toward the opinion-leader model over time. The programs were not, therefore, based on a developed theory of how they might influence international relations.

Although this book's argument applies much more broadly, I chose to focus on British government-sponsored scholarships because the research into their historical development was necessarily painstaking. Sourcing information about the historical development of government programs is a time-consuming and laborious process. The four case studies are British programs whose histories were relatively unexplored when this project began. As there was so little information about the policymaking processes which led to their creation, I had to launch new investigations[1]. I chose British scholarship programs partly from convenience, as the agencies involved were open to researchers (scholarly mobility is hardly a sensitive subject) and partly because they seemed to be becoming increasingly influenced by a "public diplomacy" agenda which emphasized opinion leadership (e.g. Fisher and Bröckerhoff 2008, Leonard and Alakeson 2000, Leonard, Stead and Smewing 2002). The British government funds several programs which distribute financial support to select foreign scholars, and a reasonable number of foreign students receive funding every year.

Nonetheless, showing that a subset of mobility programs now presented as conforming to an opinion-leader model were actually set up for different reasons has broader implications. The schemes' histories suggest an interesting pattern in the development of the public diplomacy agenda: it is *possible* for the opinion-leader model to creep into programs' operating theories over time, even if it was not a major consideration at the outset. The stories of British scholarship programs are not sufficient evidence to show that similar dynamics must be at work in the creation of other mobility programs (although the personnel involved generally had some knowledge of other programs, and I encouraged them to consider how far they thought their stories reflected broader trends). The stories are, however, sufficient to cast some doubt on the opinion-leader model. The fact that many programs in many different countries are justified in these terms does not imply that mobility programs actually contribute significantly to shaping public opinion.

Four Revealing Scholarships

The four case studies are the Marshall Scholarships, Britain's contribution to the Commonwealth Scholarship and Fellowship Plan, Chevening Scholarships, and Entente Cordiale Scholarships. All provide funding, including fees and a relatively generous stipend to cover living expenses, to foreign students wishing to study in the UK. I delved into the histories of these four programs using a combination of secondary analyses, archival evidence, and interviews. With the exception of Perraton's 2009 analysis of the Commonwealth Scholarships, there was little secondary literature available on these programs. Where possible, I tracked down and interviewed officials involved in creating the scholarship programs. Where this was impossible—particularly in the case of the Marshall Scholarships, which were created in the 1950s—I examined material held in the National Archives at Kew or else shared by the administrators themselves.

I preferred interviews to documentary evidence because I wanted to ask about the intentions behind the programs as well as the policy-making processes. I was worried that there might never have been a very significant paper trail at a high enough level to be archived, and that lower-level official records might have been destroyed.[2] The odds of obtaining interviews were of course best for relatively recently created programs, and the unusually small-scale Entente Cordiale program was included partly to fill the need for at least one vignette which could be based on interviews.

Marshall Scholarships

The Marshall Scholarship Scheme brings American postgraduate students to study in the UK, providing funds to cover their tuition and a relatively generous grant for living costs. It is funded by a grant from the Foreign Office, but the Marshall Trust based at the London office of the Association of Commonwealth Universities (ACU) administers the grants. The Scheme is unusual in that it was established by an Act of Parliament in 1953, apparently as a spontaneous gesture of gratitude by the British Government for Marshall Aid supplied by the United States in the aftermath of the Second World War (Marshall Foundation 2009). The 'official' version of the history is that the scheme was set up by senior diplomat Roger Makins for this purpose:

> The principal architect of the scheme was Roger Makins (Lord Sherfield) who, as Deputy Under Secretary in the Foreign Office supervising the American Department, arranged for the bill to be drafted and passed through

Parliament. Soon after the bill passed he was transferred to Washington as Ambassador where he was able to organize the scheme in the United States.

The idea behind the Marshall Scholarships was to build on the Rhodes Scholarships established by a private bequest a half-century earlier. The Rhodes scheme was acknowledged to be an outstanding success, but it was restricted to one British university and, in 1953–54, to one carefully defined category of male candidate. The Marshall, in Roger Makins's view, would extend the Rhodes Scholarship idea and apply it, without distinction of gender and with a wider age range, to any university in the United Kingdom. (Marshall 2009a).

While this account is accurate, the story is actually rather more complex. The Marshall Scheme is a reminder that stated objectives can be much more flexible than actual activities. Often for reasons of bureaucratic inertia (Hogwood and Peters 1983: 14–18), what officials actually do can be much more resistant to change than why they say, and often believe, they do it.

The history of the Marshall Scholarships can largely be deduced from a file of correspondence stored at Kew. This contains a series of memos circulated between civil servants in the Foreign Office America Unit, including Makins, J. N. O. Curle and to a lesser extent M. S. Russell and K. M. Anderson (Foreign Office 1952). This reveals that the Marshall Scholarships were actually created for reasons other than British desire to repay a moral debt, but these certainly do not correspond to the modern idea of using scholarships to win over soon-to-be-influential young Americans.

Foundation

A tension between two objectives, signaling goodwill and influencing attitudes, goes back to the very beginning of the Marshall story. This tension is not simply a matter of semantics: the activities that are most effective in one are not necessarily optimal for the other. For example, a program intended as a symbol of a strong relationship would probably use very different criteria to select applicants from a program designed to exert political influence through its alumni.

The Marshall Trust was conceived in the early 1950s, when various means of recognizing American support since the Second World War were already under discussion. These had come to focus on the possibility of gifting an original copy of the Magna Carta to the United States. While there had been periodic speculation on this possibility, interest seems to have been reawakened by Sir Evelyn Wrench, who raised it publicly in a letter to the *Times*(Foreign Office 1951a). Wrench was a particularly notable figure in the US-UK relationship due to his famous support for Anglo-American relations after the First World War. Wrench had arranged the creation of the English-Speaking Union, a multinational charity based in London, in the hope of sustaining a sense of transatlantic community which could be (and was) called upon in the event of another war. The ESU later supported the government's campaign to bring the United States into the Second World War by lending key personnel to the wartime Ministry of Information (Cull 1995: 7, 23–6, 29). His intervention, therefore, attracted some attention within the Foreign Office, and senior civil servant Sir Roger Makins began to take soundings from his colleagues on how Britain could signal gratitude for Marshall Aid.

The Magna Carta could have been a symbolic gift. A copy loaned to the Americans during the War for security had proved a popular attraction, and was portrayed as a symbol of the two countries' (allegedly) shared liberal traditions (Foreign Office 1951a). Unfortunately, obtaining a copy for a permanent gift proved impossible. Only four copies of the most desirable Magna Carta, the 1215 Runnymede issue, survive. Of these, two copies had to be kept in the UK according to legacy conditions, while two were owned by cathedrals. Both dioceses were unwilling to part with them, and presumably the prospect of the government applying pressure to bishops would have been politically awkward. There are several more recent, less desirable issues of the Magna Carta, but these could have been perceived as inferior gifts.[3]

This seems to have left something of a diplomatic and public relations problem for the Foreign Office. Correspondence in the files (for example, a letter from the Minister of Labor to the Foreign Secretary—Foreign Office 1951b) suggests that influential people in the British government believed a suitable gift in recognition of Marshall Aid, to be made to seem like a spontaneous gesture of goodwill, was seen as almost compulsory by the American side. The civil servants involved were put in a potentially embarrassing position. This led to a search for alternatives which could be provided within a relatively short period of time. There was concern that the 'gift' should be made once the UK was no longer obviously dependent on Marshall Aid, but given the country's financial situation in the early 1950s it was far from inconceivable that Britain might require American aid again. This created a rather narrow window of opportunity. The gesture had to come before the government could be forced to seek further aid, or else a gesture intended to build up goodwill on the American side could be seen as manipulative (Foreign Office 1951c).

Scholarships were seen as a viable alternative. There was a glamorous precedent which would increase their appeal for the American public: the Rhodes Scholarships, created by Cecil Rhodes' vast legacy to Oxford

University (see Ziegler 2008). This private endowment was clearly a model from the outset.[4] Even at that time several former Rhodes Scholars were known to have had a notable impact on American public opinion, and the original plan was to award scholarships to young Americans "of Rhodes Scholar type" who would take second undergraduate degrees. After graduation they were expected to return home and, as a bonus for the Foreign Office, act as a "leaven" for public opinion[5] (Foreign Office 1951d). Importantly, however, the files provide strong evidence that the symbolism of the gesture was seen as much more important to British interests than what the visitors might do for the transatlantic relationship in later life. In a wonderful example of what Kingdon (1984: Ch6) memorably labels the "primordial soup" of policy ideas, many suggestions were floated around Whitehall. Several would have used the gesture of reciprocity to conceal more clearly propagandistic activities. They included sending select British students to the United States and funding visits by American schoolteachers to the UK in the hope of influencing future generations, a proposal which would clearly link to the opinion-leader model. These ideas had to be squashed by Anderson, Curle, and Russell:

> It must be remembered that the object of this exercise is to make a suitable gesture of gratitude for Marshall Aid, any long-term advantage to this country arising from the gesture being incidental [. . .] The suggestion that the scheme should concentrate on U.S. teachers coming to this country [for example] would, I think, run the danger of making the scheme so obviously propagandistic and limited as to distract from its value as an expression of gratitude. (Curle in Foreign Office 1951e)

It is worth bearing in mind that these discussions were confidential at the time, and Foreign Office files are typically closed for decades. It is difficult to imagine that these remarks were tailored to American public opinion.

It was, of course, not unnoticed that scholarships would have, as J. N. O. Curle put it, "the added advantage of indoctrinating young Americans with the British way of life" (Foreign Office 1951f). However, this seems to have been considered very much a secondary issue. The scheme was established by the most high-profile means possible, an Act of Parliament establishing an autonomous Marshall Trust. The Trust's terms of reference were to be laid down in statute, and therefore publicly visible. There is of course a tradition of British mobility programs being administered by autonomous bodies, but there is usually some indirect mechanism for the government to keep control. The British Council—which administers many such schemes—is autonomous, but it receives a block grant from the government. The grant may be influenced to some degree by the Council's ability to demonstrate effectiveness in changing opinions, hence the emphasis on evaluations which are copied to the Foreign Office (British Council Interview Two). The Marshall Trust was eventually funded in a similar way (and hence needs to rely on an annual appropriation) but this was not the original intention. In fact, it was hoped that the Trust could be sustained by an endowment in which the government would simply deposit enough money to maintain a certain number of scholars every year in perpetuity. Such a plan would have made it very difficult for diplomats to use the scholarships for the political priorities of the day unless the Trust's instructions were changed by statute. This would involve a very public parliamentary debate which, if the aim was to make the scholarships more "propagandistic", could be embarrassing. The annual appropriation won out over the endowment idea in the end, but not because this logic was followed. Instead, the economic uncertainty of the time led to worries about any one-off endowment being exposed to a significant inflation risk (Foreign Office 1951g, 1951h). Had this not been a factor, it seems that the scholarships would have been insulated from Foreign Office influence. The Marshall Scholarships were created by a consensus of people who either had not thought through the long-term consequences of their actions or else genuinely did not prioritize influencing American public opinion through Marshall alumni. Given the rigorous planning process revealed by the files, the second seems rather more likely.

Marshall Scholarships Today

This history is not necessarily what someone familiar with the scheme's modern objectives might expect. The Marshall Scholarships are now very much considered part of the UK's public diplomacy effort, with the aim of creating goodwill among influential Americans and sustaining their country's alleged "special relationship" with Britain. One administrator even made an explicit statement that, while people in the ACU tended to believe that the scholarships had originally been created as a gesture of thanks, they had since had to shift toward demonstrating their usefulness in terms of impact on public opinion (Marshall Interview Two). A recent graduate of the scheme remembers being made very aware that scholars were expected to act as miniature ambassadors, and that "the whole purpose of [the] program is to bolster UK/US ties" (Marshall Interview One). The Trust's official website includes as a key component of its mission statement: "To motivate scholars to act as ambassadors from America to the UK and vice versa throughout their lives thus strengthening British American understanding" (Marshall 2009b).

This mission statement is consistent with how the program is organized. Professional diplomats are directly involved in the final selection process, with interviews held in the local British Consulates. Diplomats, by definition, are likely to be interested in diplomacy, and trained in improving relationships with foreign countries. And the selection criteria they apply are tailored to an opinion-leader model of what the scholarships are intended to achieve: "Ambassadorial Potential" is weighted equally with "Leadership Potential" and "Academic Merit" (Marshall Foundation 2013).

The ACU shows a strong desire to demonstrate a link between the scheme and the strength of the "special relationship" between Britain and the United States (Kubler 2008: 12–13). This is reflected in the evaluation criteria used for the scholarships. The ACU has commissioned a large survey of Marshall alumni, with questions apparently chosen to demonstrate the impact of the scholarships on alumni beliefs and behavior to the benefit of the United Kingdom (Kubler 2008). This was presumably designed partly to impress the Marshall Trust's sponsors, particularly the Foreign Office, at a time when the Foreign Secretary was consolidating Britain's scholarship programs (BBC 2008).

It seems likely that this change was not generated by the Marshall Foundation alone. The Foreign Office's own internal communications also reveal a distinct shift over time. The Foreign Office increasingly rationalized spending money on foreign students as a means to support conventional diplomacy. The 1985 Foreign and Commonwealth Office Internal Review of British Government and British Council Funded Award Schemes included Marshall Scholarships in category (iii):

> (iii) Schemes which are intended to help Britain win friends and influence people abroad. Most of these schemes aim to attract people taking a leading part in the future in their field of study and in their own countries generally, or who seem likely to do so. (FCO 1985 section 3.1)

At the time, category (iii) also included the FCO Scholarships and Award Scheme, and the Foreign Office contribution to Commonwealth Scholarships (discussed later), as well as the British Council Fellowships (now defunct), and Britain's contribution to the Fulbright program. The authors went on to express their hopes that the other two categories identified in the review (scholarships aimed at providing developing countries with needed skills and the Overseas Research Students Awards Scheme, designed to offset the damage to UK research capacity when overseas student fees were first imposed) would also help to win friends and influence even though this was not their *primary* purpose (FCO 1985: 3.2). This implies that for category (iii) changing attitudes was considered the main objective. The review (which, while hardly top secret, was obviously not intended for public consumption) listed the Marshall Scholarships' objective as

"To further United States/United Kingdom relations by the provision of prestigious awards to enable American scholars to study at British universities" (FCO 1985: 1.9)

The authors noted (1985: 1.9.7) that

"The standard of scholars is exceptionally high and, as their careers progress, they frequently occupy positions in American life of importance and influence [. . .] The Scheme is thus rewarding in both academic and *political* senses" (my emphasis).

The Marshall Scholarships were and are now expected to justify their claims for funding by demonstrating impact on grantees consistent with the opinion-leader model.

This analysis shows that the policy objectives of the Marshall Scholarships have drifted since their creation. The symbolic impact of their very existence, and the avoidance of national embarrassment, were seen as sufficient to justify funding in the early 1950s. Today they are expected to support diplomacy, sustaining beneficial relationships with the United States. The change is a somewhat nuanced one and it would probably be impossible to trace anyone who could identify a pivotal moment at which it occurred, even if they were still alive. But over six decades the change is very obvious.

The case also shows us that we cannot assume that programs which now justify themselves in political terms were necessarily created for this purpose, or that they have followed logical, linear historical trajectories. Government programs do not always move from identifying a problem to providing the best-available solution to it. In consequence, programs which claim to be diplomatic tools could be poorly designed for the purpose, having been created to serve some other function. They may continue to behave in similar ways even after their ostensible objectives have changed. It is not necessarily fair to assume that a program is ineffective if its mission is allegedly to change perceptions of a country abroad but no such change occurs. The program could be very effective at achieving something, perhaps something very useful, other than the objective its advocates are emphasizing—which may simply be the objective they have found most instrumentally useful to associate with it. The mission statement may change in order to maximize resources, while the program continues to use these resources to do much the same things as it always did.

The symbolic power of the existence of such scholarships as Marshall may in itself be influential. Their existence may signal British goodwill toward the (elite) section of the American population which is likely to be aware of them. But the different objectives may pull the schemes in multiple directions: the grantees who are likely to make the most diplomatic impact (for example, future politicians) may not be the same as those who will diffuse the symbol most widely (perhaps future academics). Knowing whether mobility actually does bring goodwill, and if so how, remains crucially important.

The Commonwealth Scholarship and Fellowship Plan

The Commonwealth Scholarship and Fellowship Plan (CSFP) provides financial support for nationals of one Commonwealth country who wish to pursue university-level education in another. Unlike the Marshall Scholarships, the CSFP is transnational project, but different Commonwealth members can vary their contributions to the Plan. In practice, the wealthier members have underwritten much of the cost, and the British contribution has been crucial. Britain has always funded more awards than any other country, usually far more. In 2006, Britain funded as many as 1172 out of 1560 Scholars and Fellows—and while 2006 marked the peak of Britain's proportional contribution[6] the country has consistently funded a majority of CSFP awards (Perraton 2009: 195). The British Government's motives for this contribution are interesting. As with the Marshall Scholarships, the rationalizations offered for the British contribution shifted toward an opinion-leader model over time.

Hillary Perraton's comprehensive (2009) investigation details the Plan's development from its foundation in 1960 until 2009, weaving together archival evidence with an impressive range of interviews. As his approach is very similar to my exploration of the histories of the Marshall, Chevening, and Entente Cordiale schemes, and goes into much more depth, I am comfortable relying heavily on Perraton's work with only a little extra research. Reassuringly, his findings mirror my conclusions on the Marshall and Chevening Awards.

Commonwealth Scholarships and Fellowships are academic grants, mainly at postgraduate level[7] which enable citizens of one Commonwealth country to study in another. For the British government the scheme has had two main aims. First, the CSFP was considered part of development aid, sharing British skills with developing Commonwealth countries. Second, the awards were believed to strengthen relations with the developed Commonwealth. Until 2009 this division was neatly illustrated by a division of British government funding flowing to the Commonwealth Secretariat for use in the CSFP: one chunk came from the Department for International Development (DfID) and was aimed at students from developing Commonwealth countries, while the rest came from the Foreign Office to support visitors from the wealthy Commonwealth countries (Marshall Interview Two). The Foreign Office funding is the interesting part. This was justified not on the basis that countries like Canada and Australia needed British help, but instead because bringing their citizens to the UK was assumed to bring diplomatic benefits to Britain (Kirkland 2003: ix). The Foreign Office went through a long period in which it was providing scholarships to some Commonwealth countries for diplomatic reasons. Again, this does not seem to have been the main impulse which led Britain to start contributing.

Foundation

The CSFP arose from successive meetings of Commonwealth Trade and Education Ministers in Montreal and Oxford in the late 1950s. The first class left home in 1960. While some details are hazy[8] Perraton (2009: 5–7) is clear that Canada provoked the new scheme. The new Canadian administration of John Diefenbaker suggested several ideas for Commonwealth cooperation of which more experienced British delegates were skeptical. The CSFP was only one of these, but it was considered "safer and cheaper than [the Canadians'] grander plans" such as a Commonwealth Development Bank (Perraton 2009: 6). Rebuffing all of the Canadians' ideas could be offensive, and so officials searched for the 'least-bad' Canadian suggestion. British support does not seem to have been driven by a strategic calculation of national interest, but by a search for a distraction—much as the creation of the Marshall Scholarships distracted from failure to provide a copy of the Magna Carta.

Given this half-heartedness, it may seem curious that the British government not only agreed to co-operate but offered to provide most of the money. The British commitment to provide at least half the funding for the Plan seems to have reflected a concern with national prestige (Perraton 2009: 36). The CSFP was seen as a symbol of bonds between Commonwealth countries (Perraton 2009: Ch.2). The Commonwealth was seen as much more economically and politically important in the 1950s than it is now, and Britain expected to take a leadership role (Perraton 2009: 81–3). As the Cold War developed, the Commonwealth came to be seen as one weapon against Communism[9] (Perraton 2009: 36), and British prestige within the organization was consequently linked to other foreign policy agendas. This leadership also served to signal Britain's continued interest in the Commonwealth, despite engagement with precursors of the European Union (Perraton 2009: 35). Britain was leading a joint enterprise, giving diplomats something they could point to if the relevance of this vestige of Empire were ever questioned. The possibility of CSFP alumni themselves influencing public opinion seems to have been discussed rarely, if ever.

Universities were key beneficiaries of the Plan, and their representatives were closely tied into its organization from the beginning (Perraton 2009: Ch.1). Unsurprisingly, universities supported the Plan largely for their own reasons, as a means of bringing talent into British higher education. From their point of view this may have outweighed any impact on Commonwealth relations. But in the 1950s most of the academics involved framed their support in the language of Commonwealth unity (Perraton 2009: 37). While this may have concealed self-interest, the fact that they chose to do so suggests that they believed diplomats would be most responsive to this line of argument. For the Foreign Office, the symbolism of a few elite sojourners for the Commonwealth was relevant.

Shifting Objectives

Perraton's account shows that the developed Commonwealth countries, which ultimately paid the CSFP's bills, changed their attitudes over the lifetime of the Plan. While they may have been concerned with strengthening the Commonwealth as an institution in the 1950s, they increasingly focused on how the CSFP served their own perceived national interests. Britain was foremost among them (Perraton 2009: 26–7, 61). By the end of the twentieth century, contributions to the Plan for developed countries were being justified on the grounds that it won Britain influential friends.

Perraton's conclusions are consistent with other evidence. While the Commonwealth Secretariat itself is not dependent on any one member, funding for the Plan ultimately came from member states, and officials had an interest in convincing these governments that the CSFP served their interests. A study tracing CSFP alumni (Commonwealth Secretariat 1989) reflected their interest in how influential alumni had become. As well as gathering general information about alumni careers, this very explicitly sought alumni who took part in politics, regardless of whether their activity was part-time or voluntary. Alumni who had gone into politics could be used to support a case that scholarship money was securing political influence—although the tracer study never tried to discover whether studying in the UK actually changed attitudes. By the early 1990s, British diplomats were explicitly stating that the CSFP should be making "future leaders, decision makers and opinion formers" into "influential friends overseas" by giving positive impressions of the UK (quoted in Perraton 2009: 71). Although they retained elements of Commonwealth-unity rhetoric, the civil servants funding the CSFP came to see it as a means of influencing influential foreigners (Perraton 2009: Ch5, 184). CSFP administrators were certainly aware of the political motives, as the Secretary implicitly acknowledged in his introduction to a catalogue of prominent alumni:

> Governments offer scholarships for a variety of reasons. Typically, however, they represent a balance between enlightened self-interest and a genuine desire to help others. One motive might be to 'win friends' in other parts of the world, who, if favorably impressed, *will in turn influence policy or public opinion towards their former hosts in later life.* Another might be to provide key skills to the next generation of leaders and practitioners, particularly in developing counties, as part of strategies to improve living standards there. (Kirkland et al. 2003: ix; my italics)

British contributions to the Plan were divided, with one stream directed to the developing Commonwealth as development aid and another seen as a tool for influencing developed Commonwealth countries. While their symbolic value may initially have been more important, by 2003 the developed-country awards were expected to generate well-placed alumni sympathetic to Britain. These expectations echo the opinion-leader model.

There are parallels between the shifting arguments surrounding the British CSFP contributions for developed countries and Marshall Scholarships. In both cases, scholarships seems to have been created in reaction to potentially embarrassing circumstances outside Foreign Office control— the unavailability of a Magna Carta and a Canadian delegation's over-ambitious plans for Commonwealth conferences. The symbolism of creating the awards was of greatest importance, outweighing any sympathy generated among the grantees themselves. By the turn of the (twenty-first) century, however, program administrators claimed they were shaping soon-to-be-influential grantees' attitudes toward Britain—and staked claims to support on that basis. We will return to the question of how Commonwealth Scholarships actually influenced opinions about Britain in the final chapter of this book, which reflects on the testimony of former Commonwealth Scholars about the impact their grant had on them.

The Foreign and Commonwealth Office decided to terminate its contribution to the Plan in 2008, with some attendant controversy (BBC 2008, Perraton 2009: 78–9). FCO funding was to focus on the Chevening Program and Marshall Scholarships. As the Marshall Program is a statutory creation, termination would imply considerable debate, and given that

Marshall is symbolically tied to Britain's "special" relationship the diplomatic costs could be substantial. It is one exception to a general consolidation of Foreign Office scholarships under the Chevening[10] brand, and no such exception was made for the developed country CSFP. Chevening has become particularly single-minded in its pursuit of future leaders.

Chevening Scholarships

The Chevening Program has become the largest scholarship program funded by the British government. It is a continuation of the Foreign and Commonwealth Office Scholarships and Awards Scheme (FCOSAS) which had existed since the 1980s and was renamed in 1994 (Chevening 2002).

Little knowledge of how the FCOSAS was created survives among current administrators (Chevening Interview One 2:00) but there does seem to be an assumption that it was created to secure political influence. Speculating on the scheme's early history, one senior administrator was confident that

> it would have been set up with the same principles that it has now which [are] to try and attract the future leaders from other countries [...] for a period of study in the UK, to get a good impression of the UK and to become a friend and possibly a partner to the UK in future years. (Chevening Interview One)

Again, this is not entirely correct.

Foundation

The Chevening Scholarships are a little over 25 years old, so key documents are still closed under the National Archives' 30-year rule at the time of writing. On the other hand, 25 years is long enough for all the key players in the scheme's creation to have left their posts, and many have become difficult to trace. Gathering material for this vignette was difficult, and more details will be available when the files are opened. However, I was able to locate a few key interviewees. Their recollections suggest that the Foreign Office's objectives shifted as the FCOSAS developed into Chevening, just as with the Marshall and Commonwealth Scholarships.

The Foreign and Commonwealth Office Scholarships and Awards Scheme dispensed its first grants in 1984, when the Thatcher Government was imposing severe budgetary constraint. One of the money-saving measures the government introduced early in its term was to greatly increase tuition fees for students coming from outside the EU to study in Britain.

Previous governments had in effect been subsidizing foreign students by paying part of the cost of educating non-EU students to universities, keeping costs to those students down. Removing the subsidy allowed universities to set their own fees for foreign students. Unsurprisingly, this greatly increased the cost. Equally unsurprising, the reduction in support led to discontent in countries which had become accustomed to sending their students to the UK (Perraton 2009: 60–1, Williams 1981).

Of the few witnesses to the Scheme's creation who could be traced, the best-placed[11] was adamant that the FCOSAS was created in response to this increase in fees (Chevening Interview Two). This was "absolutely" the primary cause and "it wouldn't have happened apart from that." He recalled that the fee subsidy had been removed by the Department of Education and Science and the Treasury without seriously consulting the Foreign Office. This decision antagonized some foreign governments. Creating a very public scholarship scheme was seen as a gesture which would reduce their disaffection—even though it would support far fewer students than the hidden subsidy. The Foreign Office attempted to create such a scheme repeatedly in the early 1980s (after fees had been increased) but was unable to secure funding from the Treasury until the economy had recovered and spending restrictions were eased slightly. Had the FCO been able to fund them, awards would have been offered much earlier.

Once funding was available, there was a question as to whether the FCO or the British Council, Britain's quasi-autonomous cultural relations agency, would control the awards. Both dispense funds allocated to the FCO by the Treasury, but the British Council enjoys some level of independence. There was a feeling within the Council that it would use scholarship money to develop longer-term relationships, whereas the Foreign Office might fixate on short-term priorities (Chevening Interview Three); the Foreign Office seems to have been under the impression that the British Council wanted to use the additional funding to augment its existing portfolio of scholarships (Chevening Interview Two). The Foreign Office succeeded in retaining direct control. However, this was not born of a desire to control which candidates received awards. It seems that the Foreign Office had no fixed criteria for making awards, besides academic promise, and would often delegate this decision (Chevening Interview Two). Rather, the reason for this concern to retain control was that Foreign Office ministers had been "taking the flak" for the increase in fees and were, therefore, keen that an Award Scheme designed to mitigate the diplomatic consequences of this should carry a Foreign Office branding (Chevening Interview Two). Hence, the *"Foreign and Commonwealth Office* Scholarships and Awards Scheme."

Given this, my best-placed interviewee was clear that the main aim was to smooth conventional diplomacy, and impact on the grantees themselves was a bonus.

Q: So from your point of view it was primarily about intergovernmental relations rather than the impact on the students themselves?
A: Oh, absolutely. (Chevening Interview Two 12:00)

By contrast, the modern Chevening Program focuses on the impact of mobility on grantees.

Chevening Today

From the relatively small number of awards offered in 1984, the Chevening Scholarships have developed into a major operation, recruiting students from a wide range of countries to study in the UK. Apart from the far less selective Erasmus program, to which the government contributes through the European Union, Chevening is probably the largest scholarship program funded by the British government (Chevening Interview One).

Despite its history, the Chevening Program today is heavily tilted toward the opinion-leader model. In many respects it is the closest British equivalent to the Fulbright Program, administered by the British Council and overseen by the Public Diplomacy unit of the Foreign Office, the section tasked with improving public views of Britain in foreign countries (FCO 2005: 8). Chevening seeks prospective students who will "establish a position of leadership in [their] own country within ten years of [the] Scholarship" and "who will are able to use [their] studies and experience in the UK to benefit [themselves, their] country *and the UK*" (Chevening 2013, my emphasis). The Foreign Office has retained its influence since the struggle between the British Council and FCO in the early days of the scheme (Chevening Interview Two, Three): as with the Marshall Scholarships, selection interviews are held in consulates by panels including at least one diplomat (FCO 2002, 2013). When announcing cuts to the scheme in 2008, the Foreign Secretary stressed that his staff should mitigate their impact by targeting the awards more carefully. They should place even greater emphasis on choosing candidates who were likely to become influential. The FCO would

> select more carefully to ensure our scholars really are potential future leaders, with our heads of mission having personal responsibility for ensuring their posts are getting this right. (Miliband 2008)[12]

This emphasis on recruiting future leaders, the awards' direct ties to professional diplomats trained in the pursuit of influence, and their well-publicized foreign policy objectives all fit the opinion-leader model.

The early history of Chevening does require some further investigation. In particular, it would be helpful to have some corroboration of the testimony that the FCOSAS was originally created to reduce "flak" (Chevening Interview Two) experienced by the Foreign Office. However, the pattern of scholarship programs being created as a sign of goodwill to avoid diplomatic embarrassment, and then gradually drifting toward an opinion-leader model over time, is very similar to the stories of the Marshall Scholarships and the CSFP. The account is both the most plausible and is consistent with the emerging finding about how this model has spread within the Foreign Office.

Entente Cordiale Scholarships

The Entente Cordiale Scholarships are a relatively recent creation. The scheme is a very small one, what two interviewees independently termed a "bijou"[13] program, and at the outset, it appeared that this scheme had a particularly close relationship to diplomatic objectives. It clearly originated in a specific embassy, the British mission in Paris, where we might expect personnel to be particularly focused on the diplomatic impact of their activities. In fact, the reality proved to be somewhat different. The Entente Cordiale Scholarships are somewhat exceptional in making almost no *direct* claim for public funds at all, and it is tempting to conclude that this exception proves a rule. The Entente Cordiale Scholarships were framed in rather more nuanced terms than the taxpayer-funded schemes.

Entente Cordiale Scholarships are awarded to postgraduate students crossing the Channel between Britain and France—British nationals wishing to take postgraduate courses at French universities and French graduates wishing to continue studying in the UK. The grants are raised from private and corporate contributions, but the program can legitimately be considered government-supported because the British side (the selection and support of British students in France) is administered by officials at the French Embassy in London and the French side (dealing with French grantees in the UK) by the British Council in Paris. There are officials formally tasked with administering both, although this is not their full-time job.

A *"Bijou" Program*

The Entente Cordiale Scholarships were officially launched by British Prime Minister John Major and French President Jacques Chirac at a

Franco-British summit commemorating the 90th anniversary of the original Entente between Britain and France. The first scholars were exchanged in the 1995-96 academic year. (Ambassade de France 2007, Entente Cordiale Interviews One, Four). The history of the Entente Cordiale Scholarships, and the policy-making process which made them a reality, begins some time earlier. My informants were unanimous in suggesting that the 'first mover' in the creation of the program was Sir Christopher Mallaby (Entente Cordiale Interviews One, Two, Three, Four, Mallaby Interview), British Ambassador to France between 1993 and 1996. Mallaby not only raised the idea of bilateral mobility between Britain and France at a time when the pan-European Erasmus scheme was well-established, but also came up with the novel idea of fundraising from the private sector.

Further investigation revealed that interviewees' emphasis on Mallaby's personal input was not exaggerated. As ambassador at the time he enjoyed significant personal authority, so there was little opposition within the embassy (Entente Cordiale Interview One). More importantly, he was able to raise funds through his personal contacts, reputation, and influential friends. His voluntary input continued as a trustee until 2008, and he was responsible for raising a huge slice of the scheme's income in the form of voluntary donations by corporations and philanthropists.

Private fundraising was considered due to the difficulties of obtaining, and more importantly sustaining, government funding for postgraduates. Mallaby originally hoped to substitute for government support by raising a private endowment. Raising endowment funds proved impossible (Mallaby Interview), and both he and subsequent administrators have had to resort to raising funds year-by-year from a combination of individual philanthropists and corporate sponsors in Britain and France—which, incidentally, has increased the indirect costs to the British and French governments, as staff time has to be devoted to fundraising and dealing with sponsors every year (Entente Cordiale Interview Three). Using private finance for an educational scheme raised many eyebrows at the time, particularly in France where education had traditionally been almost exclusively the remit of the state (Entente Cordiale Interview Three, Mallaby Interview). Despite annual fluctuations it has always been possible to raise enough money to provide for a reasonable number of scholars from private sources. The Entente Cordiale Scholarships Trust, which actually receives funds and pays the scholarships, is run as a private charity, so the funds are not gathered through the embassies' bank accounts. However, senior public officials in Britain and France are ex-officio trustees. Much of the actual administration and pastoral care for scholarship recipients is provided by the British Council and CROUS (an agency which looks after the pastoral needs of students in France), agencies which are unlikely to turn away funding for supporting international students given that this fits very well with their overall objectives. The Entente Cordiale scheme can thus be seen as an expression of one notable individual's wishes, to a far greater degree than would normally be the case for a government program. Mallaby's objectives for the scheme appear inseparable from the original aims of the Entente Cordiale.

Mallaby's background included both close personal ties to France and an ongoing interest in linking education to diplomacy. His most personal links to France date back to his years as an undergraduate at Cambridge University, many decades before being posted to the British Embassy in Paris. He not only spent time at the Sorbonne on a language placement as part of a French and German degree, but also met the future Mrs. Mallaby, a French student learning English at one of the Cambridge language schools. Relations between the two countries might have been of particular interest, especially when he became responsible for aspects of that relationship at diplomatic level. But Mallaby also had a long-standing interest in linking education with diplomacy, and had helped to facilitate academic courses focused on Britain at German universities before he ever arrived in Paris.

The 1980s were a period of some unease in Franco-British relations (Wright 2000: 333–6), and doubtless a frustrating time for already-convinced advocates of a close bilateral relationship. In his position as British Ambassador, Mallaby experimented with many other schemes to improve Franco-British relations at an informal level (for example, an abortive attempt to produce joint television series—Mallaby Interview) of which the Entente Cordiale scholarships have proved the most enduring. Coming into being toward the end of his time in Paris, and near his retirement from government service, the scheme seems to have been partly the result of a desire to leave a "legacy" (Mallaby Interview, Entente Cordiale Interview Four) with the potential to improve a relationship about which he personally felt strongly (Mallaby 2004: 265–7). This developed from Mallaby's frustration with (in his view) unwarranted suspicions between the two countries at elite level:

> ... differences and misunderstandings have persisted. You find them in conversations about the other country on both sides of the channel, and sometimes in parliamentary debates or in arguments between the two governments. (Mallaby 2004: 265)

The Entente Cordiale Scholarships were seen as antidotes to this situation in two respects. The creation of the scholarships was well-publicized and linked to a "benign" anniversary to signal that the Franco-British relationship was "on a firm foundation and on the up" (Entente Cordiale Interview One).

> It's the kind of thing that governments do to ensure that there is attention [...] in the right quarters to the underlying strength of a relationship which might otherwise be taken for granted. (Entente Cordiale Interview One)

In addition, an ongoing influence was expected because grantees, who were selected on the basis that they were likely to become future elites, would enhance their knowledge of another country through personal exposure:

> What I'm really thinking about is a [future] British Cabinet meeting where a minister knows the other country really well, or the editorial board of the FT on a Monday morning—or the *Economist*—and somebody there knows the other country really well. That's my [...] perfect picture for the future. (Mallaby Interview)

The Entente Cordiale mission statement, perhaps unsurprisingly, echoes this sentiment:

> **Its ambition** is not only to enable the most outstanding students of both countries to study or carry out research for a year on the other side of the Channel, but also to promote contacts and increase exchanges between tomorrow's decision-makers in the United Kingdom and France and to **build an influential and widespread network of alumni and sponsors**. (Entente Cordiale 2013, emphasis in the original)

This emphasis on increased knowledge and interaction differs subtly from both the original and contemporary aims of the other three programs. It is clearly linked to changes in grantees' future behavior, but not necessarily through more positive attitudes. An attitude change model was not considered appropriate to the Entente Cordiale Scholarships, reflected in a hostile reception given to my hypothesis that the scheme was intended to influence scholars' subsequent political attitudes. The key player in the scheme's creation explicitly rejected changing political attitudes as a goal of the scheme:

> If you imagine saying to yourself 1) is this a person who sees the world through the perspective of the centre-left in France; 2) is this a person who's likely to be susceptible to removing their position through a year in Britain, I just feel uncomfortable with the whole idea because I'm getting into participating in French democracy. (Mallaby Interview)

However, this objection did not mean that alumni were not expected to impact on Franco-British relations as a result of their experiences: there was even a hope that they might influence government policy. The same interviewee was very clear on this:

> I won't claim that there is a particular decision of the British government that would have gone another way if the scheme hadn't existed. It's too soon for that. The time may come when there's somebody [for example] on the editorial staff of the *Financial Times* or, in France, *Le Monde*, whose series on an aspect of Britain has really caught—made waves in the other country. It will be that—things like that will happen. But I think it's too early to claim it. (Mallaby Interview)

The difference is more subtle in that increased understanding, rather than a more positive attitude, was expected to bring about the change.[14] This focus on increasing exchangees' understanding appears to have been retained, and is echoed by more recent administrators (Entente Cordiale Interview Three, Entente Cordiale Interview Four):

> We wouldn't expect for example a French civil servant to explicitly push—you know—British interests. I mean, that's not what their job is about. But we'd expect them to be sympathetic to those interests and we'd expect them to have perhaps a deeper understanding of them [. . .] why they're saying what they're saying even if you don't agree with what they're saying [. . .] I think it is just really more having an understanding. It's not a kind of propaganda exercise that we're, you know [laughs] trying to convert them to the other side. (Entente Cordiale Interview Four)

This model of how the Entente Cordiale Scholarships affect international relations differs from the expectations which surround the Marshall, Commonwealth, and Chevening programs. Those programs are expected to emphasize the production of alumni who have positive views of the UK. The distinction is subtle but may nonetheless be significant, and it is interesting to consider why the Entente Cordiale's objectives differ from the others'.

The Entente Cordiale scheme differs in two important respects. It is funded from private contributions and its objectives are understood slightly differently. It seems likely that these differences are related, which may offer a clue as to why the opinion-leader model has diffused.

The Entente Cordiale's unconventional funding stream seems to make it unlikely that the program would be eliminated directly by an order from the British Treasury or French Finance Ministry. The costs to the governments are opportunity costs of lost staff time which will not appear as budget items. While, for obvious reasons, there are no figures with which we could make an exact comparison, these costs must work out to be many orders of magnitude smaller than the costs of disbursing government grants to students, particularly since the Entente scheme is so small compared to the others.

Many policy ideas are subjected to significant compromises on their path to implementation because multiple interests need to be appeased in order to create a "coalition" with enough power to implement them as policies (Hogwood and Gunn 1984: 50–1, 206; Hogwood and Peters 1983: 78–80, 227–9). If the Entente Cordiale Scholarships had been funded in cash, then other government agencies, particularly the Treasury and Finance Ministry, would have sought assurance that the money was being spent wisely. Using private funds circumvented much of the need for negotiations with other government agencies. Consequently, there was less need to construct a coalition of officials in favor of the scheme than might have been the case had it been consuming significant public resources. Private sponsors might have their own agendas, but these will be different from those of other public agencies.

The Entente Cordiale Scholarships do not have to bid for public funds in order to survive, but are able to bring in money from outside the finite resources of the Foreign Office. They have retained a subtly different objective based on the personal views of their most influential creator. There is a much greater emphasis on increasing understanding of France or the UK among their alumni, rather than necessarily sending them home with more positive views. This is one piece of circumstantial evidence that pressure to justify the use of public money encourages claims that giving foreigners grants for extended visits improves their attitudes toward the donor country.

Patterns of Objectives

In combination, these vignettes suggest a pattern of drift toward the opinion-leader model over time. In each of the first three cases, scholarship schemes seem to have been created primarily as a signal of goodwill and to evade potentially embarrassing diplomatic situations—such as the unavailability of a Magna Carta, unwelcome Canadian suggestions for Commonwealth projects, and increases in overseas student fees by other government departments which did not consult the Foreign Office. Their declared objectives have drifted over time. The fourth and most recent case, of the Entente Cordiale Scholarships, is subtly different. This scheme is unusual in that instead of bidding for public funding, its founder raised money from the private sector. Since the scheme did not appear as a budget line, its survival depended primarily on private fundraising rather than on official support. The objectives of the three schemes supported directly by the FCO have converged around an opinion-leader model even though they were created and designed for different purposes. This pattern suggests that objectives shifted because it was easier for schemes to secure funding if they were presented as means of influencing foreigners. Put crudely, the convergence suggests that the idea of using scholarships as tools for "winning influential friends" was easy to "sell" within government.

A crucial distinction which needs to be made here is between *creating* a program and *operating* it. In all four cases, different rationales were provided for the programs' creation and operation. Winning over grantees would be a benefit of *operating* the program. For every year that the program runs at a given level of resources, there would seem to be a similar added chance of impressing an exchangee who will go on to bring diplomatic benefits. Doubling the number of grantees would double the odds of including someone who will go on to be, for example, an influential diplomat in the future.[15] By contrast, many of the arguments which surrounded the creation of the programs applied specifically to *creation*. If the aim of a scholarship program is to signal goodwill, then it clearly does so in the first year in which it operates. The sponsoring government is very publicly engaged with it, and it is likely to attract publicity. Once the program has been running for several years, the positive signaling effect of running it for another year is less obvious. Once the issue and the personnel who set up the scheme have moved on and management has been passed to a new generation of officials, there is no longer a clear link to the will of political leaders, who have simply inherited a scheme, and publicity is likely to become harder to attract. The signaling function of long-established programs, inherited along with all the many other policy inheritances which new officials acquire, may not be clear.

Even if the diplomatic benefits flowing from some programs are no longer clear, there could still be significant costs to terminating them. Actively ending them might well be interpreted as a negative diplomatic signal. It would also carry the costs that Hogwood and Peters (1983: 14–8) identify in terminating any government program. Influential beneficiaries and supporters, which these schemes are designed to recruit, as well as staff who have invested their careers in the program, may be hostile to change. However, even if inertia were an important reason for continued support of a program, it would seem reasonable for administrators to keep suggesting benefits from their activities. This does not require any speculation that officials responsible for the programs made conscious decisions to change their arguments. The natural personnel changes as previous administrators retire or are redeployed will affect the balance of arguments about why a program is doing what it does. New generations of administrators have to rationalize their activities for themselves, and will not necessarily follow the rationalizations offered by their predecessors. However, in order to bid for resources to maintain their programs administrators must claim that doing so brings some benefit.[16] If they cannot, we would not expect the programs to survive and expand when they have to compete with other activities for a share of limited government budgets. Thus there is always a need for administrators to tell a story about the benefits a program brings. For international scholarships and exchange programs these stories seem to have converged on the opinion-leader model.

From the point of view of administrators who inherit responsibility for such programs, explaining their careers as historical hangovers would presumably be rather unsatisfactory. First, it seems reasonable that they may have a psychological need to feel that their work has a very important purpose. A clear causal link between their programs and the future of international relations would support that feeling. Second, there are career incentives for them to seek to expand the resources channeled to their program, which usually involves making a case that the program is delivering benefits in the present and will do so in the future (there may also be social incentives). Third, they may find themselves in the role of administrator because they are personally convinced that exchanges are a good thing. A belief that international mobility is good, and a desire to see opportunities expand, is likely to lead someone to such a career. All but one of the British officials I interviewed for my accounts of the Chevening and Entente Cordiale Schemes had previously received scholarships to go abroad and (unsurprisingly given their subsequent careers) they seemed enthusiastic about the experience.

Administrators are likely to encounter difficulties in making a case for expansion of their programs on the basis that setting them up sent useful signals. The best they could hope for would be stagnating support. To make a case for expansion, they would need to argue that the marginal benefit of adding another grantee to the program outweighed the marginal financial cost of supporting them. In other words, if supporting an extra student were to cost £10,000, they would need to argue that this generated more than £10,000 worth of benefit to the sponsor. It would be difficult to do this on the basis of signaling good intentions. With signaling, the greatest benefit would come from setting up an exchange. The goodwill benefit from funding the first dozen scholarships would be significant, whereas the marginal benefit of adding a second dozen would be much less. The marginal impact of additional spending falls very quickly as the numbers involved increase.

If scholarships are rationalized in terms of potential impact on recipients, the marginal benefits are much clearer. If there is an impact, doubling the number would (almost) double the diplomatic benefits. This offers a viable case for expansion.

For the programs which relied on public funding, a case which suggested marginal benefits developed from an opinion-leader model. The Entente Cordiale's survival did not depend on convincing other officials that scholarships were a worthwhile use of money, but on raising funds from private donors with different agendas. Accordingly, administrators were under less pressure to impress other officials in a position to authorize funding. The fact that the others did suggests that they were pushed toward the opinion-leader model because it made them more likely to attract funding. Of course, it is always possible that the Entente Cordiale Scholarships may come to be rationalized within an opinion-leader framework in the future.

This case is necessarily circumstantial. It fits with key observations. The justifications offered for spending money on international scholarships have changed over time. The change has been from justifications which would not show a marginal benefit from adding another grant to one that would. It is reasonable to assume that program administrators will favor the addition of extra grants, and the expansion of their programs. This should lead them to favor justifications which show a marginal benefit when they have to choose how they justify their existence. The justifications chosen by all three of the programs which had to compete for government funds are essentially the same, whereas the one program which does not depend on public money diverges slightly.

Because of the generational succession which takes place within bureaucracies,[17] explanations for the increased appeal of the public diplomacy model over such a long time frame must remain slightly speculative. No one interviewee is likely to be able to capture the development of the public diplomacy agenda over time. The mechanism I have suggested does not rest on conscious choices made by individuals, and so it would be difficult to prove definitively that this is the explanation for objective drift.

The fact that this pattern can be observed in the British Foreign Office does not necessarily mean that it is widespread in other foreign ministries. Investigations into other countries would be needed to show that. However, finding such a dynamic in one country is significant, and not only because it suggests the possibility that it is a widespread pattern elsewhere.

These stories illustrate a broader point: when governments fund mobility, this is a result of interactions within complex bureaucracies. In such bureaucracies, we cannot assume that a decision to do something is supported by evidence that it is a good idea. Resources can be allocated to an activity independently of evidence that it actually achieves the objectives it is intended to. Bureaucracies can keep doing the same thing and change the story about why they are doing it just as easily as they can change what they do in response to evidence on whether it achieves its objectives—probably much more easily. The opinion-leader model could be attached to mobility programs even if it does not adequately describe social reality. The fact that it is ubiquitous does not mean it is accurate, or that there is convincing evidence to support it.

The model could have become widespread *even if the assumptions underpinning it are incorrect* because it is a useful tool for securing funding. We emphatically *cannot* infer that mobility generates positive attitudes simply because officials tasked with facilitating mobility say that is what their programs are for.

We need empirical research to know whether mobility actually does lead to attitude change. While there has been a significant volume of research on this question, that has not been shown convincingly.

3

How Strong Is the Evidence of Political Impact?

Mobility programs that were created for other reasons may have drifted toward the assumptions of the opinion-leader model, regardless of whether the evidence shows that mobility actually contributes to political change. While these beliefs appear to be spreading quite widely, this does not necessarily mean that there is a wealth of evidence that paying for people to cross borders secures influence for the sponsors. The question of whether and how mobility affects politics remains important.

A fair number of researchers have set out to discover whether mobility changes attitudes, which then in turn leads to political change (the essence of the opinion-leader model). Unfortunately, many of them have chosen strategies poorly-suited to the task.

What kinds of political change might mobility bring about?

Mobility might encourage an internationalist outlook, or change people's attitudes to specific countries, or both (Abrams and Hatch 1960). We may not be able to completely separate these two: they have intermingled since at least the early twentieth century, and probably much earlier (Arndt 2005). Interest in whether mobility nurtures more cosmopolitan attitudes in general continues to this day (Sell 1983, Golay 2006). But there is probably some truth in Flack's (1976) assertion that the emphasis has shifted in line with the climate in international relations. In the immediate aftermath of the world wars, schemes tended to be set up with the stated goal of helping people realize their common humanity (e.g. American Field Service 2007). With the onset of the Cold War, cultural relations became a competition to convince foreigners of a particular sponsor's goodwill—or the superiority of its social system (Aspden 2004, Saunders 2000).

Regardless of which outcome sponsors might desire, it is far from self-evident that international contact can generate it. The rationale usually boils down to some variant of the "contact hypothesis," that bringing people from different backgrounds together diminishes tensions and increases mutual appreciation (Allport 1958). Discussion of this hypothesis in the psychological literature long ago moved toward a more sophisticated understanding. Contact can sometimes have these effects, but only under certain conditions (Amir 1969). The impact of international contact probably varies depending on perceptions of relative status, and overseas visitors do not necessarily feel adequately respected (see e.g. Morris 1960). It is not clear that most mobility programs provide the conditions in which contact has been found to improve intergroup perceptions, and it is almost certain that not all of them do. Gudykunst (1979), for example, asserts that meaningful change only begins to occur after two years' exposure to another culture; very few programs maintain foreign visitors for even two years.

Mobility will affect different people in different ways, perhaps moving them in opposite directions. Producing anecdotal success stories is not terribly helpful, because for every success there might be more disasters (or vice versa). It would be more helpful to get a sense of whether mobility brings about positive changes in more visitors and negative changes in fewer. Teichler and Maiworm (1997: 24) suggest a set of criteria for designing an "ideal" study to establish this. Although there are quite a large number of studies on how international mobility affects people's attitudes, many of them are imperfect according to these criteria. And even knowing whether desirable changes outnumber undesirable ones does not tell the whole story, because the impact of positive changes might be considerably amplified over the grantee's subsequent career while negative changes affected only that one visitor (or vice versa). No single study really addresses the possibility of such "differential multiplication" (my phrase), which later interviews suggested was a real possibility.

How We Could Know

Mobility programs represent an attempt by governments to alter the political environment they face. They do so by applying a direct stimulus which might not otherwise occur. The Canadian, or French, or British, or Chinese, or American government pays for a foreigner to visit. If the government had not provided a grant to facilitate this, she might have stayed at home and her life would have been different. At least in theory, the hope is that the differences in how her life develops will, in some way, benefit that government. In a sense, the government is sponsoring a natural 'experiment.'

For an experimental stimulus to be judged effective, first, a *ceteris paribus* ("if everything else was held constant") *change* must occur between the beginning and the end of the experiment[1] and, second, the change must *result from the stimulus* so that it would not have occurred without it.

People who choose to go abroad are self-selecting, and they tend to be relatively open to foreign countries before they go abroad (Murphy-Lejeune 2002). Simply discovering that they tend to have cosmopolitan view afterward would hardly be surprising (Demetry and Vaz 2002). Furthermore, it seems plausible that the experiences the host government facilitates may influence political development regardless of whether it occurs in a student's home country or abroad. For example, gaining more education, especially higher education, tends to be associated with more cosmopolitan views regardless of whether students attend the college in their home town or fly to another continent. (Carlson and Widaman 1988: 3, Jacobsen 2001). Military service might also be a potent socializing influence (see e.g. Jennings and Markus 1977), so simply finding that soldiers who take part in officer exchange programs change would not show that the mobility caused those changes—they might also have developed in the barracks of the town where those soldiers grew up (Atkinson 2010). Showing that change happens is not useful if similar changes could have occurred without the intervention: that would represent a *post-hoc, ergo proctor-hoc* fallacy.[2]

What kinds of changes would satisfy expectations? Our earlier examination of the discourse surrounding mobility (e.g. House of Commons Foreign Affairs Committee 2006) links the programs to potential benefits for governments that sponsor them. This implies a third criterion for a mobility program to be judged effective—some *behavioral* change must occur. Attitude change may be necessary for success, but it is unlikely to be sufficient. Behavioral changes, unlike purely attitudinal changes, could potentially be politically salient. If participants change their attitudes or perspectives this would be academically interesting, but it is difficult to see how governments could derive the promised benefits from purely psychological changes. Changes in behavior, such as voting patterns, could indirectly benefit foreign governments. Such changes could occur among participants or other individuals to whom they communicate a changed perspective, but behavioral changes would need to occur somewhere and it seems implausible that they could occur purely among third parties and not among participants. There has been a dearth of evidence about the effects of exchanges on political behavior. Dekker, Oostindie, and Hester's literature review (1993: 241) reports only one study showing an effect on "international political behavior or intentions" (this suggested that increasing Dutch schoolchildren's contact with other Europeans also increased their willingness to vote in European Parliament elections). Simply assuming that changed attitudes must translate into changed behavior is dubious.

Therefore, it makes sense for analyses to seek evidence of changes in behavior.

Finally, the psychological literature on the contact hypothesis suggests that different individuals (and perhaps classes of individuals) will react differently to mobility. There is a general consensus that, even if the contact hypothesis is valid, only some participants will experience positive changes (Amir 1969) and some will inevitably react negatively (Mitchell 1986: Ch. 15). There are plenty of historical figures, such as F. W. DeKlerk (Dizard 2004: 206-7), who acquired pro-Western views while visiting Western countries, but there are also many examples of former students, notably Ho Chi Minh, who became hostile to the countries which educated them, and others whose reaction was more complex, including Nicolas Sarkozy (Scott-Smith 2011). The outcome depends on the social context, made up of an array of factors, such as relative social status and self-esteem of the individuals being brought into contact (e.g. Morris 1960) and their patterns of social interaction (e.g. Murphy-Lejeune 2002). These are not the kinds of variables we can simply plug into a pre-determined model, and so the impact on individuals is difficult if not impossible to predict. Given this diversity, a degree of statistical representativeness seems to be a necessary ingredient for a successful study. At some point we need to examine *large samples* of participants. I am not claiming that large-*n* research is superior across the social sciences and, in fact, it may not be sufficient to tell us everything we need to know about the political impact of mobility programs (Scott-Smith 2008). But the diversity of experiences does make it a necessary step if we are to have any sense of whether one individual's movement in one direction is outweighed by another's movement in the opposite direction.

When we talk about a desirable outcome, we can only be talking about a desirable *net* outcome. A net improvement would mean that, among a group of participants, attitudes and behaviors would become more desirable overall. Individuals might become disillusioned, but the net effect could be positive if they were balanced out by others who became more positive, either because the positive changes outnumbered the negative or because they were more intense. A net effect can only be evaluated on a statistical level.

Gathering some evidence at a statistical level has another crucial benefit: it can allow research to support both negative and positive conclusions. Proving a negative is logically problematic, but analyzing large samples can suggest the probability that there really is no meaningful effect (the null hypothesis). While qualitative analyses can provide in-depth knowledge of selected cases, and potentially offer new insights which go beyond the researcher's expectations, they are less suitable for assessing net effect.

These criteria imply that a lot of the information we should be looking for can come from a study comparing two groups. One would be a group of participants, another an initially similar control group who stayed in their home country. In experimental language, the group going abroad is the 'treatment' group, the group staying in their home country the 'control.' Measuring both groups' attitudes and behaviors before and after the treatment group went abroad should reveal net, *ceteris paribus* change (Carlson and Widaman 1988: 2–3, Teichler and Maiworm 1997: 24).

Existing Evidence

As I have stressed, the history of some of these programs suggests that many were not created as part of a rational plan to improve international relations, but rather their existence was rationalized in those terms much later. Although I cannot estimate how common these kinds of retrospective rationalizations may be, this does mean that we cannot assume the programs are actually effective at doing what they are supposed to. Although there have been many investigations of what actually happens when we pay people to live abroad (Bochner et al. 1977, Eide 1972, Golay 2006: 12-3, Ch.2, Sell 1983), much of the evidence remains surprisingly weak.

Many of the authors who have discussed international mobility are simply not interested in its political consequences. This is quite understandable: these programs are interesting for many other reasons. Living abroad can have a profound impact on the individuals involved, which interests sociologists, anthropologists, and psychologists because of their impact on individuals' interpersonal skills (e.g. Wilson 1993) and social development (e.g. Murphy-Lejeune 2002). Because so many students and academics travel for educational reasons, several scholarly journals, such as *Intercultural Education*, the *Journal of Research in International Education*, *Studies in Higher Education*, and the *Journal of International Students* carry extensive discussions of how mobility affects international students' learning. These changes might well be beneficial, but links to international relations are tenuous.

Of the studies which do consider the political consequences of mobility, not many can tell us about the net impact.

There are plenty of historical accounts of mobility programs, often based on the memoirs of officials who have spent their careers organizing them (e.g. Arndt 2005, Dizard 2004, Espinoza 1976, Fairbank 1976, Ninkovich 1981). Authors typically believe that their activities were effective (or else that they were undermined only by inadequate support from politicians) but they are not strong evidence that mobility programs *in general* produce desirable net effects. These kinds of *post-hoc* accounts tend to be biased in their examples of former students, favoring noteworthy alumni and usually success stories; they also focus on atypical programs and tend to neglect cases in which programs produced equivocal results (Henderson *et al.* 1973 being an exception). For example, since the end of the Cold War there has been particular interest in how exchange programs have helped bring down hostile regimes, particularly the Soviet Union. Yale Richmond's fascinating (2003) history of exchanges with the USSR is typical.[3] It relies on testimony from an unsystematic sample of former students who visited the USSR from the West, gathered many years after the event. The account focuses on 'notable' individuals who developed strongly pro- or anti-host sentiments (and may also have been selected to go abroad) precisely because they already had atypical characteristics. Although Richmond makes a good case for his particular argument, that Soviet citizens who visited the United States were influenced in their subsequent careers,[4] this is not strong evidence that exchanges generally lead to political change. Historical studies are very useful for analyzing the macro-level impact on society as a whole, but not for demonstrating net change in groups of individuals who were neglected by scholarship of the time.

Similarly, a large number of studies collect and synthesize testimonials from alumni (e.g. Arndt and Rubin 1993, Dudden and Dynes 1987, NCIV 2000, Nye 2004 para11). A lot of this evidence is essentially anecdotal—alumni choose to participate after the experience, so they are unlikely to be representative. Success stories are both more likely to be asked to testify and more likely to be willing. This is not helpful for evaluating net effect.

On the other hand, interview evidence can be very helpful when researchers try to select their interviewees systematically. Bochner 1973, Kharlamova 2005, Murphy-Lejeune 2002, and Useem and Useem 1967 are good examples, and I will be drawing on interview evidence extensively in my analysis. Again, however, it is difficult to use interviews as evidence of net effect. Researchers have interviewed hundreds of sojourners, mainly international students, and gathered a range of positive and negative experiences and attitudes. But depth interviews are subjective processes, led by interviewers' questions, and by their very nature different semi- and unstructured interviews take different courses.[5] They do not provide quantifiable data which can be added and subtracted to get a sense of whether positive changes outweigh negative ones. They can provide very useful qualitative evidence, and have led to some very influential hypotheses, but interviews *alone* cannot demonstrate net effect.

Survey Research

The classic approach to these kinds of questions is a longitudinal survey. Surveys are a frustrating tool because they limit the responses subjects can offer, and in so doing sacrifice some of the richness of response we get from interviews. On the other hand, they allow for representative samples of large groups and generate answers which can be aggregated and compared.

A fair number of surveys have been conducted, particularly in the 1950s, 1960s, and 1970s when this was a fashionable method. Not all of them are very helpful.

Many surveys simply ask returning travelers whether, *in retrospect*, their opinions or behavior changed (Ayabe 1977, Bochner 1973, Teichler and Maiworm 1997). Funding agencies often use this approach (e.g. State Department 2006) to shown that alumni changed their views. But these kinds of questions may cause grantees to tell the evaluators what they expect to hear. Questions are often phrased in terms of whether any change has occurred, rather than whether such change is significant or is likely to be enduring. They do not encourage respondents to report negative change. Alternatively, researchers could ask returning travelers for their opinions and then compare their views with those of the rest of the population, most of whom will not have lived abroad. Over the past few years the Erasmus Student Network has used this approach in surveys of Europeans who study in a European Union state other than their home country. The 2007 edition looked at their attitudes to Europe (ESN Interview, ESN 2007), and showed that students returning from another European country are more pro-European than the rest of the population (ESN Interview). But it is impossible to know how much this is due to self-selection rather than actually going abroad. Probably this group was somewhat more pro-European before leaving home!

Yet another approach which gives only part of the information we need is to ask returning sojourners both what their views were before they left and what they are now. An example is Teichler and Maiworm's (1997) study of European Erasmus students, the product of an impressively large, detailed evaluation funded by the European Commission. Teichler and Maiworm asked thousands of students about their knowledge and opinion of the host country before and after their time there, but they only asked them once, after they had already returned. Their memories of what they thought up to a year earlier may not have been reliable (Carlson and Widaman 1988: 5). In any case, the overall impression is hardly of dramatic changes in opinion; the average change for all the questions they asked was not considered statistically significant (Teichler and Maiworm 1997: 130).

We have good reason to doubt that retrospective surveys like these can be reliable (Bochner 1981: 18). Lamare's (1975) review of educational socialization studies draws a distinction between studies based on asking students whether, in retrospect, they felt a given experience had influenced them, and studies which attempted to measure attitudes before and after. Retrospective studies seem to be much more likely to indicate that experiences are influential than "before and after" designs. Students looking back at their experience are quite likely to label it as influential even when panel studies suggest it is not.

Before-and-after panel studies offer more reliable evidence. They avoid respondents needing to recall their own opinions in the past. Expecting people to remember such complex information as the details of their own opinions may be unreasonable. Attitudes can form from the accumulation of subtle, unremarkable experiences. And when respondents are asked about politics in relation to their time abroad, their more general feelings about that may interfere. Retrospective studies cannot avoid this because they are necessarily asking about change during a period in which living abroad almost certainly dominated respondents' lives. And respondents have a well-known psychological, possibly subconscious, tendency to present qualities they perceive as socially desirable (Converse 1964, De Vaus 2002: 108, 130). They might want to seem aware of and sensitive to their surroundings, to show the changes that would be expected of an intelligent visitor. With panel studies this is far less likely as it would involve remembering the answers given many months earlier.

Panel Surveys

Hence, it seems as if we need evidence from before-and-after panel studies. That said, many of the panel studies which have been tried do not actually yield such evidence. Design choices can make their results ambiguous, usually because any attitude change they identify might be better explained by other factors. This points to the importance of making fair comparisons between the mobile and non-mobile.

One common scenario (e.g. Carlson and Widaman 1988, Golay 2006, one group in Marion 1974, 1980) is that the sample contains American undergraduates who have gone to "study centers" established by American institutions in European cities. As Golay notes (2006: 56), these can be protective environments which isolate participants from the host culture. Faculty and students who choose to be assigned to overseas study centers probably have particularly internationalist outlooks, so the students will be surrounded by other Americans who have unusually internationalist outlooks. And students following a different curriculum should develop more cosmopolitan views regardless of whether they have contact with foreigners—Hensley and Sell (1979) found that a group of American students enrolled in a course on international organizations taught by a charismatic lecturer increased their "world-mindedness" scores[6] much more than a group which actually visited an international organization in Switzerland! In any case, this is a different situation from being immersed in a foreign culture alongside host nationals.

Finding a suitable control group is very important to putting together a good panel study. Without one, it is difficult to claim that travelers would not have experienced the same changes had they continued to study in their home countries.

The most obvious way to create a control group would be to recruit some students who simply stayed at home while the treatment group went abroad. King and Ruiz-Gelices (2003) have tried to avoid waiting for students to age by comparing different groups, and sending out questionnaire only once. Their approach used a group of students who had not yet gone abroad as a surrogate for younger versions of students who had just returned, and compared the attitudes of students about to depart on exchanges in the early 2000s with the attitudes of alumni who actually did go abroad many years earlier. While their comparisons are ingenious, this technique has obvious weaknesses given the myriad of uncontrolled (cohort) differences between the generations. A much safer and simpler approach is simply to recruit a non-equivalent[7] but contemporary control group of students who are not going abroad, measure their attitudes (and behavior) before the treatment group go abroad and compare the changes.

Emmanuel Sigalas's (2008, 2010a, 2010b) study of students participating in the European Union's Erasmus program is, to the best of my knowledge, the only existing study with a convincing controlled panel design. Sigalas questioned one group of Erasmus students visiting the UK, one group of British Erasmus students going abroad, and a group of British students remaining in the UK on how far they considered themselves to be European.[8] Both groups of students were asked identical questions at the start and at the end of the academic year in which the Erasmus students went abroad.

Sigalas's results complicate the idea that mobility generates positive sentiments. He found no evidence that any group became more supportive of further European integration, and Erasmus students who came to the UK actually became less proud of being European. The British students who went abroad did show greater attachment to Europe, increased contentment with British membership of the European Union, and more positive attitudes to other Europeans, but confusingly some of these changes were echoed by the control group for no obvious reason (Sigalas 2008: 188–90).[9] The fact that such a well-designed study gathered such ambiguous results should give us cause to be skeptical about the impact of international mobility.

Of all the previous studies of mobile students' political development, Sigalas's comes closest to meeting Teichler and Maiworm's (1997: 24) criteria for an "ideal" study of whether exchange participants' political views are altered by the experience. However, it focuses on a relatively narrow set of attitudes. Sigalas's aim was primarily to find out whether the Erasmus program generates pro-European sentiment, and he paid less attention to the broader diplomatic agenda of using mobility to promote national diplomatic agendas. As a result, the questionnaire was also very obviously focused on Europe, possibly making respondents who had just returned from abroad aware of which responses were expected. Sigalas did not attempt to link changes in attitudes to changes in behavior, and did not follow students for more than a few weeks after their return. My new study (which actually overlapped with Sigalas's) is both broader and considers the experience of going abroad within its longer-term context.

Sigalas's timing was constrained by circumstances, which was unfortunate because past work on student mobility, in particular, shows that international students' attitudes fluctuate significantly over time (presumably this is also true of other mobile groups, but existing research has focused on students). Sigalas had to distribute many of his first-wave questionnaires in September or October, when Erasmus students had already arrived in the host country. By this time they might already have had important socializing experiences and almost certainly would have spent part of their summer educating themselves about circumstances in the host country. This might well have influenced their pretest responses. Many of the second-wave questionnaires were completed immediately when the students returned home (Sigalas 2008: 140–2). Distributing surveys so soon afterward may produce results which do not represent the longer-term settling of students' attitudes, because the "U-curve" hypothesis suggests that students' attitudes are likely to fluctuate erratically immediately after returning from abroad (Klineberg 1981: 125, Useem and Useem 1967).

The "U-curve" hypothesis was first identified by DuBois in 1953 (Klineberg 1981: 125), but has been greatly elaborated by in-depth interviews with international students (see Useem and Useem 1967). The original hypothesis was that students' attitudes to a host country tend to change in a predictable pattern: initial euphoria at the new environment is soon overtaken by disillusionment at the practical problems they encounter, but attitudes then become more positive again as the students start to feel at home in their new environment. It is at this point, in most cases, when they are sent back to their home country. The U-curve has been revisited several times (Murphy-Lejeune 2002) and refined into a W-curve in which students experience a second, less dramatic but still pronounced U when they return to their home countries. Importantly, the W-curve implies that students' responses immediately after they return home will not reflect the long-term impact on them—attitudes take some time to settle. Ideally, panel studies should take this into account when timing the questionnaires.

One further lesson from past work is that students' experiences while abroad will affect how their responses change. Not everyone who crosses a given border has the same experiences. Salter and Teger's very small (1975) panel study of American students visiting Europe led them to hypothesize a "generalization of affect" when they found that 13 students who spent nine weeks of their vacation on construction work alongside locals developed negative attitudes, while 22 (rather more fortunate) classmates who traveled comfortably as tourists developed more positive attitudes. While Salter and Teger's study was probably too small to allow for much generalization, and in any case a nine-week visit is very different from living in a country long-term, the generalization of affect seems intuitively plausible. Marion (1974, 1980) goes further. His panel of ninety students taking part in the University of Colorado's study abroad program was uncontrolled, but in any case the students' responses showed little net change. Rather than simply accept this, however, Marion then split the students into groups which proved resistant and susceptible to change. Although the sample as a whole showed little change, he found that there was a pattern of change concentrated among the students who had the most intense interactions with host nationals. Marion's work has important implications for my research design, and so I will be discussing the details when we consider diversity in Erasmus students' experiences (Chapter 6).

In summary, there is still a lot we do not know about the political impact of international mobility. The net effect of mobility on large groups seems to be crucial to governments' expectations, but many studies suffer from design problems which mean that they cannot really detect net changes. Studies that are better designed tend to show ambiguous results. The U-curve suggests that we will get more reliable results if we can compare travelers with controls well before they leave their home countries and well after they return. If only some visitors consistently show attitude changes, it may be possible to isolate them from their less affected peers.

In response, I have conducted a rigorous new empirical study.

4

How Can We Detect Short-Term Impact (and What Does That Mean)?

Mobility programs rarely attract established elites: top decision-makers are rarely able to take extended breaks from their high-profile jobs. Instead, they try to select *future* elites, relatively young professionals with promising trajectories (which explains why so many programs target top-performing students). For this to work, mobility would need to have a long-term and enduring impact.

Unfortunately long-term effects, by definition, cannot be observed for a long time. I have shown that before-and-after measurements are much more reliable than retrospective questioning, but obviously it was not practical to wait for decades between rounds of surveys. Instead, I combined two types of evidence. In Chapter 8 I discuss retrospective interviews with mature decision-makers who went abroad decades earlier. However, given the evidence that retrospective reports may be distorted in various ways, it would be dangerous to rely on these reports alone.

This chapter considers the shorter-term impact of studying abroad. Although we cannot assume that short-term change is enduring, it seems unlikely that longer-term impact would not be preceded by changes while abroad or soon after returning home. It is based on before-and-after surveys of students from France, Sweden and the United Kingdom who received Erasmus grants to study abroad during the 2007-8 academic year. I will follow this by reporting on my interviews with some of these Erasmus students, examining the interaction between their experiences while abroad and the development of their views, on the premise that students who share certain experiences may alter their views while others do not. While the surveys address the question of net impact, the interviews provide qualitative depth.

My Surveys

We need to know more about this net effect of mobility on political attitudes and behavior over the relatively short term—between going abroad and a few months after returning. To do so, I ran a small pilot survey of fully funded postgraduate students in 2006–7, and followed this with a larger panel of students on the European Union's Erasmus program in 2007–8. After both of these I selected some of the participants for in-depth interviews.

Pilot

The pilot was on a relatively small scale, but recruited from an elite group funded for overtly political reasons. These capital-intensive programs tend to support relatively small numbers (and, of course, participation in the surveys was far from 100 percent) but, on the other hand, the political ambitions attached to them are explicit.

I recruited Marshall Scholars coming to Britain from the United States, as well as German students funded to study in the UK and British students funded to study in Germany by the German Academic Exchange Service (DAAD). Both of these are highly selective scholarship schemes, which pay for the tuition and living costs of relatively small numbers of high performers seeking postgraduate degrees abroad. To make sure that any change was linked to living abroad, I recruited a control group made up of fully-funded postgraduate students at the Universities of Pennsylvania, Leeds and York, and a selection of advanced students at German universities approached directly through a social networking site.

The pilot did not show a pattern of significant change among the groups who went abroad relative to those who remained in their home countries. I have included more detail of the pilot surveys and their results in an online report (Appendix One). These results should not be taken as evidence against the opinion-leader model, as there are several reasons why the pilot might not have shown much change—even if mobility usually does change attitudes. The sample size was relatively small, with only 26 respondents completing both before-and-after surveys. Only 13 of the mobile scholars and 11 controls answered most of the questions. This makes it difficult to draw meaningful conclusions. The surveys could have been underpowered, so even if there had been changes in the response pattern the small number of cases would prevent a statistical analysis from revealing this. However, this hardly means that the pilot was not valuable. My plan had always been to interview some of the participants before the main survey began in 2007, which meant that the pilot had to be terminated prematurely in spring 2007 to give me time to analyze the feedback and interviews before the larger panel began. This is problematic given what we know about U-curves in attitudes—the pilot groups might not have settled on their final trajectory, so even if I had gathered more responses I would still have needed a second panel. The interviews also suggested another possible explanation for the lack of change: many of the students included were quite advanced postgraduate students and often relatively old. They may have had more mature political attitudes than the typical participant in a mobility program, and so may have been less likely to alter their attitude in response to new environments.

The interviews gave richer qualitative data than I could obtain from the survey results. They helped to identify significant aspects of the students' experience missed by the questionnaire as well as to refine hypotheses, particularly about aspects of such students' lifestyles that might have a significant impact on their socialization, for use in future rounds. The interviews also provided an opportunity to explore the questions which related specifically to the host country (the second page of the survey), the results for which could not be subjected to meaningful statistical analysis because very few responses were received on those questions.

The numbers eventually interviewed were very small—only three students who expressed willingness proved eligible to take part, with several others ruled out because they had not submitted a full set of questionnaires. However, the interviews proved very useful, particularly when backed by survey results which reminded the respondents of how they had felt a year earlier. Although the pilot was not terribly helpful for drawing conclusions about the net effect on a group, the open responses to the survey and subsequent interviews suggested several hypotheses about the kinds of political change which we might expect. Interviewees also had interesting ideas about the circumstances in which political change is most likely.

Scholars Had Well-Developed Political Views Before Going Abroad

One striking finding was that all three interviewees had very strong interests in political affairs well before they began their time abroad (DAAD Interview One, Two; Marshall Interview One)—one was willing to state that "it's practically my life in some ways" (Marshall Interview One). While questions about levels of interest in politics coming from an academic interviewer might be seen as normatively loaded, this interest was obviously genuine, with all three interviewees demonstrating a wide-ranging political knowledge in the course of the interviews. It was also consistent with their reported behavior, such as previous work for politically-oriented think tanks (Marshall Interview One) and political activism. At least in the case of the Marshall Scholarships, for which an interest in political affairs seems to have been a significant factor in selection (Marshall Interview One, Two), this should not come as a great surprise. Although the DAAD seems to have selected students primarily on academic performance and potential (DAAD Interview Two), it did seem that the effect, at least in the social sciences, was similar: high academic achievers tend to take an interest in political issues. Both DAAD interviewees came from arts/social science backgrounds, but these also form a major segment of the DAAD's grantees. It seems reasonable to assume that many of the elite grantees recruited by Marshall and the DAAD will have had unusually sophisticated understandings of politics before they were selected for awards.

This interest in political affairs has significant consequences for the research. In one of the interviews, the interviewee even explicitly suggested (without direct prompting) that the politically-engaged students receiving highly selective scholarships might be less likely to change their attitudes than others simply because they already had strong fixed opinions (Marshall Interview One). All three interviewees had traveled extensively, and two of them pointed to specific examples of experiences which they believed had influenced them more than their current studies: one had spent time in a deprived part of Africa (DAAD Interview One), while the other had been in the Middle East during a military conflict (DAAD Interview Two).

It is quite possible that younger undergraduates would not share these characteristics, so their political attitudes would be more malleable (Scott 1956), and overseas travel (facilitated by a government) might be formative for them in the same way that these interviewees believed their time in Africa and the Middle East had been. This suggested that younger students might experience changes which would not be shared by many participants in the pilot study.

Limited Contact with Host Society (But Plenty with Third-Country Students and Academics)

Another finding also suggested that the students included in the pilot may have been atypical in ways that reduced their susceptibility to attitude changes. It appeared from the interviews that students involved in these programs can have very limited contact with members of the broader host country society. In two cases (Marshall Interview One, DAAD Interview

One) the interviewees struggled to describe a meaningful relationship with any host nationals who were not university students or employees. Both were quite open about this ("my social life kind of revolves around the university"—Marshall Interview One) and implied that this was not unusual for people in their social circles. In the third interview (DAAD Interview Two), the only people mentioned were a few Irish flatmates[1] who worked in Dublin but outside the university. Although one or two of them may have been relatively close acquaintances, none seemed to be close confidantes. A married interviewee (DAAD Interview One) also pointed out that having a family had a dramatic effect on contact with host nationals. It seems plausible that married students, for example, may have less time to socialize with other students or host nationals, or may travel back to their home countries regularly. The students included in the pilot may have been more likely to find themselves in this position because they were relatively mature.

A related feature of the students' social lives, which they seemed to consider typical, was that they had more contact with other students from their home country or third countries (that is, neither the home nor the host country) than with host country nationals. In relatively cosmopolitan university environments it would not be unusual to encounter third-country nationals as housemates and classmates. There was some suggestion that this might have altered their perceptions of those students' home countries.

Following Marion's (1974, 1980) and Selltiz et al.'s (1962, 1963) work, students who have contact with a variety of people from the host country are probably more likely to be changed by going abroad. Although we do not know how much contact the other Marshall and DAAD grantees had with the host population, these findings did emphasize the importance of checking how much contact participants in the larger panel had with the host population (see Chapter 7). After all, many mobility programs fund scholarships, and students may well be the largest beneficiaries of government-sponsored mobility, but universities and colleges can be social bubbles where students and scholars interact almost entirely with each other. If these few interviewees' experiences are typical, it would perhaps not be surprising if academic mobility had little effect on attitudes—scholars can move thousands of miles in space and yet continue to spend their time with much the same kinds of people as they would have had they stayed at home.

At the very least, this pattern of socializing might also (at least partly) explain why I found so little attitude change in the pilot. Mature, well-socialized postgraduates (particularly if they have existing family ties) might be less likely to form links with host nationals.

Information Gains Seemed to Be More Pronounced Than Attitude Changes

Taking the interviews as a whole, one striking theme was that they tended to stress how much knowledge they had gained about the host country, and indeed third countries, rather than how far they had changed their attitudes to it. As one interviewee put it, the experience "refined my political views" (Marshall Interview One) rather than fundamentally altering them, exposing a few existing beliefs as "naïve" due to contact with people who had experienced the reality of life in other countries. Increased knowledge could simply be more obvious to the students involved than subtle changes in their attitudes, so this may not be an entirely accurate reflection of the reality. Nonetheless, the idea that knowledge could increase independent of attitude change—and might have a political impact—is intriguing. Even if no changes in attitude are found, the learning experience of going abroad may in itself have important consequences, a theme reflected in my conversations with founders of the Entente Cordiale Scholarships (see Chapter 2). Interviewees' reports of how going abroad affected them seemed more consistent with the Entente Cordiale aim of increasing knowledge and understanding of the host country than the attitude-change model which seems to have permeated official discourse. Of course, it would not be sensible to generalize from these few interviews alone.

These three interviewees were clearly not a probability sample of the survey respondents. However, it seems very plausible that in some respects their experiences and backgrounds should reflect those of other elite scholarship recipients, who are an unusual group of people. In particular, they tend to be high academic achievers, relatively mature, and have spent much of their adult lives in universities debating social issues. It would not be surprising if going abroad had less impact on their political views than on the views of other students, or soldiers, schoolteachers, police officers, physicians, or any of the other groups who can receive funding to live abroad. Accordingly, the next phase of the project tested a sample of younger, less elite, perhaps less politically- engaged, primarily undergraduate exchange students.

The pilot informed this study in many ways. I took some care to broaden the classic approach of seeking changes in attitudes, adding in questions which would reflect changes in behavior and increased knowledge. The pilot also showed that the social experience of mobility is much more complex than simply *being* abroad: we need to know how people actually live once they are there.

Tracking Erasmus Students

The 2007–8 survey followed (as its treatment group) a much larger number of students going abroad under the auspices of the European Union's Erasmus Program, who received partial funding in mobility grants from the Union. Erasmus helps European students to spend part of their course attending universities or colleges in other European Union member states.

This might seem an odd choice. Not only is Erasmus dominated by undergraduate students, while mobility programs include a range of different backgrounds, but it is normally presented as an educational program rather than a diplomatic tool. Again, conventional wisdom is deceptive. Erasmus does have a political objective, albeit an unusual one, and its sheer size means that it draws in a wide variety of Europeans.

Erasmus as a Political Project

Erasmus has an unusual design. While fundamentally it is a network of bilateral exchanges between European universities, the funding—over €450 million in 2013 (European Commission 2013)—is not provided by national governments. Instead, the money comes from the European Commission, the executive branch of a supranational organization of which most (but not all[2]) of the countries whose universities and colleges take part are members. Erasmus students are different from the elite scholarship holders involved in the pilot. The vast majority of Erasmus grants are given to undergraduates who are spending a year abroad as part of a degree course in their home country, and they generally receive a relatively small grant which only partially covers their living expenses (Boomans et al. 2008). Grants ranged from €275 to €375 per month in 2013, with one-off mobility grants of up to €900 available to some students; there is also an arrangement for offsetting tuition fees in the countries which charge them (British Council 2013). This is a substantial amount of money (especially within a student budget!) but probably not enough to cover the entire cost of a year's study. Instead, the key to Erasmus is that the Union guarantees that assessments those students pass while they are abroad will be accepted as contributing to qualifications from their home institution.

Clearly, Erasmus is intended to attract mass participation, rather than a small number of likely future elites who are expected to wield unusual influence in the future. The comparatively huge numbers of students taking part every year (Corbett and Footitt 2001: ix) made it easier to recruit a sufficiently large sample to allow for a solid statistical analysis. The program provides very visible benefits to Europe's universities. But Erasmus is funded as part of a political agenda, which extends back to the early days of idealism about European unity and can be interpreted through an opinion-leader model.

There are many possible explanations for the EU's support of student mobility, not all of which are political. Different analyses prioritize different explanations, and the Commission has tended to stress the educational and economic benefits of Erasmus in its publicity. If political objectives are not the most important, then on one level this does not make Erasmus an irrelevant case: whether or not participants are influenced is still relevant to the broader question of how mobility changes attitudes. On the other hand, how far Erasmus is intended to alter attitudes (and if so, how and to what) is an interesting question in itself. In my view, the evidence suggests that political change is a primary objective, but the changes in how officials rationalize Erasmus over time tell us a lot about the EU—and probably about public policy making more broadly (Corbett 2005, Wilson 2011).

One established strand of argument holds that Erasmus is designed to foster a sense of European identity among participants, and so it contributes to support for common European institutions. Petit (2007) identifies three schools of thought on what drives European integration: the intergovernmentalist, the neofunctionalist, and an unnamed position I will call the supranationalist that she herself endorses in respect of European education policy.

Put simply, or even simplistically, the intergovernmentalist position holds that the governments of member states encourage the transfer of competencies to the European Union when it serves their own national interests to do so. National officials have problems, and see the EU as part of a solution.

The neofunctionalist position holds that the European Union acquires powers over certain policy areas because of a "spillover" effect: in order to effectively implement one policy at Union level, other related policies in different areas need to be coordinated at Union level. The Union grew out of a project which shared coal and steel production between a few of the early member states. We might explain European integration as spreading from one policy area to another, as integrating any sector resulted in problems that could only be solved by further integration. For example, cooperation on coal and steel production would eventually affect transport (the products had to be moved on standardized tracks) workers' welfare, competition policy, and so on.

In education policy both of these approaches would seem to predict fairly similar outcomes in many situations (although the explanation for why things happen may well be different). For example, once the member states had agreed that a single market was in their interests, they had to concede that free movement of labor within Europe would help the market to operate efficiently. The spillover effect in education was that in order for professional workers to move freely there had to be recognition of their qualifications in other EU countries. Pressure for comparable education systems, and hence qualifications, across the continent was a driving force in the increasing standardization which has led to the Bologna Process of convergence in degree schemes across Europe. Alternatively, member states may have been more interested in their universities' international competitiveness, given increasing competition for academic talent from North America married to a belief that higher education can solve economic and social problems (see e.g. Teichler 2004: 19, 22). However, the supranationalist position would be that education policy has been steered purposefully in a direction which is likely to encourage the development of a European identity among its citizens, much as national consciousness is promoted partly through universal education in a classic nation-building process (Anderson 2006, Petit 2007: 4–7). This argument seems to imply that there is a conscious desire to forge a European national identity somewhere within the European policy-making process. Certainly, former policy-makers have enthused about a role for higher education as "one of the key elements in European integration" (Neave 1991: 37).

These positions do not seem to be either contradictory or mutually exclusive, and it may well be that all are involved to greater or lesser degrees at various points in the policy-making process. The complex coalition-building and bureaucratic maneuvering required to pass a policy through the European Union's system of checks and balances can provide incentives to relabel objectives, presenting a program as being intended to do different things depending on what is politically palatable at the time. The process which ultimately led to the emergence of Erasmus in its current form has taken several decades, during which there have been many changes in the personnel involved; different officials have been committed to student mobility for different reasons (Corbett 2005). However, the implications of a supranationalist position for understanding how the Erasmus Program is expected to impact on students taking part would seem to be different from those of an intergovernmentalist or neofunctionalist account. A supranationalist position alone would suggest that one objective of Erasmus is to create a sense of being "European" rather than bearing only a national identity. Simply spreading good practice between universities and supporting the pragmatic mobility implied by the common market are rather more prosaic—if worthy—aims.

One myth about the Erasmus Program is that it was created entirely in response to legal rulings (Adia 1998 Ch. 4, Sprokkereef 1995: 341–3). In particular, it is very tempting to portray Erasmus as an attempt to blunt the impact of the European Court of Justice ruling on the case of *Gravier* vs. *City of Liège* (European Court of Justice 1985). This story initially appears to support the view that a European dimension in education was promoted by the neofunctionalist concept of "competency creep"—the gradual acquisition of broader and broader powers by supranational components of the EU, such as the Commission—when maintaining national control over non-vocational education proved legally unsustainable. This was established in a succession of legal precedents (Gould 1989), all of which have roots in the *Gravier* ruling. Gravier, a French student taking a course in cartoon drawing at a college in Liège (in neighboring Belgium) protested at being charged a special fee applied to all non-Belgians studying in the country's public educational institutions. Previous European treaties had established that mobile European nationals had to be granted equal access to vocational *training* by other member states as a complement to the single market in labor (Sprokkereef 1995: 340-1) but national governments had not been keen to relinquish control over *education* (Neave 1991: 37). Was a course in cartoon drawing vocational? In the *Gravier* case, the Court of Justice adopted such an expansive definition of "vocational training" that almost all tertiary education could be included, preventing discriminatory fees from being charged to nationals of other European countries. One interpretation is that Erasmus was an attempt by national governments to divert the massive free (non-exchange) movement of students across borders into less controversial controlled exchange schemes.

However, recent research shows that the chronology of European education policy is not compatible with the notion that the *Gravier* ruling caused Erasmus (although it may well have catalyzed the process). Much of the groundwork for such a scheme had already been laid by 1985 and had captured many powerful imaginations within the European Commission (the EU's executive bureaucracy). Senior officials were seeking a convenient opportunity to expand existing (relatively small-scale) mobility schemes. While the *Gravier* ruling may have helped weaken opposition from national governments to large-scale student exchange mobility within Europe, there was already pressure for a scheme on the model of Erasmus long before the *Gravier* judgment, which was more significant (Cheiladaki-Liarokapi 2007: 18–20, Corbett 2003: 178–9). The Court of Justice decision should not be seen as the ultimate cause. Rather, it provided a convenient tool for actors who already supported the policy to fend off opponents. Their motives are important.

In fact, recent research on the origins of Erasmus includes several strands of circumstantial evidence consistent with a supranationalist position. Three stand out.

First, there is clearly a desire within the European Commission to help to form a European consciousness, expressed explicitly in the movement for a "People's Europe" in the early 1980s, but probably going back further (Adia 1998: Ch. 4, Papatsiba 2005: 175). The Commission freely advertises that "One of the main objectives of the European Union is to introduce European citizenship" (European Commission 2001: 9). Furthermore, this concept of citizenship does appear to be conceived in terms of particular shared European attitudes, rather than simply the holding of common legal rights. The Commission funds regular Eurobarometer surveys which focus on issues of European supranational identity, continuously monitoring Europeans' loyalties. This long-running survey of European public opinion pays particular attention to how far people show traits of European citizenship, including belief in a common European culture and identity (Eurobarometer 2008, European Commission 2001: 10–2).

Second, a hope among some European policy makers that Erasmus could endow its alumni with a sense of European identity (or at least a willingness to cross borders within Europe) seems to have been one of several factors driving its creation (Corbett 2005: Ch. 9, Neave 1991: 38). There are many possible justifications for the Commission to support Erasmus. In her review, Papatsiba has identified four broad groups of arguments: two are economic, one narrowly educational, and one directly related to supranational consciousness. The economic arguments link Erasmus to European prosperity. Erasmus might help alumni themselves cross intra-European borders during their future careers, lubricating the common European labor market. Mobility could also allow the transfer of skills, techniques, and technology within Europe dynamizing the economy. The educational case is that international mobility helps students to acquire such personal characteristics as independence and intercultural sensitivity. The supranationalist argument, of course, is that mobility contributes to a sense of European identity, and ultimately leads alumni to calculate costs and benefits in European terms, rather than evaluating all political issues in terms of national interest (Papatsiba 2005: 174).

The supranationalist idea was not exactly kept secret from member states, but there may have been some diplomatic discretion given the ever-present controversy about creation of a "European superstate" in certain countries. At times the construction of a European consciousness has featured prominently in European discourse, and has been closely tied to mobility. The *Adonnino Report* on the creation of a "People's Europe," which preceded the expansion of existing exchange programs into Erasmus by only a few months, listed identity at the top of its arguments for an expansion of exchange schemes:

Action at Community level to encourage exchanges of young people between different Member States helps to promote the identity of Europe for young Europeans. (Committee on a People's Europe 1985: 5–8)

While the four categories have fluctuated, the political dimension of Erasmus has generally been given less emphasis than the economic case (Papatsiba 2005: 184) in the Commission's official documents. If it is genuinely of secondary importance then this does not undermine my suggestion that Erasmus can be judged, in part, on its contribution to feelings of "Europeanness"—but in any case there are grounds for believing that this secondary position in official publications does not reflect its relative importance to many of the policy makers involved. There are grounds to believe that the original rationale for Erasmus was to support integration (ESN Interview) but the scheme was "re-branded" and economic rationales were emphasized later in the process for reasons of political expediency (Corbett 2003: 182). In the economic climate in which Erasmus had to operate in its early years, it made strategic sense for personnel who aimed to increase student mobility in Europe—regardless of their motives—to tap the anxieties of political elites about Europe's economic decline relative to other major powers. By contrast, talking about Europe as a political project has provoked resistance in the past. Presenting Erasmus as a tool for building European unity is unlikely to be the path of least resistance for officials seeking finance.

Reviewing European education policy as a whole, Corbett (2003, 2005) has identified several "policy entrepreneurs" within the Commission who came to their roles with the view that a pan-European education policy was desirable, even while member state governments were more skeptical. In the early years of European integration this was generally a product of wartime experiences and hopes for reconciliation (Corbett 2003: 158–61) but even in more recent times several key players have been motivated by a desire to instill a concept of European solidarity in the next generation—perhaps reflecting their own pro-European sentiments (2003: 175–6, 184–5). These individuals, given their existing commitment to European cooperation in education, were advocates for educational initiatives including student mobility and were willing, on occasion, to promote educational initiatives as solutions to other problems posed to them.[3] There is at least a strong circumstantial case that the promotion of European identity among young elites was a primary concern (Papatsiba 2005: 177). Desire to promote supranationalist sentiment certainly appears to have been one factor driving the process which eventually led to Erasmus, even if the more politically-palatable objective of increasing the efficiency of the European labor market has dominated the official publications. From the perspective of the policy entrepreneurs, a shift in the views of Erasmus students toward favoring integration and an increased sense of their own identity as Europeans would presumably fulfill many of their ambitions.

Not only have leading figures in forming European education policies had supranationalist ideas, but there seems to be a continuing consciousness that Erasmus may be contributing to the formation of a European identity. The team responsible for coordinating Erasmus and the EU's other educational mobility programs is housed within the European Education, Audiovisual, and Culture Executive Agency, which is also the agency responsible for promoting European citizenship (EACEA 2008). The parallel Directorate-General within the European Commission itself also combines responsibility for Erasmus with responsibility for European citizenship and lists as its mission:

> To reinforce and promote lifelong learning, linguistic and cultural diversity, mobility and the engagement of European citizens, in particular the young. (European Commission 2008)

Erasmus students are, unknowingly, taking part in an experiment in shaping political loyalties. This experiment is based on an assumption that helping them to live in another European country will influence their attitudes to the European project. But while Erasmus has a distinctive political agenda, it is still founded on mobility between pairs of countries. If mobility changes attitudes, we should be able to see changes in Erasmus students too.

The Erasmus Panel

I set out to recruit a sample of Erasmus students who would help me test these ideas. Again, the basic research design selected a group of students who were going abroad thanks to Erasmus. I asked them to complete a survey at the start of their time abroad and then to complete another, almost identical, survey on their return. To ensure that I was not just picking up the effects of these students becoming older and more mature, I also recruited students who remained in their home countries and asked them to complete surveys at the start and at the end of the academic year. The surveys were made available online using the Bristol Online Survey project's software and servers (Bristol Online Surveys 2013), and students were recruited by sending them emails with links to the appropriate survey page. I produced several different copies of the survey, some in English, others in French, so that Erasmus and control students from different countries could be identified.

Recruiting Erasmus Students

Erasmus is a huge network of bilateral exchanges between more than 4,000 universities and colleges in 33 countries (European Commission 2013). It would not be possible to survey all of them. My research strategy was based on inviting Erasmus students to complete online surveys, which required some means of getting email messages to them. As there is no central database of email addresses (and even if one existed, actually using it would raise ethical issues) my research strategy relied on institutional gatekeepers—the administrators of individual exchanges—to help me distribute emails which directed students to my surveys. Securing their cooperation and sustaining good relations took some time. It would not have been practical to include students from all the countries involved.

I drew samples of participants in the Erasmus program[4] from three countries: the United Kingdom, France and Sweden. Gaining cooperation from gatekeepers within universities was one of the most challenging aspects of this research. I already had promises of help from British universities, and France was Britain's largest partner within Erasmus. At the time, movement between Britain and France was among the largest streams within Erasmus, with France hosting 2,146 periods of study by British students, while French students spent 4,567 in the UK[5] (Socrates Erasmus Council 2007). I was also looking for pairs of countries whose inhabitants showed different patterns of responses to survey questions on social attitudes, and responses to the most recent round of the European Social Survey had shown that residents of the two countries differed on several important attitudes (ESS 2007).

I wanted to increase the size of the sample, and also get a sense of whether British students going to France might be in some way atypical. The easiest way to do so was to ask Erasmus coordinators in British universities with which I had already established relationships to send emails to students going to another country. According to the Socrates Erasmus Council figures (2007) Spain was the second most popular destination for British students, attracting 1,654 study periods in 2004-5, and therefore seemed a sensible second choice target. Germany, incidentally, was the second largest source country for Erasmus students in Britain (3,089), but I had problems finding a German university willing to cooperate.

I arranged to include Swedish students coming to Britain later in the process in order to boost the numbers of survey respondents and diversify the samples. The agency coordinating Sweden's Erasmus effort was willing to cooperate, and it was possible to recruit a control group at the University of Linköping. Sweden, incidentally, had a helpful practical advantage, since significant numbers of students understand English well enough to follow the questionnaire without another translation of the survey. While I would have translated if necessary, this could potentially have introduced translation error and, of course, would have taken up extra time and resources.

Recruiting Control Students

Once the countries from which Erasmus students were to be drawn had been selected, controls had to be recruited from the same countries. These were students and scholars who did not take part in Erasmus, and including them allowed me to be sure that any changes I found in the Erasmus students were genuinely caused by going abroad. Based on my past experience with the pilot and other studies which had tried similar approaches (e.g. Lazenby-Taylor 2005), I was confident that this could be done relatively easily in British universities, but unfortunately recruiting suitable controls in other countries proved to be tricky.

United Kingdom
I recruited a control group of students who continued their studies at British universities in the 2007–8 academic year by forwarding invitation emails to students at the Universities of Reading and Leeds. These institutions were chosen because they had been large contributors to the Erasmus Program in previous years, and they seemed likely to have student bodies relatively typical of British universities as a whole. Their campus atmospheres have not been particularly politically-polarized and they do not have a reputation for being hotbeds of radical activism. Like most of the major Erasmus contributors they are fairly selective in their student intake, but they are not extremely elite institutions.

No Erasmus students from either of these universities were included in the survey. This was partly in order to avoid potential confusion if there were to be any students eligible for the control as well as the treatment group, but also to minimize the possibilities for treatment and control students to come into contact with each other. The responses of the control group might be affected if they were aware of being controls in a project primarily targeting Erasmus students. Given that most British Erasmus students who are not language specialists go abroad during the second year of their degrees (third year in Scotland) the survey was targeted at students who were approaching the end of their first year.[6]

Sweden
Sweden has relatively few higher education institutions and most of them were called before settling on the University of Linköping, which was the

only institution willing to cooperate. While the university would not pass on messages to their students, administrators were willing to sell a sample of email addresses. This was unexpected, but I did purchase paper copies of the email addresses of around 1,000 first-year students at the university and used them to send invitation emails to a random sample on the survey start date. Having contact details for so many students locked in my desk raised obvious confidentiality concerns, so I destroyed them soon afterwards. While Linköping was chosen largely due to these practical constraints, it seemed likely to be reasonably representative of Swedish universities. Linköping is a selective but not elite institution, situated in a medium-sized city roughly in the centre of the more populous southern part of Sweden, and there is no reason to believe that the political atmosphere was particularly extreme.

France
Recruiting a suitable control group in France proved much more difficult. At the time, it seemed that many French universities did not provide email addresses to students in the same way as their British and Swedish counterparts. Academic departments seemed not to keep email lists and suggested calling central administration; the administrative departments were generally unwilling to cooperate. Conversations with numerous French universities suggested that recruiting a control group in this way was unlikely to succeed. Somewhat reluctantly, as the deadline for the survey approached I had to resort to a more creative approach—using a social networking site to recruit controls.

To do this, I used the StudiQG.fr website to distribute personal messages modeled on the invitation emails to randomly-selected students at a range of French universities. StudiQG.fr was a networking site which linked social acquaintances, and vaguely resembled the much better-known Facebook.com in its design. The key difference was that StudiQG.fr specialized in French students. The network had members at a range of French universities, and it was possible to estimate how far they had progressed into their degree from personal information provided in their profiles. I randomly selected students who appeared to be second- or third-year undergraduates at several different French universities (using the characters of their surnames) as French students tended to take Erasmus periods after spending two or three years at their home universities.[7] Each of the students had to be contacted individually through their personal profile, and it was simple to check on other aspects of their identities before including them in the sample. For example, StudiQG users who appeared to be staff or foreign students studying in France were excluded (StudiQG was a subsidiary of the more popular German StudiVZ.net, and so some users seemed to be German visitors who had transferred their accounts). Students who appeared to be future Erasmus students would often have joined user groups referring to this, and so could be excluded from the control group.

By creating a blank StudiQG profile for myself, which gave no information about me beyond what I provided in the cover letter to the other groups of participants, I was able to send individual messages to other users. This meant I could recruit enough French students using StudiQG to provide a feasible control group, although there were significant trade-offs involved.

Advantages and disadvantages of recruiting through a social networking site

To the best of my knowledge, social networking sites have not as yet been used to systematically recruit survey participants in quite this way in major academic studies. The approach does raise several methodological issues, which may well become important in the future as social networking sites expand and perhaps become more tempting targets for researchers. My experience suggests that it is possible to recruit in this way, but there are several significant disadvantages.

Social networking sites do have several advantages over traditional means of recruiting survey participants. Most obviously, users are likely to advertise much more information about themselves than can be obtained from more conventional sampling frames. A typical StudiQG page was likely to include personal details such as the owner's name, date of birth, nationality, hometown, sex, university, how long the owner has been enrolled there and subject of study (as well as a photograph). Many users also chose to advertise facts such as their relationship status, interests, taste in literature, part-time jobs and, potentially interesting to researchers, a simple description of their political views (in terms of "left," "right," "green," and so on). The site also allowed members to join interest groups and identify their "friends," whose locations are advertised. This feature helped to identify some students who had previously studied abroad and would not, therefore, make suitable controls. A less obvious but perhaps more important benefit of StudiQG as a sampling frame was that (to some extent) it verified the profile owner's identity, because it was only possible to obtain a profile using an email address issued by a higher education institution.[8] Access to institutional email accounts is generally closely controlled and available only to individual students, so it is reasonable to assume that the respondents were registered at an appropriate college or university. In this respect, it is possible to be much more certain of the respondent's identity than when distributing surveys through the postal system, for example, in which case forms might be collected by anyone sharing an address. StudiQG was used across France, so the controls were not all recruited from one (possibly atypical) institution.

From my point of view, however, the site simply offered one of the few legal means of contacting selected students by email (or a messaging system very similar to email) which did not require the cooperation of a "gatekeeper" working in a university. With all the other groups in the pilot study, messages had to be forwarded to students by an administrator in a funding body or a university. In France it was simply impossible to find a cooperative gatekeeper willing to forward emails to students. Removing the gatekeeper from the process gave me much more control over the distribution and timing of the survey.

There are, however, several disadvantages to recruiting respondents in this way.

Although profile owners' institutional affiliations can be known with some certainty, there are no checks on any other information they choose to display about themselves. While most of the information made available is probably true, there is no way to confirm this other than by checking individual profiles and forming a judgment about whether the contents are plausible. It is also unlikely that the owners of StudiQG profiles were representative of the broader French population, or even French students, a serious problem for any study attempting to draw cross-sectional conclusions about a broader population. However, the fact that the respondents were not representative of the broader population did not prevent them from being useful in this study, as I was interested in *change* in views and behavior. Finally, StudiQG was designed to prevent large numbers of unsolicited messages from being sent through its system, and various safeguards were in place to prevent messages from being copied to multiple users. This meant that an individual message had to be written to each user invited to take part, which was labor-intensive.

I had experimented with social networking sites for recruitment before, using a similar strategy to invite a few German students to take part in the pilot. The experience had not been encouraging, which was part of the reason for my hesitancy about using StudiQG for French students. The German students I contacted through a networking site in the pilot had a low response rate even for an online survey, with 212 invitations yielding only 13 completed first-round surveys (Hewson et al. 2003: 82–3). They proved even less likely to complete a second questionnaire, with all of 13 dropping out over the year. Attrition was also unusually high for French control-group students in the main study, with 52 students completing the first-round questionnaire in 2007, and only 20 completing the follow-up in 2008. While this was enough for a viable statistical analysis, the process was difficult and unpredictable.

Ethics
Although my activities were perfectly compatible with the sites' regulations, there are a few ethical issues surrounding this strategy. The sites are not intended as venues for surveying and the invitations are, ultimately, unsolicited messages which can be perceived as inappropriate in internet "culture" (Bryman 2004: 484). Two of the students who received invitations replied to express their disapproval. However, sending unsolicited messages in some form is part of almost all survey-based research designs, and is considered ethically justifiable within the academic community—provided that the research is worthwhile. It is not obvious that sending messages through, for example, StudiQG is more disruptive than sending questionnaires by post, which is commonplace. There are familiar issues about the sheer volume of unsolicited email received by the average internet user, but this tends to be a problem with messages delivered directly to email accounts, usually automated emails copied randomly to millions of addresses. StudiQG's internal system was largely free of such messages, and given the labor required to send a hundred or so individual messages, it seems unlikely that mass messaging will become a significant problem. The fact that most internet users are so used to ignoring unwanted emails might well help them to ignore unwanted survey invitations sent through social networks. The barriers to recruiting in this way are largely practical rather than ethical.

Timing

Panel studies like this need to be timed quite carefully. We know from the existing literature that there can be a period of extreme attitude fluctuation (the "W-curve") immediately after students return to their home countries. Foreign students arriving in universities have been known to form bonds with the host country, which can affect their attitudes surprisingly soon after their arrival, and so the first round was sent out before they arrived (Selltiz et al. 1963: 195–8). Accordingly, invitations to complete the two questionnaires were actually distributed at the end of the 2006–7 and beginning of the 2008–9 academic years. The start and end dates were the 8th of May and the 8th of July 2007 for the first questionnaire, and the 1st of October and 30th of November 2008 for the second. The one exception was the distribution of the first questionnaire to British students studying in Spain, who were added in during the data collection window: their invitations went out on the 23rd of May and the close date, the 24th of July, was later to compensate for this. "Thank-you" notes, which would also have served as reminders, went out on the 20th of June 2007. This meant that data collection in both the 2007 and 2008 rounds extended for exactly two months, with submissions accepted between the 8th of May and 8th of July 2007, and 1st of October and 30th of November 2008. Collecting responses over a relatively long period did raise the possibility that some event might have occurred during the two-month window which affected respondents' attitudes, but this does not seem to have been a major problem.

Completion time

Survey responses were being accepted over the course of two months in both 2007 and 2008. One possible threat to the validity of the data collected was that during these relatively extended periods of data collection other environmental influences might have affected respondents' views. If changes in the environment were influencing attitudes, this may have led to responses collected toward the end of the data collection period being systematically different from those collected at the beginning, generating a spurious relationship.

Dramatic political events affect the political views of informed citizens. In the spring of 2007 there was no one obvious factor which might have been affecting respondents' views. Data collection in 2008, however, coincided with a period of significant turmoil in the global economy, transition from a period of sustained economic boom to the apparent beginning of a major recession, and major government interventions in private industry—including the effective nationalization of several private banks. This affected public opinion (Pew Research Centre 2008). The future economic prospects of students expecting to graduate in the next year or so had suddenly became significantly less secure during the data collection period, which might have increased (or indeed decreased) their support for government intervention in the economy.

I checked whether respondents who completed the survey later in the data collection period differed from those who completed it at beginning on several variables for which this was particular concern. These considered economic affairs and the government's role in the economy. For each of these variables I computed a 'difference' variable by subtracting the scores in 2007 from scores in 2008, and used a Pearson correlation to test whether the changes over the year correlated with time taken to submit a completed survey in 2008.

The correlations were:

"How far do you agree or disagree with the following statements? Government should take measures to reduce differences in income levels" correlation of .076, 2-tailed Sig = .263.

"How far do you agree or disagree with the following statements? When jobs are scarce, employers should give priority to citizens over immigrants" correlation of -.028, 2-tailed Sig = .678.

"In terms of political matters people talk of "left" and "right." How would you place yourself in comparison to most people in your (home) country?" correlation of .051, 2-tailed Sig = .478.

None of these was close to the .05 significance threshold at which I would be concerned, so I concluded that how long respondents took to complete the survey did not distort the pattern.

Analysis

For the first round, invitations to complete the questionnaires were distributed to the gatekeepers for all British and Swedish students and the French Erasmus students and, judging from the timing of responses, they seem to have been passed on quickly. French controls were contacted directly using StudiQG.fr messages. For the second round, in 2008, I contacted students directly using email addresses they had provided in 2007. With the second round I was anxious to maximize response rate, and was no longer dependent on gatekeepers, so respondents who did not complete the questionnaire within a few days of this email were sent a series of reminders. For each of the reminder emails, a sentence was added at the end giving the reminder email's number out of five (e.g. "This is the second reminder of five") to emphasize that they would continue to receive reminder emails until they completed the survey. I also promised to enter all respondents into a prize draw for £100, €125, or SEK1200 as appropriate. To sum up, respondents to the first round were exhorted to complete the second round with as much urgency as I thought I could justify.

Attrition

Despite all these attempts to maximize the response rate for the second wave, this survey suffered considerable attrition between 2007 and 2008. Overall, only 46.9 percent of the Erasmus students and 54.9 percent of the control students who completed the first questionnaire provided valid responses to the second. However, 99 Erasmus students and 145 controls still completed both questionnaires, which was enough to allow for sensible comparisons between the two groups.

Table One presents the figures.

A small number of Erasmus students who completed both questionnaires were excluded from this table and the analysis because they did not appear to be nationals of the country in which they were studying. For example, they might have been Irish students studying in France who chose to take an Erasmus year in Britain. Given that they would already have had extensive experience of living and studying abroad, Erasmus might have less of an effect on them. However, repeating the analysis with these students included did not affect the overall pattern of results.

Attrition is common in all panel designs and not necessarily cause for concern in itself. Provided that enough respondents complete both questionnaires to allow for a meaningful comparison (i.e. the numbers are large enough to allow for adequate statistical power) it is not unreasonable to simply base the analysis on respondents to the second questionnaire—provided that the drop-outs are similar to the respondents who eventually complete both questionnaires. What would be problematic would be a situation in which different kinds of respondents were more likely to drop out between the rounds. Attrition would bias the results if, for example, respondents to the first round who had less cosmopolitan attitudes were more likely to drop out. It is, of course, impossible to predict directly how those respondents' attitudes might have changed over the course of the year. Given the limited information available, the most I can show is that they did not differ systematically in terms of initial positions or demographic characteristics—and this was generally true. To test for attrition bias, I split the respondents to the first questionnaire into

Table 4.1 Overall attrition, Erasmus panel

	Erasmus Students		
	Number completing 2007 questionnaire	Number completing 2008 questionnaire	Attrition (%)
UK to France	97	56	42.3
UK to Spain	7	3	57.1
France to UK	81	33	59.3
Sweden to UK	26	7	73.1
Total	211	99	53.1
	Control Groups		
	Number completing 2007 questionnaire	Number completing 2008 questionnaire	Attrition (%)
UK	189	113	40.2
France	52	20	61.5
Sweden	23	12	47.8
Total	264	145	45.1

those who did and did not go on to complete the second. I then compared the two groups' responses to the first (2007) questionnaire.[9] For most of the questions, there were not significant differences between respondents who eventually completed both questionnaires and those who completed the 2007 questionnaire but dropped out of the study. Chi^2 tests showed significance values comfortably above the $p = .05$ threshold at which I would have become concerned. This indicates that attrition bias was not a serious problem.

There were two questions which were exceptions to this pattern, in that there did appear to be statistically significant differences between the students who completed both questionnaires and those who completed only the first. These could have been familywise errors. I looked for differential attrition by conducting separate Chi^2 tests on a large number of questions, and each statistical test conducted has a possibility of generating a type I error. A type I error means that the test shows a "significant" relationship when in reality there is none (a false positive). Setting $p = .05$ as the significance threshold, for example, means there is a one-in-twenty chance of a type I error for every test. If the analyst then runs more than twenty tests, as I did, the odds are that at least one "significant" result will show up, even when there is really nothing to be concerned about.[10] Nonetheless, the two questions which did show significant differences were intriguing. One was a question asking respondents to place the political party they support on a left-right spectrum. I am confident that this was a spurious relationship.

The other was a measure of respondents' overall attitude toward the host country. It is plausible that this might be related to whether respondents have the motivation to complete the survey.

Because differential attrition would significantly affect what the survey results mean, I have included attrition diagnostics along with the findings on individual questions.

Method of Analysis

The surveys were designed to detect change in the attitudes and behaviors of exchange students by comparing them with a control group. Most of the questions were asked twice of each respondent. The analysis depends on two independent variables. One indicated whether the student was an Erasmus participant or a control, while the other indicated the time of response, distinguishing between individual respondents' answers in the first questionnaire and the second. Crucially, these were dummy (dichotomous) variables.

Dummy variables are by definition categorical—that is, there were only two possible responses or else multiple possible responses which could not be listed in any meaningful order. This meant I could only use statistical tests which deal with categorical independent variables. For the questions which were asked at both time points, I used two methods of statistical analysis to compare changes in attitudes within the two groups. These were Chi^2 tests and Split-Plot Analyses of Variance.

For some of the questions, students' responses were also categorical (or at a nominal level of measurement). For example, if I was asking whether they agreed or disagreed with a statement, and the responses were "yes" or "no" (or "I don't know"), there is no meaningful way of arranging the possible responses in a meaningful sequence. For these, I calculated the changes in students' responses over the year and then counted the number of exchange and control students who changed their responses over the year. A Chi^2 test simply shows how likely it is that the pattern I found would have occurred by chance if there were really no meaningful pattern of change. A "significant" result on these tests meant that one group was more likely to change than another, and the pattern is highly unlikely to have occurred by chance. I set the probability threshold at $p = .05$, meaning that there would need to be less than a one-in-twenty chance that the pattern could have arisen by chance before I would label it as "significant" divergence between the two groups.

For example, if there is no relationship between whether a student went on exchange and whether their agreement with a statement changed between 2007 and 2008, the same number of exchangees as controls would probably change their responses over the year. If twenty times as many exchangees changed their views as controls, this would be very unlikely to be a coincidence, and the test would show a significant relationship.

Where students' responses were made on a scale, I used the Split-Plot Analysis of Variance (SPANOVA, also known as mixed between-within ANOVA) technique. These were questions to which responses could be arranged in a meaningful order (for example, from "agree most strongly" through degrees of agreement to "neutral," and through degrees of disagreement to "disagree most strongly").[11]

Split-Plot ANOVA divides the data into two groups and then detects convergence or divergence between the group means over time.[12] SPANOVA is used to test three hypotheses for each dependent variable:

1. There is a significant between-groups main effect. This would mean that the mean responses for Erasmus students were significantly different from non-Erasmus students' mean responses in both 2007 and 2008.
2. There is a significant within-groups main effect. The within-group variable was time. A significant result would mean that the mean responses of all students in 2008 were different from their responses in 2007.
3. There is a significant **interaction** effect. The interaction term is crucial to this study because it shows whether the Erasmus students' views changed *relative to* the non-Erasmus controls. If studying abroad were making Erasmus students more pro-European, then we would expect a significant interaction term which represented divergence in the responses of the two groups over the course of the year.

Where I report a significant interaction between time (2007/2008) and group (Erasmus/control) this may well mean that studying abroad led to a change.

Statistical Power

If a test shows a "significant" result, we know that any divergence it detects is unlikely to be due to simple chance. However, we also need to briefly consider the opposite possibility—that my analysis may reveal no divergence in a situation where going abroad really did have an effect.

Statistical power is a measure of how likely a test is to wrongly suggest that the experiment had no effect, when in fact it did (a type II error). Collecting too few responses is the major cause of low power. If the number of cases falls too low there is a risk that the (natural) experiment will be entirely underpowered, without enough cases for an analysis of the results to be meaningful. Low power would indicate a high probability of making a type II error, which in this case would mean concluding that exchangees did not diverge from controls when in fact they did, simply because too few responses were collected.

Fortunately, natural experiments analyzed with Split-Plot ANOVA can score highly on statistical power even with a relatively small number of cases. They certainly need many fewer surveys than the nationally-representative opinion polls with which most political scientists are probably more familiar. I did not need many hundreds of cases to produce adequate power. In a before-and-after design any changes are occurring within the same individuals, which eliminates a great deal of random error and all the sampling error.[13] There are a multitude of factors which could influence individuals' responses besides exchange participation, but most of these are likely to be similar for the same individuals at different times. For example, social class might have influenced several responses to the survey, and it was never directly measured. However, different individuals selected at random are much more likely to differ in social class than an individual respondent in 2008 is to differ from him- or herself in 2007. This makes it reasonable to draw conclusions from much smaller numbers of responses.

My calculations—discussed in the box below—showed that with 99 Erasmus students and 145 control students we can be very confident that SPANOVA tests will be adequately powered. The conventional cut-off is 0.8 (Cohen 1977), meaning we can be 80 percent confident that the tests would detect meaningful divergence between the groups. Here, the statistical power greatly exceeds that level.

Calculating Power

The power of a given experiment can be determined by established formulae based on a combination of the number of observations (survey responses) and the likely *effect size*. For the exchange/time interaction, the effect size represents a standardized measure of how much impact being an exchangee rather than a control had on students' responses. A large expected effect size is associated with high power, because dramatic changes are more likely to be detected than smaller ones. For example, if a few exchangees dramatically changed their responses—say from "I agree" to "I very strongly disagree"—while there were only tiny fluctuations among the controls, the effect would be large. Similarly, a large number of responses were associated with greater power than a small number. As a general formula, power = A (number of observations) x B (effect size), where "A" and "B" represent mathematical functions.

Conventionally, power analysis is conducted before an experiment begins to ensure enough subjects are recruited to avoid being underpowered. In this situation, researchers can choose a desired level of power, and are able to infer the required number of cases by making an educated guess as to the likely effect size based on the existing literature (Bausell and Li 2002). Obviously that approach would not work for me because I did not directly control recruitment. Gatekeepers within universities distributed the invitations, and I could not control the number they sent out. I also expected high attrition.

Under the circumstances, a more realistic approach was to *retrospectively* estimate the effect size which could have been detected at a given power given the number of responses.[14] In this case,

effect size = [power ÷ A (number of observations)] ÷ B.

When a Split-Plot ANOVA is used, the "number of observations" term is equivalent to the number of responses from the smaller of the two groups (treatment and control). In this case, fewer Erasmus than non-Erasmus students responded, and so the effect size which would be detectable was calculated from the number of Erasmus responses and a preselected power. Conventionally, publishable research is expected to meet a minimum power threshold of 0.8, in other words to have an 80 percent chance of detecting an effect of a given size and only a 20 percent chance of making a type II error (Cohen 1977, Bausell and Li 2002).

As Cohen (1977: 16–7) points out, it is never strictly safe to state that *no* effect occurs in reality, simply because no significant results have been detected in an experiment: it is logically impossible to prove a negative. What an adequately powered experiment can show is that there is unlikely to have been an effect of a specified size in reality. If tests with high power (>0.8) are consistently showing no evidence of any impact then this suggests that either there is no effect or else the effect is very small. At this point, it is worth putting the statistical calculations back in the political context. If the objective of a program is to bring diplomatic benefits by changing attitudes, then it presumably needs to have a fairly substantial impact to be worth the cost. If a test with a high power is detecting no impact, then this cannot rule out a minor impact with any certainty, but it is very unlikely that a large impact would be missed.

With 99 exchangees responding to both the 2007 and the 2008 survey, a Split-Plot ANOVA on the results of this survey experiment is actually quite a powerful test. The power tables supplied by Bausell and Li (2002: 296–7) indicate that many fewer than 99 observations would be needed for the test to meet the conventional 0.8 power threshold for a "small" effect size (0.3). The precise figures depend on the correlation between the respondents' answers in 2007 and their answers in 2008, which varied a little between questions. The higher the correlation, the fewer cases are needed to achieve a given power. Bausell and Li provide figures only for correlations where Pearson's r is 0.4 or 0.6. The correlations were greater than 0.4 on all of my questions (most were around 0.6). At $r = 0.4$, only 53 cases would be needed to reach the 0.8 threshold for an effect size of 0.3. In fact, the power level was greater than 0.9 (or a 10 percent false-negative rate) that would require only 71 cases. At $r = 0.6$, only 36 cases would be needed to reach 0.8 for an effect size of 0.3, and this study included twice as many cases as would be needed to gain a power level of 0.9 (48 cases).[15]

In other words, 99 responses were far more than were needed for adequate power. Where this "experiment" does not show change, it is reasonable to suspect that going abroad either affected only a very small proportion of exchangees or else had only a trivial impact on the attitudes of students who were affected.

5

Short-Term Impacts of Erasmus Mobility

The panel study of contemporary Erasmus students was the main source of new information about how mobility affects political outlooks and behavior *in the short term*. The much smaller-scale pilots fed into this panel of surveys. I developed a questionnaire which combined questions tied specifically to the political impetus behind Erasmus—the sustenance of a European consciousness—with others tapping attitudes to the host country and more fundamental moral values. This chapter presents the central findings from those surveys of Erasmus students. Given the political agenda which fed into Erasmus, which I outlined in the previous chapter, many of these results may be surprising.

To complete the surveys students had to follow a hyperlink in the invitation email to a dedicated website. Although most of the questions remained the same, I produced multiple versions of the questionnaire and assigned each group a different version. Each treatment group was matched to a corresponding control, and both of these received questionnaires which were completely identical in the first (2007) wave, apart from being stored in different locations and accessed with different weblinks. The British students going abroad were matched with British students staying in the UK, French Erasmus students with French non-Erasmus students, and Swedish Erasmus students with non-mobile co-nationals. In the second (2008) wave the questionnaires were identical for the first two pages, but for the Erasmus groups I added a third page to ask in far more detail about their experiences during the year. The questionnaires were kept as similar as possible to make comparisons between them as easy as possible. There were two major differences. First, several questions on the second and third pages referred to a host nationality, and this had to be adjusted to fit the host nationality of that nationality's Erasmus students. For example, the Swedish Erasmus students all went to Britain, so for them and the Swedish controls several questions were asked specifically about attitudes toward Britain and the British. Second, the French students all received their questionnaires in French. The core questions were translated into French because the control group of French students was likely to contain many who either could not or would not understand English sufficiently to grasp the subtleties of the questions. Providing the questionnaire in English alone would most probably have limited participation to students who were particularly confident in the language, minimizing the numbers in a group which was difficult to recruit and skewing the sample. However, the Swedish version of the survey was delivered in English. It was much more common for Swedish undergraduates to have a high-level understanding of English, a language which has a significant role in Sweden's higher education and internet access (Hult 2004: 183–4).

All versions of the questionnaire followed the same basic pattern. The first-wave (2007) version (the British Erasmus students' version of which is reproduced as Appendix Two) was presented on two pages: the software only accepted submissions when both pages had been viewed, although it was possible for respondents to choose not to complete individual questions. Although the software did not support the complete randomization of responses, the order of responses varied throughout the questionnaire so that, for example, the pro-European position could appear at the top or bottom of a list of options or left or right of the screen. This was done in order to minimize response sets (Smith 1967) and encourage respondents to think about each question individually.

I used established survey questions where possible, from Eurobarometer, the European Social Survey and World Values. These questions had already been tested and passed through some form of quality control. They had also been used on a statistically-representative sample of the population. Given the limited resources available, it was not feasible to recruit representative samples from the different countries involved. By using questions from existing surveys, I could know whether any changes in the Erasmus students represented convergence with host-country students[1] or indeed the general population. Eurobarometer, European Social Survey and World Values questions are designed to be asked in a wide range of countries, and I used only questions on which there are differences between European countries. The wording also needed to be simple enough for a self-completion questionnaire.[2]

Each block of questions tested a different kind of impact that going abroad might have had on the Erasmus students. For simplicity, I am presenting them in the order in which they appeared to the respondents.

Contact Details and Tracer

The first question asked respondents to input their email address as a username, which was needed to match first- and second-wave submissions. This could easily have become an unmanageable task if many were unlabelled. Most respondents did include a functioning email address, and those who did not were removed from the analysis.

Cognitive Mobilization

How often do you talk about politics with friends and family?

- Frequently
- Sometimes
- Rarely
- Never
- Don't know

When you hold a strong opinion, do you ever find yourself persuading your friends, relatives, or fellow-workers to share your views?

- Never
- Rarely
- From time to time
- Often
- Don't Know

Table 5.1 Attrition diagnostics on cognitive mobilization

Questions	Attrition Diagnostics			
	Chi2 value	Degrees of freedom	Asymp sig	Problem?
How often do you talk about politics with friends and family?	4.489	3	.213	No
When you hold a strong opinion, do you ever find yourself persuading your friends, relatives, or fellow-workers to share your views?	5.306	4	.257	No

The substantive questions began with two questions designed to gauge how likely respondents were to discuss political issues and how likely they were to convince others of their positions. They are designed to rate respondents' potential participation in politics (Eurobarometer 2002: 164). This is crucial to the opinion-leader model because one of the possible "multiplier" effects rests on social communication (British Council Interview Two 7:00, Mitchell 1986). As mobility is usually only available to relatively few individuals, it is important that they spread any change in their views among their social circles, and discussion is one means by which they could do so. Might Erasmus make them more likely to persuade others?

These questions have been regularly featured in Eurobarometer surveys and are slightly rephrased versions of Inglehart's Cognitive Mobilization Index.

There was no sign that going abroad significantly affected either how often respondents discussed political issues or how persuasive they were. SPANOVA analyses of the two variables reveal no significant divergence between Erasmus students and controls. On the measure of how often respondents talked about politics, the interaction term was $F (1,217) = 2.566, p = .111$. As p was greater than .05, this shows no significant divergence between the groups. Similarly, on the persuasiveness measure, the interaction was $F (1,214) = 2.081, p = .151$. It is therefore unlikely that going abroad increased Erasmus students' (self-rated) persuasiveness.

The analysis also provides information about whether the students as a whole changed over time. This within-subjects main effect of time for talking about politics was $F (1,217) = 1.570, p = .212$, while for persuasive ability the within-subjects effect was $F (1,214) = .968, p = .326$.

The between-subjects main effects, which detect how far exchangees' responses differed from the controls' regardless of when the measurement was made, were also insignificant: $F (1,217) = .551, p = .459$ for discussing politics, and $F (1,214) = .063, p = .802$ for persuading others. As neither of these crossed the $p = .05$ threshold either, no significant difference between the exchangees and controls was detected.

Overall, Erasmus seems to have had no significant impact on cognitive mobilization. Levels of cognitive mobilization did not change over the year, and they did not differ significantly between the Erasmus and control groups.

European Versus National Identity

The next block of questions tested whether taking part in Erasmus would make respondents feel more European. This was judged firstly by a "Moreno question"[3] setting up European identity in opposition to a national identity the respondent had chosen from a drop-down menu—in which the nationality of their "home" university was the default.

Do you see yourself as

- This Nationality and not European
- More this Nationality than European
- Equally this Nationality and European
- More European than this Nationality
- European and not this Nationality?
- Don't Know

There was no sign of divergence in whether students considered their European identity more or less important than their nationality. The interaction between group and time showed no significant effect, with F (1,165) = .011, p = .915. These results suggest there was not divergence or convergence between Erasmus students and controls during the study, so Erasmus cannot be said to have increased participants' sense of European identity. Given the political rationale for the European Commission to be subsidizing Erasmus students, that might be considered a disappointing result.

The within-subjects main effect of time was insignificant, F (1,165) = .54 with a significance of .46. On the other hand, the between-subjects main effect of group was significant at p < .001, F (1,165) = 13.2 with an associated effect size (Partial Eta Squared)[4] of .074, a more-than-moderate effect (Pallant 2007: 208). These results indicate something which should not come as a shock: on average, Erasmus students considered themselves considerably more European than control students did. However, this was true from the beginning and there was no significant change in the groups' positions over the year. Erasmus did not *cause* this sense of European

Table 5.2 Attrition diagnostics on Moreno question

Questions	Attrition Diagnostics			
	Chi² value	Degrees of freedom	Asymp sig	Problem?
Do you see yourself as (This Nationality and not European / . . . / European and not this Nationality)?	3.401	5	.638	No
How attached do you feel to Your city/town/village?	1.413	3	.702	No
How attached do you feel to Your region?	.320	3	.956	No
How attached do you feel to Your country?	1.507	4	.825	No
How attached do you feel to Europe?	4.086	4	.394	No

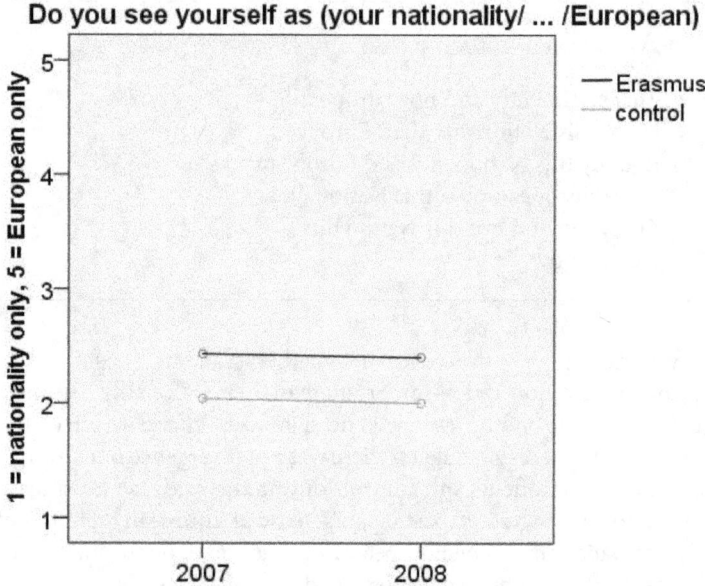

Figure 5.1 Group means on the Moreno question do not diverge

identity, but the Erasmus students were a self-selecting group who already felt more European than most students.

Territorial Attachment

I then asked respondents to rate their absolute levels of attachment to their home towns, regions and countries as well as Europe. This allowed me to identify respondents whose placement on the Moreno scale was volatile because they identified only weakly with both Europe and their chosen nationality, but also because the Erasmus experience might make students more outward-looking in general, shifting their attention away from purely local identities. Compelling respondents to consider European and national identity in opposition to each other would give a measure of the relative importance of the two, particularly if they claimed to identify strongly with both. However, the pattern turned out to be fairly similar, with little evidence that Erasmus made students much more or less attached.

People may feel different degrees of attachment to their town or village, to their region, to their country, or to Europe.
How attached do you feel to . . .

	Not very attached	Fairly attached	Not very attached	Not at all attached	Don't Know
1. Your city/town/village?	O	O	O	O	O
2. Your region?	O	O	O	O	O
3. Your country?	O	O	O	O	O
4. Europe?	O	O	O	O	O

Attachment to City/Town/Village

There was not a significant interaction between exchange participation and respondents' attachment to their home town, with $F(1,223) = 2.3$, $p = .13$ for the interaction. The main effects for time and group were both insignificant, $F(1,223) = .838$ for which $p = .361$ and $F(1,223) = .45$, $p = .50$ respectively. Respondents' level of attachment to their home town does not seem to have been in any way related to the Erasmus experience.

Attachment to Region

Level of attachment to the respondent's home region also seems to have been unrelated to Erasmus. The interaction did not approach significance, with $F(1,223) = .17$, $p = .68$. The main effect for time, coincidentally, had precisely the same values, while the main effect for group was $F(1,223) = .44$, $p = .51$. These figures indicate that Erasmus students' level of attachment to their home region did not differ from controls,' and neither group's attachment changed significantly over the year.

Respondents were also asked to type in the name of their region to check whether they were defining the term in the same way. For example, it is conceivable that Wales might be defined as a country or a region, depending on political outlook, and this might lead to respondents identifying much more strongly with some "regions" than others. However, given the lack of change either way this turned out not to be important.

Attachment to Country

Erasmus students' attitudes to their home country do not seem to diverge from the controls' as a result of their time abroad, as the interaction term is insignificant: $F(1,223) = .014$, $p = .91$. The main effect for time is identical. The main effect for group (whether the respondent is an Erasmus student or a control) comes closer to significance but does not reach the .05

significance threshold, with F (1,223) = 3.427, p = .065. While the results do not show that Erasmus students differed from controls on this measure with much certainty, it would be unwise to rule out the possibility that there was a genuine difference between the groups. If there were a genuine difference, it would indicate that the Erasmus students were slightly less attached to their home country before and after going abroad, the mean difference being about 0.2 on a four-point scale. Again, however, this is not a particularly interesting finding, as it should hardly come as a surprise that students who volunteered to live abroad were less nationalistic than others.

Attachment to Europe

For attachment to Europe, the group/time interaction was not significant: F (1, 217) = .32 with a significance score of .57. This indicates no significant divergence or convergence between the two groups' attachment to Europe during the year—again, perhaps a disappointing result for European elites seeking to construct a supranational identity.

For the main effects, the within-subjects (time) effect was also insignificant, F (1, 217) = 1.06, sig = .31 but again there was a highly significant between-subjects effect, F (1, 217) = 27.2, p <.001 which represented a substantial effect (Eta^2 = .11). In layman's terms, Erasmus students were much more attached to Europe at the start of the study and remained so.

World Values

This block of questions was designed to find out whether Erasmus affected students' fundamental political outlook. In particular, I was looking for convergence of students' values with those common in the host country. If students are being socialized into the host culture, their opinions on certain issues might converge with the dominant attitudes in the host country, as they may have been won over by convincing arguments and discussion going on around them. Thinking about socialization in this way is slightly circuitous, but it does have certain advantages for a panel study. The respondents need not be aware of the hypothesis that their views will converge in order to place themselves on value scales, and because the questions aim at fundamental values they can be disassociated from the experience of going abroad or attitudes to foreigners (which are likely to be sensitive points immediately following students' return). Indeed, it is quite possible that students in the treatment group would have been unaware from these questions alone that the questionnaire was related to their sojourn.[5] To take advantage of this, these questions were high on the first page.

Other studies have tried to gauge students' levels of internationalism, or "world-mindedness," by posing direct questions about attitudes to foreigners (e.g. Golay 2006, Carlson and Widaman 1988). While the concept is important, these kinds of questions could be perceived as normatively loaded. Established worldmindedness scales in particular tend to ask respondents to agree or disagree with items, such as "Concern with the problems of Third World countries" and "Respect for historical and cultural traditions and achievements of nations other than your own" (Golay 2006). Some responses would seem to have greater social desirability than others, particularly for students recently returned from foreign countries. It did not seem sensible to rely solely on these measures, but my values questions offered a subtler test.

The World Values questions are unlikely to be influenced by loyalty, and so net shift here would be convincing evidence that mobility shapes attitudes. We do not need to worry that the findings are conflating contentment with attitude change (a concern raised by Salter and Teger 1975). It is extremely unlikely that respondents could be aware of how their views would be *expected* to change: they would need to be aware of the hypothesis that the questions are trying to tap, know the mean responses in the host and home countries, and remember their initial response a year later. On the other hand, the questions are quite abstract and might show no evidence of change even if respondents were quite strongly influenced by their experiences. Given that these

Table 5.3 Attrition diagnostics on World Values

	Attrition Diagnostics			
Questions	Chi^2 value	Degrees of freedom	Asymp significance	Problem?
It would be better for experts, not politicians, to make major decisions according to what they think is best for the country. (Disagree strongly / ... / Agree strongly)	5.749	4	.219	No
People in my country should be more tolerant of unconventional lifestyles. (Agree strongly / ... / Disagree strongly)	8.861	4	.065	No
Government should take measures to reduce differences in income levels. (Disagree strongly / ... / Agree strongly)	3.986	4	.408	No
It would be better for my country if more people with strong religious beliefs held public office. (Agree strongly / ... / Disagree strongly)	2.681	4	.612	No
When jobs are scarce, employers should give priority to citizens over immigrants (Disagree strongly / ... / Agree strongly)	2.043	4	.728	No

are very fundamental attitudes, lack of change here was never intended to be evidence that Erasmus had no impact at a less profound level.

I asked respondents to place themselves on a series of Likert scales indicating how far they agreed or disagreed with a series of statements taken from the World Values Survey (2000). Like most of the World Values questions, these formed parts of scales aiming to tap core political beliefs, but I did not include the full sets of questions with which these were designed to be used as they would have filled up a huge slice of the questionnaire.

Experts Versus Politicians

How far do you agree or disagree with the following statements?

It would be better for experts, not politicians, to make major decisions according to what they think is best for the country.

- Disagree strongly
- Disagree
- Neither agree nor disagree
- Agree
- Agree strongly

Erasmus did not seem to have any effect. The interaction term is insignificant—$F(1, 219) = 2.4$, $p = .13$—indicating that the groups' attitudes did not diverge significantly while the Erasmus students were abroad. The main effects were also insignificant. The main effect of time at $F(1, 219) = 1.89$ had a significance value of .17, while the main effect of group was $F(1, 219) = .37$. Erasmus students did not differ significantly from control students, and this did not change over time.

Tolerance

People in my country should be more tolerant of unconventional lifestyles.

- Agree strongly
- Agree
- Neither agree nor disagree
- Disagree
- Disagree strongly

There was statistically significant divergence between the groups on tolerance of unconventional lifestyles, although curiously not in the direction we might expect. The interaction value was $F(1, 218) = 5.7, p = .018$, which is quite statistically significant. However, the divergence seems to have been largely due to convergence in attitudes between the groups. While the Erasmus students' mean score moved from 2.03 (standard deviation = .730) to 2.27 (standard deviation = .951), the controls' mean score moved from 2.41 (with a standard deviation of .960) to 2.35 (standard deviation of .967). As a high score on this question represented stronger disagreement, it appears that the Erasmus students became marginally less keen on their compatriots showing tolerance of unconventional lifestyles, whereas the controls moved in the opposite direction, as Figure 5.2 (below) illustrates.

Despite its clear statistical significance, the effect size for the interaction was fairly small, with a partial Eta^2 of .025. This implies that, while there is only a very small chance that there was actually no convergence, the impact of this change on the mean attitude was quite small. What we are seeing is that only a few students shifted their responses, and they are not moving far on the scale.

The main effect for time did not reach significance, $F(1, 218) = 1.97$, $p = .16$, but the main effect for group did, with $F(1, 218) = 4.36, p = .038$. On average, control students agreed with the statement significantly more than Erasmus students.

These results are difficult to explain. Given normal statistical uncertainty, it is possible that the figures do not accurately reflect the reality of the situation, but an interaction would be very unlikely to reach $p = .018$ if there were not a genuine effect. The year abroad may have altered Erasmus

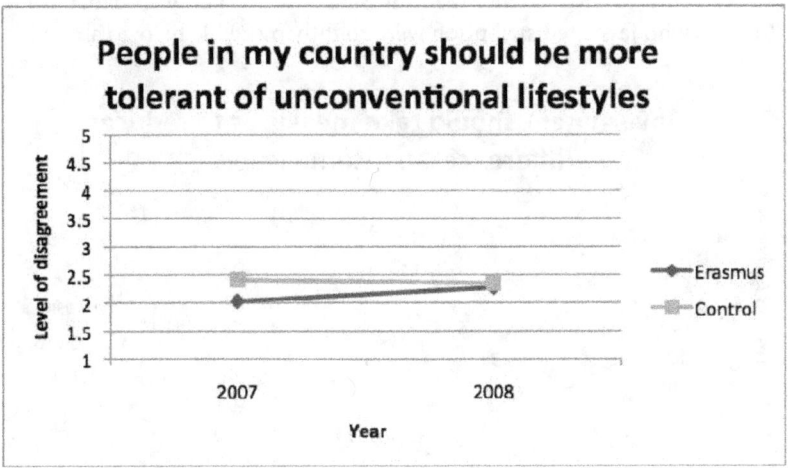

Figure 5.2 Group means for tolerance converge

students' perceptions of how tolerant people in their home countries actually are, although the impact was modest.

Income Equality

> Government should take measures to reduce differences in income levels.
>
> - Disagree strongly
> - Disagree
> - Neither agree nor disagree
> - Agree
> - Agree strongly

Studying abroad does not seem to have affected respondents' attitudes on this measure, with an insignificant interaction between being an Erasmus student (or not) and time: $F(1, 220) = .10, p = .75$. Similarly, there was not a significant main effect for time, with an $F(1,220)$ score of $.03, p = .86$. However, there was a significant main effect for group, $F(1, 220) = 4.58$, $p = .033$. This was substantively a fairly small effect (partial $Eta^2 = .02$) but still seems to indicate a genuine difference between Erasmus students and controls in both 2007 and 2008. A high score indicates a high level of agreement, and so the Erasmus students' higher average score, illustrated in Figure 5.3, indicates that they were more in favor of redistributing income. However, there is no evidence that this was caused by going abroad. Rather, students who favor redistribution were slightly more likely to go abroad.

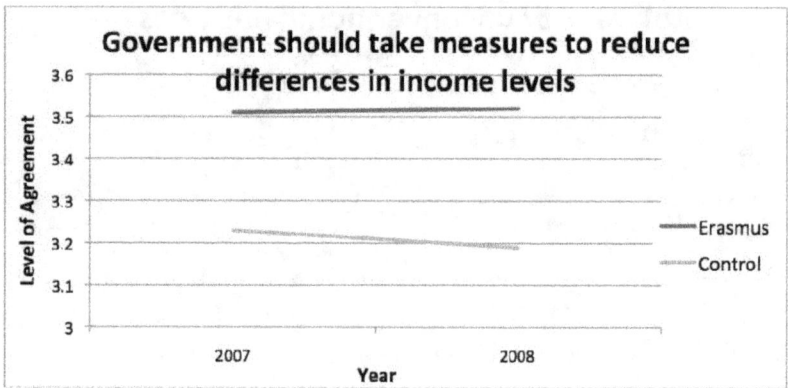

Figure 5.3 Views on redistribution did not diverge significantly

Religion in Officials

It would be better for my country if more people with strong religious beliefs held public office.

> ○ Agree strongly
> ○ Agree
> ○ Neither agree nor disagree
> ○ Disagree
> ○ Disagree strongly

There was not a significant interaction on this variable between date of response and whether the respondent was an Erasmus student, with the interaction term $F (1,218) = 1.603, p = .207$. The main effect for group was insignificant, $F (1, 218) = .88, p = .35$, but there was apparently a significant main effect for time, with agreement by respondents in both groups less likely to agree in 2008 than 2007. While the main effect for time passed the significance threshold, $F (1, 218) = 4.8, p = .03$, the effect size was small (partial $Eta^2 = .021$ suggesting that the change accounted for just over 2 percent of variance—Pallant 2007: 208).

The possibility that attitudes to religion in public life changed among students generally over the year is interesting. It is quite easy to guess at possible explanations related to the ongoing "War on Terror" and declarations of faith by increasingly unpopular political leaders in both Britain and the United States, but these would merely be speculation. For my purposes, the most important finding here is that there was no relationship between this change and the Erasmus Program.

Citizen Preferences in Employment

> When jobs are scarce, employers should give priority to citizens over immigrants.
>
> ○ Disagree strongly
> ○ Disagree
> ○ Neither agree nor disagree
> ○ Agree
> ○ Agree strongly

The interaction between time and Erasmus participation for attitudes to the employment of immigrants was $F(1, 219) = 2.80$, $p = .096$. Although there may have been some sign of divergence, and it would have shown up a "significant" if I used a $p = .1$ probability threshold, but this interaction did not reach the more conservative $p = .05$ threshold. Furthermore, while the divergence was partly due to Erasmus students becoming more favorable toward employing immigrants, there was a similar movement in the opposite direction among the control group. Thus, this result provides very little evidence that Erasmus participation affected students' support for immigrants' employment. The main effect for time was not significant, $F(1, 219) = .007$, $p = .94$, but the main effect for group was highly significant, $F(1, 219) = 13.99$, $p < .001$. Erasmus students were significantly less likely to approve of discrimination against immigrants in both 2007 and 2008.

Voting Behavior

The next block of questions dealt with voting intentions. First, respondents were asked whether they would vote if a General Election were held in the next week, a slightly-modified version of a classic and conventional voting intentions question.

Given low and falling turnout in elections across Western Europe, it seemed very likely that the sample would contain many students who would choose not to vote, and intent to vote is a question which is notoriously prone to social desirability bias. Many respondents will claim that they are likely to vote even if they are not (Karp and Brockington 2005: 825–6). I tried to minimize this social desirability effect by raising the possibility that they would choose not to vote explicitly at the beginning of the section.

Respondents who intended to vote were asked to identify the party or candidate they were likely to vote for, and this was a free-text response. Given all of the possible voting choices which could be made by students in a multinational survey, attempting to constrain them to a predefined list was likely to miss some possibilities, even if coding responses beforehand would save time in the analysis stage (the parties eventually had to be assigned numerical codes manually). To allow for a quick test of whether Erasmus students were more likely to change their voting intentions, a closed-response question was added asking whether they had changed their voting intentions since the last election, and why. In many cases 2007 undergraduates would have been too young to vote in previous elections, but the proportion of those who could who then changed their positions would provide some indication of whether Erasmus was impacting on voting intentions.

Table 5.4 Attrition diagnostics on party politics

Questions	Attrition Diagnostics			
	Chi^2 value	Degrees of freedom	Asymp significance	Problem?
Did you vote for [your currently preferred] party (or independent candidate) at the last General Election?	.619	1	.681	No
In political matters people talk of "the left" and "the right." Where would you place [your preferred] party/candidate in comparison to most of the main political parties in your country?	**13.849**	6	**.031**	**Possibly**
In terms of political matters people talk of "the left" and "the right." How would you place yourself in comparison to most people in your (home) country?	10.730	6	.097	No
Would you say this party or candidate is in favor of or opposed to development toward a European political union?	5.333	6	.502	No
Are you in favor of or opposed to development toward a European political union?	5.976	6	.426	No

The two following questions aimed to ascertain whether such changes moved their preference to the left or right of the political spectrum and to test the working hypothesis that Erasmus students might come to favor more pro-European parties. Finally, I asked respondents to place themselves on a left-right scale to check whether this matched their party preference. Voting preferences might be determined by factors besides identifying with a party's ideological standpoint.

Abstention

If there was a General Election in your country next week, do you think you would vote?
- Yes
- No

As this was a yes/no question (measured at a categorical level), I could not use SPANOVA. Instead, I computed the change in responses over time and cross-tabulated this with the respondent's group. The resulting Chi^2 statistic was 1.79 at 2 df, $p = .41$, so there was no significant correlation between being an Erasmus student whether a respondent would vote in a hypothetical election.

Voting Preference

> a. If you would vote, which party (or independent candidate) do you think you would vote for?

As responses on this question were collected in a free-text format, they had to be manually coded for statistical analysis. I created a dummy (dichotomous) variable which indicated simply whether respondents' preferences had changed.[6] To find out whether Erasmus students were more likely to change their party preference, I cross-tabulated this with the dummy variable which showed whether or not the respondent was an Erasmus student. Surprisingly, this revealed no significant relationship between the two. The conventional Chi^2 returned a value of 1.3 at 1df, $p = .26$, so there was no evidence that Erasmus participation affected party preference.[7]

Changes in Voting Preference

> b. Did you vote for this party (or independent candidate) at the last General Election?
>
> ○ Yes
> ○ No
>
> If no, why not?
>
> ○ I did not or could not vote at the last General Election.
> ○ I used to favour another party, but my position has changed.
> ○ I used to favour another party, but the parties' positions have changed.
> ○ Other *(please specify)*:

Table 5.5 Erasmus/Non-Erasmus status and change in voting intentions

			\multicolumn{3}{c}{Changed vote if voted?}		
			No	Yes	Total
Erasmus student?	Yes	Count	33	33	66
		Percent	50.0%	50.0%	100.0%
	No	Count	41	27	68
		Percent	60.3%	39.7%	100.0%
Total		Count	74	60	134
		Percent	55.2%	44.8%	100.0%

This showed whether Erasmus students were more likely to report, *in 2008 only*, that they had changed their voting intentions since the last election. In this case, $Chi^2 = 1.02$, $p = .31$, which—unsurprisingly—also shows that Erasmus students were no more likely to change their preferences than controls.[8] However, asking this question explicitly not only allowed for respondents to have trouble remembering their preference from a year earlier, but also allowed me to ask *why* any change had taken place, and to see whether any students who did change had been in the habit of changing their votes between elections before 2007.

This did actually reveal a significant correlation, $Chi^2 = 11$, $p = .004$, but a quick check revealed that this was probably a spurious relationship. Controls were less likely to have voted before, as more of them were British and there had not been a General Election in the UK since 2005 (when most of the sample would have been too young to vote). To account for this, I calculated a new variable which showed whether respondents' voting intentions as reported in 2008 differed from their intentions in 2007. This variable excluded all the students who reported in 2007 that they had not voted, or could not vote, in the last General Election. Erasmus students were not significantly more likely to show a change on this new variable than controls ($Chi^2 = 1.44$, $p = .23$). More of the remaining Erasmus students in the sample did change their positions, but the correlation was not strong enough to be statistically significant.

Very few respondents chose to type anything for the "other" response, and those who did raised no issues which were obviously related to Erasmus.

Left/Right Placement of Preferred Party

> **c.** In political matters, people talk of "the left" and "the right." Where would you place this party/candidate in comparison to most of the main political parties in your country?

> - Far to the Right
> - To the Right
> - Slightly to the Right
> - In the Centre
> - Slightly to the Left
> - To the Left
> - Far to the Left
> - Other *(please specify)*:

The interaction between time and Erasmus participation did not meet the standard probability threshold for this study, although at $F (1, 187) = 3.32, p = .07$ it would have met a less conservative $p = .1$ threshold. In any case, the effect size would have been very small, with a partial Eta^2 of .017 indicating that any "Erasmus effect" accounted for less than 2 percent of variance. The main effect of time was similarly insignificant, $F (1, 187) = 2.7, p = .102$, as was the main effect for group, $F (1, 187) = 2.3, p = .13$. These results do not provide sufficiently strong evidence to claim that being an Erasmus student affected respondents' preference for left- or right-wing parties.

The picture is slightly more complicated because there was differential attrition on this question, with students who gave certain answers on the first questionnaire more likely to drop out of the survey. Respondents who completed both questionnaires tended to support more left-wing parties. Drop-outs were

Table 5.6 Differential attrition on party placement

		Party Placement							
		Far to the Right	To the Right	Slightly to the Right	In the Centre	Slightly to the Left	To the Left	Far to the Left	Total
Attrition Retained	Count	1	17	31	26	43	47	3	168
	% within Attrition	.6%	10.1%	18.5%	15.5%	25.6%	28.0%	1.8%	100.0%
Drop-out	Count	5	41	29	51	51	47	8	232
	% within Attrition	2.2%	17.7%	12.5%	22.0%	22.0%	20.3%	3.4%	100.0%
Total	Count	6	58	60	77	94	94	11	400
	% within Attrition	1.5%	14.5%	15.0%	19.3%	23.5%	23.5%	2.8%	100.0%

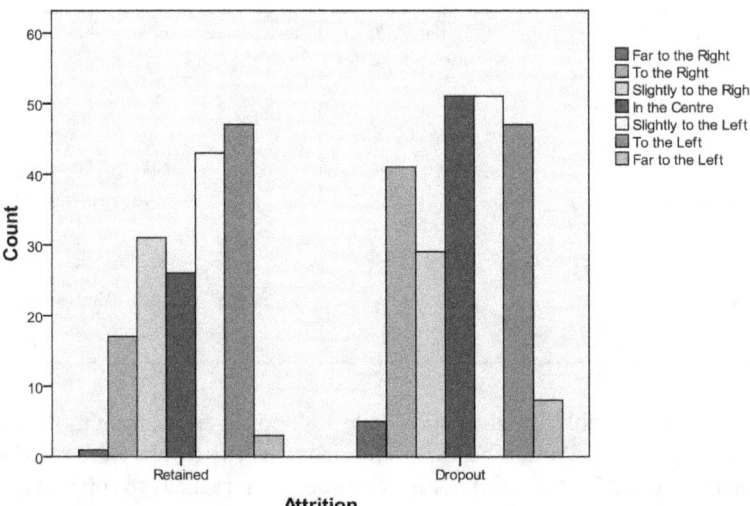

Figure 5.4 A chart summarizing the differential attrition in party placement

more likely to support parties they described as "to the right" of the political center, as shown in Table 5.6. This may be worth investigating, since the pattern of responses came relatively close to the probability threshold.

There is not an instantly obvious theoretical reason for this to be the case, suggesting that the finding may have been a family-wise error. a significance value of .031 is unlikely to have come about by chance on any single test, but it is far from impossible that one test would reach this significance level when so many of them were run on the survey results. However, it is also possible that the relationship between attrition and party preference is a spurious one, and that an unidentified factor relates to both attrition and party preference independently of each other.

Some investigation suggests that this was probably the case. The third factor is likely to be the national group from which the students were drawn. French students had a higher attrition rate than other nationalities and were also more likely than most to identify themselves as supporters of right-leaning parties (French parties in the Gaullist tradition are not particularly shy of that label).

The apparent attrition bias on this variable was a classic example of a spurious relationship: being French led to both a higher likelihood of dropping out of the survey and a higher likelihood of supporting a right-wing

Table 5.7 French students' support for right-wing parties

		Party Placement							
		Far to the Right	To the Right	Slightly to the Right	In the Centre	Slightly to the Left	To the Left	Far to the Left	Total
French Erasmus Students	Count	0	19	9	11	14	21	1	75
	%	.0%	25.3%	12.0%	14.7%	18.7%	28.0%	1.3%	100.0%
French Control Students	Count	0	8	5	7	8	13	4	45
	%	.0%	17.8%	11.1%	15.6%	17.8%	28.9%	8.9%	100.0%
All Students	Count	6	58	60	77	94	94	11	400
	%	1.5%	14.5%	15.0%	19.2%	23.5%	23.5%	2.8%	100.0%

party (and possibly "Right" and "Left" had different connotations for French students). We can be fairly confident that the results were not distorted, and that Erasmus did not make students more likely to support left- or right-wing parties.

Preferred Party's Position on European Integration

> d. Would you say this party or candidate is in favour of or opposed to development toward a European political union?
>
> ○ Strongly in favour
> ○ In favour
> ○ Slightly in favour
> ○ Neutral
> ○ Slightly opposed
> ○ Opposed
> ○ Strongly opposed

There was no significant interaction between group and time, $F(1, 184) = .19$, $p = .67$, indicating that Erasmus and control students' preferences for pro- or anti-European parties did not converge or diverge. The figures for the main within-subjects effect of change over time were actually identical to those for the interaction, $F(1, 184) = .19$, $p = .67$; again, there was no evidence of the average position of an Erasmus or a non-Erasmus student changing over time.

The main effect for group was significant, $F (1, 184) = 6.23, p = .013$. Again, it should not be surprising to learn that Erasmus students were a little more likely to favor parties they considered pro-European before they set out. The effect size was relatively small, with $Eta^2 = .033$. What this pattern does not show is any evidence that Erasmus made students more likely to support pro-European parties.

Personal left/right placement

In terms of political matters people talk of "the left" and "the right." How would you place yourself in comparison to most people in your (home) country?

- Far to the Right
- To the Right
- Slightly to the Right
- In the Centre
- Slightly to the Left
- To the Left
- Far to the Left
- Other (*please specify*):

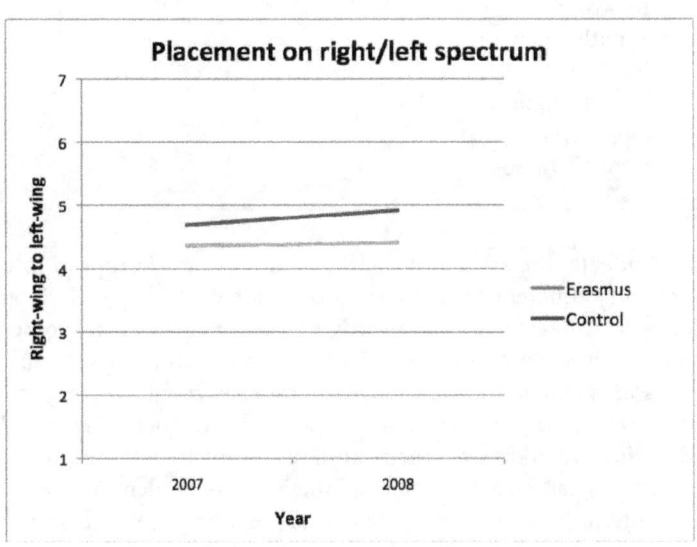

Figure 5.5 Divergence in left-right placement appears to be insignificant

A Split-Plot ANOVA did not detect significant divergence between the Erasmus and non-Erasmus students in how they placed themselves on a left-right spectrum, $F (1, 196) = 1.57$, $p = .21$. On the other hand, there appear to have been significant main effects for both group and time, which would imply that both groups changed their left/right placement over time, and also that the two groups differed from each other at both time points.

The main effect for time was only marginally significant, $F (1, 196) = 3.96$, $p = .048$, and substantively small, $Eta^2 = .020$, so it is conceivable that considering this to be evidence of change in the students' aggregate political views would be a familywise error. The main effect for group seems more reliable, $F (1, 196) = 4.56$, $p = .034$, but again it has a small effect size, $Eta^2 = .023$. Apparently, the Erasmus students thought of themselves as slightly more left-wing than the controls did before they left home.[9] The pattern is illustrated above.

Personally in favor of more European political union

Are you in favour of or opposed to development towards a European political union?

- ○ Strongly in favour
- ○ In favour
- ○ Slightly in favour
- ○ Neutral
- ○ Slightly opposed
- ○ Opposed
- ○ Strongly opposed

Asking students directly about their attitudes toward European integration was very different from the European identity questions. Supporting European integration is an overtly political characteristic, going well beyond merely feeling European. Similarly, pro-European students will not necessarily choose to vote for a pro-European party, since it is perfectly possible to choose a party for reasons other than its stance on Europe. This question directly addressed their attitude toward the European Union, whose officials had recently facilitated the Erasmus students' travels.

The pattern, however, is similarly disappointing. Again, there was no significant interaction between being an Erasmus student (or not) and change over time, with F (1, 218) = .62, p = .43. There was no sign of convergence or divergence in attitudes toward European political union during the year.

There was no significant main effect for time, with F (1, 218) = .069, sig = .79. On the other hand, the main between-subjects effect yielded F (1, 218) = 19.9, p < .001, with a more-than-moderate effect size, partial Eta^2 = .084. Erasmus students were noticeably more favorable toward further European political union, and they remained more pro-European.[10] But Erasmus seemingly had little effect.

International Affairs

Although these questions referred to international relations, they were actually chosen because of the possibility of convergence between French and British respondents. The NATO/EU/governments question had been asked in a special Eurobarometer (54.1) and revealed that French citizens were much more likely to favor a role for the EU in national defense, while their British counterparts preferred this to be a responsibility of national governments (Manigart 2001: 11–2). Similarly, Eurobarometer results have tended to show British respondents to be dramatically more likely to consider the United States a force for peace than French respondents (Eurobarometer 2003: B.8).

Table 5.8 Attrition diagnostics on foreign affairs

Questions	Attrition Diagnostics			
	Chi^2 value	Degrees of freedom	Asymp significance	Problem?
In your opinion, should decisions concerning European defense policy be taken by National Governments, by NATO, or by the European Union?	1.650	3	.648	No
On balance, would you say that the United States tends to play a positive or a negative role in preserving peace in the world?	4.395	3	.222	No
3. Do you tend to agree or disagree that the European Union should develop a common immigration policy toward people from outside the European Union?	.852	2	.653	No

This section also included another question intended to uncover changes in support for European integration, this time on a specific policy issue. The possibility of a common European immigration policy had been controversial in 2007–8. I could have asked about a large number of other policy areas, but that would probably have made my interest in the European Union too obvious to the respondents. There was a lively debate on immigration at the time, and Erasmus students' recent personal experience of mobility within Europe might have affected their views.

European Defense

> In your opinion should decisions concerning European defence policy be taken by National Governments, by NATO or by the European Union?
>
> ○ National Governments
> ○ NATO
> ○ The European Union
> ○ Don't Know

Again, I was largely interested in whether responses changed over the year. To find out, I subtracted responses to this question in 2007 from responses in 2008 and recoded all non-zero responses as 1, creating a dummy variable showing whether or not respondents had changed their views. This dummy variable did not correlate significantly with the dummy indicating whether or not the respondent was an Erasmus student (Chi^2 = .89 at 1df, p = .35.)[11] This result indicates that Erasmus students were no more likely to change their position on which of these organizations should be primarily responsible for European defense than students who remained in their home countries.

This headline result might potentially be concealing shifts between individual categories. To make sure this was not the case, I recoded the dummy variable to include only changes in which "The European Union" was one of the responses. Repeating the analysis under these conditions still did not show a significant relationship between students having taken part in Erasmus and having changed their views on whether the EU should play a role in European defense (Chi^2 = 1.1 at 2df, p = .57).[12]

The United States

> On balance, would you say that the United States tends to play a positive or a negative role in preserving peace in the world?
>
> ○ Positive
> ○ Negative
> ○ Neither positive nor negative
> ○ Don't know

Similarly, there was no significant association between a respondent being an Erasmus student and changing his or her view on whether the United States is a force for or against peace. The Chi^2 value in this case was 3.8 at 4 df, with $p = .43$.

A Common Immigration Policy

> Do you tend to agree or disagree that the European Union should develop a common immigration policy toward people from outside the European Union?
>
> ○ Agree
> ○ Disagree
> ○ Don't know

Surprisingly, the experience of studying in another European country also had no discernible effect on respondents' views on whether the EU should have a common immigration policy. I calculated changes by subtracting responses in 2007 from responses in 2008, and checked whether Erasmus students were more likely to change than controls. A Chi^2 value of 2.1 at 4 df, $p = .72$ indicates that it is highly unlikely that there was a

Table 5.9 Attrition diagnostics on demographics

	Attrition Diagnostics			
Questions	Chi^2 value	Degrees of freedom	Asymp significance	Problem?
Are you male or female?	3.744	2	.154	No
How old are you?	20.253	18	.319	No

relationship between being an Erasmus student and changing position on whether the EU should have a common immigration policy.

Demographics

Although respondents often find demographic questions boring, a few needed to be asked. They were placed at the end of the survey to maximize the chances of obtaining answers (McColl et al. 2001: 180)—respondents who are nearing the end of a questionnaire seem to be driven to complete it even if the final questions are less interesting than others.

These responses also showed that gender and age were not significantly related to a respondent's odds of dropping out.

For obvious reasons, I only asked the students' ages, genders, subjects of study, and whether they had any other degrees, once. However, I was curious as to how far they would report increased confidence in foreign languages. Being fluent in foreign languages probably helps students fit in, and becoming more fluent is clearly an important benefit of the program.

How well would you say you speak English?

- I do not speak English
- I speak very little English
- I speak reasonable English
- I speak good English
- I am fluent in English

The questionnaire included such four questions about respondents' ability in English, French, Spanish and German. All Erasmus students went to English-, French- or Spanish-speaking countries; German was included for comparison. The first question was about the respondent's home country's language, with the host language next, then the other possible language, and finally the reference language for comparison. For example, British Erasmus students going to Spain would be asked about English, then Spanish, then French, then German. As Swedish was not an option, I have excluded Swedish students from the analysis.

Home Language

As expected, Erasmus had little effect on the respondents' fluency in their home country's language. There was no interaction between time and group for British and French students' knowledge of their home country's language, $F(1, 199) = .000$, $p = .99$. There was no significant effect for group, $F(1, 199) = .000$, $p = .99$.

From a *statistical* point of view, there does appear to have been a significant main effect for time, $F(1, 199) = 4.87$, $p = .03$, but this was not an important *substantive* difference. With an effect size, partial Eta^2 of .028, this corresponds to an increase from 4.975 to 5 in average response on a five-point scale. The vast majority of respondents already rated themselves as "fluent" in 2007, and these figures represent one Erasmus and one control student moving from the "good" to the "fluent" category, which is hardly exciting news.

Host Language

On the other hand, the interaction and both of the main effects were highly significant for the host language. Perhaps unsurprisingly, Erasmus participants became much more confident. The divergence over time was dramatic, $F(1, 198) = 45.5$, $p < .001$, partial $Eta^2 = .187$. The main effect for time was even more dramatic, $F(1, 198) = 51.5$, $p < .001$, partial $Eta^2 = .207$, while the main effect for group was exceptionally large, $F(1, 198) = 165.7$, $p < .001$, partial $Eta^2 = .46$. These results represent a divergence pattern: Erasmus students began with a much greater knowledge of the host country language, and this advantage was greatly reinforced as illustrated below.[13]

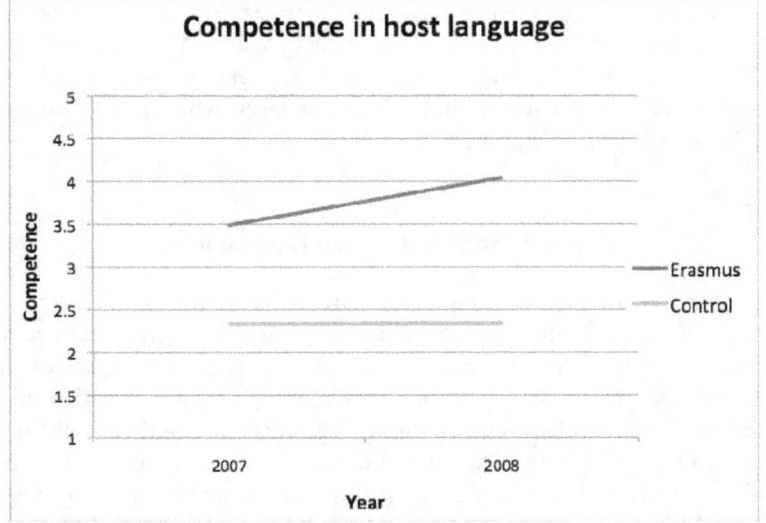

Figure 5.6 Erasmus students' knowledge of the host language increased

Third Language

Did Erasmus participation have any effect on students' confidence in other languages? Going abroad might well bring students into contact with other foreigners besides host nationals. The third language was Spanish, except for the very small number of British Erasmus students in Spain (for whom the third language was French). Unfortunately, the interaction term here was insignificant, $F(1, 199) = .058$, $p = .81$. Erasmus students did not diverge significantly from the control group.

On the other hand, the main effect for time did pass the significance threshold, at $F(1, 199) = 5.13$, $p = .025$, with a small substantive effect, partial $Eta^2 = .025$. The main effect for group was also significant, $F(1, 199) = 25.2$, $p < .001$, and this had a much larger effect size (partial $Eta^2 = .11$). This pattern indicates that Erasmus students began with a higher average level of the third language, but the two groups' fluency increased similarly over the year.[14] There was increase among the Erasmus students, but it cannot be attributed to Erasmus as it was mirrored among the control group.

German

Oddly, the pattern for German was rather different. The interaction term was not significant, at $F(1, 198) = .18$, $p = .67$, but in this case the main effect for time was also insignificant, $F(1, 198) = .004$, $p = .95$, and so was the main effect for group, $F(1, 198) = .022$, $p = .88$. The fact that Erasmus students' self-rated ability in German did not increase, while their ability in the host language did, reinforces the impression that immersion in the host country caused improvement in the host language—which is a pleasing, if perhaps unsurprising, finding.

Public Administration and Host Country

I used the second page of the questionnaire mainly to ask questions which had to refer specifically to the host country. I wanted to separate these questions out of concern that the respondents not be sensitized to the aim of the study by mentioning the name of a host country—a country with which the Erasmus students might well have developed an emotional relationship. This page addressed two broad themes: whether students acquired policy ideas from the host country, and whether students' overall feelings about the host country changed over time.

Policy Transfer

The first section was designed to find out whether the students who went abroad developed a deeper understanding of how public services were provided in the host country, and whether they saw opportunities to adopt ideas from the host country. Some interviews following the pilot had suggested this was likely. The rationale lies in theories of "policy learning" (see Rose 1991) in which policy ideas spread internationally as a result of individuals imitating policies they have observed working effectively in another country. The adoption of policy ideas from other jurisdictions is labeled variously "policy transfer," "lesson-drawing," and "policy diffusion," each of which implies a slightly different model of how similar policy ideas spread among countries (see Dolowitz and Marsh 2000). However, the basic idea that people need to be made aware of how things are done in other jurisdictions is common to all models. In order for policies to be adopted from other countries, someone must be aware of alternatives to the status quo being pursued elsewhere.

Exchangees will be directly exposed to the operation of public services in their host countries, and are likely to discuss past experiences with host-national friends (Bochner et al. 1977, Marshall Interview One). This may lead to changed attitudes. Historically, many governments have sent students abroad specifically to acquire practical and administrative ideas they can implement on their return home: the Meiji regimes of nineteenth-century Japan are a particularly striking example[15] (Arndt 2005, McConnell 2000: Ch. 1). Some modern programs, such as the Harkness Fellowships and parts of the Fulbright program which target established professionals, support mobility specifically to stimulate policy learning, and some of the rationalizations of Erasmus also depend on the transfer of useful ideas between European countries.

As usual, learning would not, in itself, imply that mobility has a direct impact on which policies are actually executed in the future. For changes to affect policy they need to be multiplied, either because the visitors themselves go on to positions of influence or because they disseminate the impact widely among their compatriots. It does seem intuitively plausible that students do become increasingly aware of the strengths (and weaknesses) of other countries' system. But of course the rationale for this research is that things that seem intuitively plausible are not always true—and the counter-intuitive results I have presented so far show how important it is to question common sense.

Although this line of reasoning seems to imply that internationally mobile students should become interested in how things are done in their host country, the policy-learning literature has tended to focus on active civil servants and politicians rather than students who might develop into civil servants and politicians in the distant future. In fact, to the best of my knowledge, before this study no-one had used an approach like this to explore how internationally-mobile students react to policy ideas they see implemented in the host country. Unfortunately, this meant there was no bank of tested questions available and I had to develop new ones. I tested these in the pilot and received broadly positive feedback from my interviewees (DAAD Interview Two, Marshall Interview One). Of course, only a few interviews followed the pilot, and the interviewees were elite postgraduates visiting different countries.

I gave some thought to how I could best express "the ways things are done" in host countries before settling on specific questions about "public services." Of course, it is quite possible that students' learning would have expanded well beyond public services, and they might have come across interesting ideas about banking, retail, advertising, or a range of other activities. However, the policy literature in political science—for obvious reasons—has tended to focus on techniques of governance. Conversely, the questions were phrased quite loosely, referring to wide policy areas ("the health-care system" and so on) rather than very specific issues. I simply had little information about what respondents might find attractive, so the closed-response options were designed to set respondents thinking in broad terms. I included open-text responses to collect specific ideas. With such open phrasing it is possible that different respondents interpreted the questions differently, and considered different things to be part of the health, education, and legal systems. Given the time-series design, this would not threaten the usefulness of the results—provided that individual respondents interpreted the terms consistently over time.

Comparative Policy Approval

How would you compare the following in your country and in France . . .					
	My country's system is better	The French system is better	The systems are of equal quality	Don't know/ undecided	Not applicable - I am from France
a. Health-care system?	O	O	O	O	O
b. Compulsory Education (school) system?	O	O	O	O	O
c. Higher Education (university) system?	O	O	O	O	O
d. Legal system?	O	O	O	O	O

The first table on the second page of the survey collected a large amount of information, and the aggregate results were very complex. It would be difficult to summarize all the changes without giving a misleading impression,[16] but exchangees were significantly more likely to change their opinions. More Erasmus students shifted their positions on schools (58 percent of Erasmus students changed their answers as opposed to 42 percent of the controls, Chi^2 = 4.9 at 1df, p = .026), universities (61 percent versus 37 percent, Chi^2 = 12 at 1df, p = 0.001), and the legal system (42 percent versus 29 percent, Chi^2 = 4.2 at 1df, p = 0.039). Oddly, while the statistical pattern did not show up in responses on health care (Chi^2 = .031 at 1df, p = .86), individual members of the panel I met in person were fascinated by it, and some of the most vivid stories I heard were about comparisons between health-care systems. The responses to this question, combined with the open-text answers, were most useful in guiding interviews, and some Erasmus students' own stories about their learning process are recounted in the following chapter.

Policy Transfer: Host to Home

Of course, having an opinion on how two countries' public services compare does not necessarily mean that students will become advocates of policy transfer. To find out whether they had taken this further step, I asked respondents whether they thought it would be good for their country to operate some public services more like the host country did. This question had three valid responses, "yes," "no," and "don't know," testing two working hypotheses. The first was that studying the foreign country would lead some students who previously thought that their country would not benefit from importing policy ideas to change their position, leading to a shift in

Table 5.10 Attrition diagnostics on policy transfer from host

Questions	Attrition Diagnostics			
	Chi^2 value	Degrees of freedom	Asymp significance	Problem?
Do you think it would be good for your country if some public services were delivered more like they are in [host], rather than as they are now?	7.779	3	.051	No
Do you think it would be good for [host] if some public services were delivered more like they are in your country, rather than as they are now?	2.542	3	.468	No

Table 5.11 Change in approval of copying host country policies

			Change in Approval		
			No	Yes	Total
Exchangee?	Yes	Count	46	40	86
			53.5%	46.5%	100.0%
	No	Count	93	45	138
			67.4%	32.6%	100.0%

students from the "no" to the "yes" category. The second hypothesis was that students who had not previously had a clear idea of whether policy transfer would be desirable would formulate more clear opinions as a result of exposure. This was expected to lead to a shift from the "don't know" category to one of the others, although it would be difficult to predict which of these categories was likely to prove most attractive.[17]

> Do you think it would be good for your country if some public services were delivered more like they are in France, rather than as they are now?
>
> o Yes.
> o No.
> o Don't Know.
> o Not applicable—I am from France.

To answer these, I first created a dummy variable which showed whether there had been *any* change in response between 2007 and 2008. There was a significant association between this variable and whether the respondent was an Erasmus student. The table below shows that students who had gone abroad were more likely to change their response over the year (Chi^2 = 4.35 at 1df, p = .037).[18]

However, this analysis removed all the information about the direction of change. To explore this, I isolated movements between the "yes" and "no" categories and excluded "don't know" responses. This included only respondents who chose either "yes" or "no" in both 2007 and 2008. This analysis did not give a significant result, with Chi^2 = 1.03 at 1df, p = .31.[19] Although more Erasmus students shifted from being in favor of transfer to being opposed, the numbers who actually changed between these categories were very small.

By contrast, Erasmus students were much more likely than controls to move out of the "don't know" category. The final results indicate a significantly greater movement from "don't know" to "know" among Erasmus students, Chi^2 = 6.48 at 2df, p = .039. Curiously, control students were quite likely to move in the opposite direction.

This seems reasonable. Erasmus students are being directly exposed to governance in another country, and that should lead them to form an attitude toward its policies. This reasoning does not predict whether the attitude will be positive or negative. Erasmus students were more likely than controls to develop a firm opinion on whether their country should import policy ideas from the host country. However, they did not seem to move consistently toward imitating the host country. In fact, by the end of their year abroad, Erasmus students did not seem to be significantly more likely to support transferring specific policies than students who had stayed at home, a pattern summarized in Tables 5.12 and 5.13. The experience formed more concrete opinions, but did not necessarily create more advocates for transfer than it did skeptics.

Table 5.12 Change between yes/no responses, policy transfer from host

			Change in approval "yes" and "no"			
			No to Yes	No change	Yes to No	Total
Exchangee?	Yes	Count	5	36	9	50
			10.0%	72.0%	18.0%	100.0%
	No	Count	5	35	3	43
			11.6%	81.4%	7.0%	100.0%

Table 5.13 Changes from "don't know" to all other responses, policy transfer

			Movement to or from "don't know"			
			Don't know to know	No change	Know to don't know	Total
Exchangee?	Yes	Count	18	60	8	86
			20.9%	69.8%	9.3%	100.0%
	No	Count	14	101	23	138
			10.1%	73.2%	16.7%	100.0%
Total		Count	32	161	31	224
			14.3%	71.9%	13.8%	100.0%

Nonetheless, thinking about this in the broader political context suggests that these changes may be significant for future policy, even if Erasmus students are moving to positive and negative positions in roughly even numbers. Lack of awareness is itself a potential barrier to adopting a policy (Rogers 1995). Some Erasmus students will go on to positions of authority. When they are there, they may be influenced by their observations of other countries—perhaps they will even try to implement ideas they first encountered abroad. If they become convinced that other ideas are inappropriate, they are unlikely to try to implement those. But they are similarly unlikely to try to implement ideas they never encountered and which are unfamiliar. I explored this possibility in the interviews with alumni of mobility programs who have, in fact, gone on to find themselves in this position, and their reports in the final chapter suggest this learning may be important.

Specific Policy Areas

To find out which policies respondents could envisage being transferred, they were again presented with the predetermined list of policy areas (healthcare, compulsory education, higher education and the legal system) and prompted on whether they thought changes would be beneficial in these areas. Experience from the pilot had been that, while these categories captured most of the comments respondents wished to make, there was also a range of miscellaneous issues which they identified but which would be hard to categorize. Accordingly, I added a self-completion option so that respondents could mention any issues that did not fit the predefined categories.

The information collected here was intended primarily as a guide for the semi-structured, in-person interviews which followed the survey, rather than for a statistical comparison of the groups. One striking pattern was that the most commonly-chosen policy area where Erasmus students wanted to see transfer was higher education. Direct personal exposure to the higher education system of a foreign country was, of course, something that Erasmus students had in common. The post-panel interviews showed that this

Table 5.14 Approval of transferring specific policies to home, after the Erasmus year, not significantly associated with Erasmus status

	Erasmus	Control	Chi^2 at 1df	p
Healthcare	23 of 88 (26%)	25 of 138 (18%)	2	.151
Compulsory Education	23 of 88 (26%)	31 of 138 (23%)	0.4	0.53
Higher Education	20 of 88 (23%)	20 of 138 (15%)	2.5	0.11
Legal System	6 of 88 (6.8%)	6 of 138 (4.3%)	0.65	0.42

a. Do you think it would be good for your country to become more like France in any of these policy areas?

(select all that apply)

☐ Healthcare ☐ Compulsory Education ☐ Higher Education
☐ The Legal System

b. Do you want to mention any particular changes which could be made in your country which you think would be beneficial?

passive learning through personal exposure had an important role to play in shaping interviewees' ideas. Erasmus did give students more solid opinions on the desirability of policy transfer from their former hosts to their home countries.

Policy Transfer: Home to Host

Conversely, mobile students might see the potential for policy ideas to travel in the other direction, from their home country to the host country. The questionnaire treated this possibility in exactly the same way, and I checked first for the formation of clear attitudes, and then whether respondents who had opinions tended to change from "yes" to "no." Respondents were then prompted on the same four policy areas and allowed a free-text space to raise any other possibilities they had considered.

> Do you think it would be good for France if some public services were delivered more like they are in your country, rather than as they are now?
>
> o Yes.
> o No.
> o Don't Know.
> o Not applicable—I am from France.
>
> a. Do you think it would be good for France to become more like your country in any of these policy areas?
>
> (select all that apply)
>
> ☐ Healthcare ☐ Compulsory Education ☐ Higher Education
> ☐ The Legal System
>
> b. Do you want to mention any particular changes which could be made in France which you think would be beneficial?

Again, I considered first whether there was any change in response and second whether this reflected movement between the positive and negative categories or increased certainty. Again, Erasmus students showed more change ($Chi^2 = 4.65$ at 2df, $p = 0.31$) as shown in Table 5.15.

Table 5.15 Changes on policy transfer, home to host

			Change in Approval		
			No	Yes	Total
Exchangee?	Yes	Count	43	36	79
			54.4%	45.6%	100.0%
	No	Count	90	40	140
			69.2%	30.8%	100.0%

However, again the significant shift was from the "don't know" category to a firm "yes" or "no." There was no significant movement between "yes" and "no" answers ($Chi^2 = 0.1$ at 2df, $p = 0.95$, Table 5.16), but Erasmus students were more likely to move out of the "don't know" category than students who remained in their home countries ($Chi^2 = 12.2$ at 2df, $p = 0.002$, Table 5.17). This matches the overall pattern of students who went abroad becoming more confident that they could express an opinion, rather than necessarily becoming enthusiastic about policy transfer.

The pattern of change was similar when students were thinking about transfer from home country to host as when thinking about transfer from host to home, but overall Erasmus students seemed more likely to be able to think of specific examples of policy areas where the host country could benefit from imitating their home country.[20] There was a particularly clear approval of transfer when they considered higher education policy. Nearly 46 percent of Erasmus students thought that some transfer would be desirable after they had returned, as opposed to just 12 percent of the students who stayed in their home countries ($Chi^2 = 33$, $p < 0.001$). Returning students were also significantly more likely to believe that the host country should adopt some ideas about compulsory education (21 percent versus 4 percent, $Chi^2 = 15$, $p < .001$), and health care (38 percent

Table 5.16 Yes/No movement on policy transfer from home

			Change in approval "yes" and "no"			
			No to Yes	No change	Yes to No	Total
Exchangee?	Yes	Count	2	45	1	48
			4.2%	93.8%	2.1%	100.0%
	No	Count	3	90	2	95
			3.2%	94.7%	2.1%	100.0%

Table 5.17 Know/Don't know movement on policy transfer from home

			Movement to or from "don't know"			
			Don't know to know	No change	Know to don't know	Total
Exchangee?	Yes	Count	29	53	7	89
			32.6%	59.6%	7.9%	100.0%
	No	Count	18	98	18	134
			13.4%	73.1%	13.4%	100.0%

versus 20 percent, $Chi^2 = 8.9$, $p = 0.003$), but there was not a significant association on the legal system. This reflected some reservations about governance in the host countries, which cropped up again during in-person interviews.

Overall, these measures showed Erasmus students developing clearer opinions on the potential for transfer—thought-out reservations as well as enthusiasm. That clarity might prove important as they develop into their future careers.

Host Country

To end the questionnaire, I asked four questions specifically about the host country. This is perhaps the most intuitive approach to forming questions about the impact of mobility: simply ask respondents directly what they think about the host country (e.g. Selltiz and Cook 1961). If students who have lived in a foreign country report that they like it better after living there, that is clearly encouraging. Of course, these questions only capture one dimension of the experience, and inevitably name a country which may trigger emotional reactions. These questions were placed toward the end of the questionnaire so that other responses were less likely to be influenced by vivid associations with the name of the host country; Salter and Teger (1975) have shown that these associations can color responses to more abstract questions, but trying to avoid them entirely would miss something very important. Asking the questions but isolating them at the end of the questionnaire was a compromise.

Table 5.18 Attrition diagnostics for host country attitudes

	Attrition Diagnostics			
Questions	Chi^2 value	Degrees of freedom	Asymp significance	Problem?
Regardless of whether you agree with [host]'s foreign policies, how well would you say you understand why it pursues them?	1.168	4	.883	No
How well would you say you understand [host] people?	2.151	4	.708	No
How interested are you in learning more about [host]?	6.466	6	.373	No
How would you sum up your opinions about [host]?	13.161	6	.041	Possibly

The first two questions aimed at Erasmus students' level of understanding of the host country. I included two self-ratings of understanding: understanding of why the host country chooses its foreign policies and understanding of the host country's citizens. Increasing understanding is a key objective for many sponsors of international mobility (British Council Interview Two), even if there is less agreement on what behavior and attitude changes would be desirable. These are obviously self-rating measures, and I included no test of whether respondents' perceptions of their own understanding were accurate. The rationale for asking about interest in learning more about the host country was that in interviews (e.g. Marshall Interview Two) administrators of exchange programs would often claim that building long-term interest in their countries was an important objective. Interest in learning more, even after a year's immersion, could indicate the beginning of an enduring relationship which would reinforce the short-term impact. Finally, respondents were tested on the most obvious impact of any international mobility: a change in exchangees' attitudes to the country in which they studied.

Differential attrition was not a concern for three of these questions, but it was possible for the last question—perhaps the single most important. I have been very careful in interpreting responses to that question.

Understanding of Host Foreign Policy

> Regardless of whether you agree with France's foreign policies, how well would you say you understand why it pursues them?
>
> o Very well
> o Well
> o A little
> o Very little
> o I do not understand at all

There was a highly significant divergence between the Erasmus students and the control groups in their self-rated understanding of why the host country selected its foreign policies, $F(1, 218) = 7.8, p = .006$. This divergence was highly significant—meaning it was very unlikely I would have detected a pattern like this by chance if there were actually no divergence between Erasmus and non-Erasmus students in reality – but substantively it was fairly small ($Eta^2 = .035$) so on average Erasmus students' responses were only moving 'a little further from the controls'.

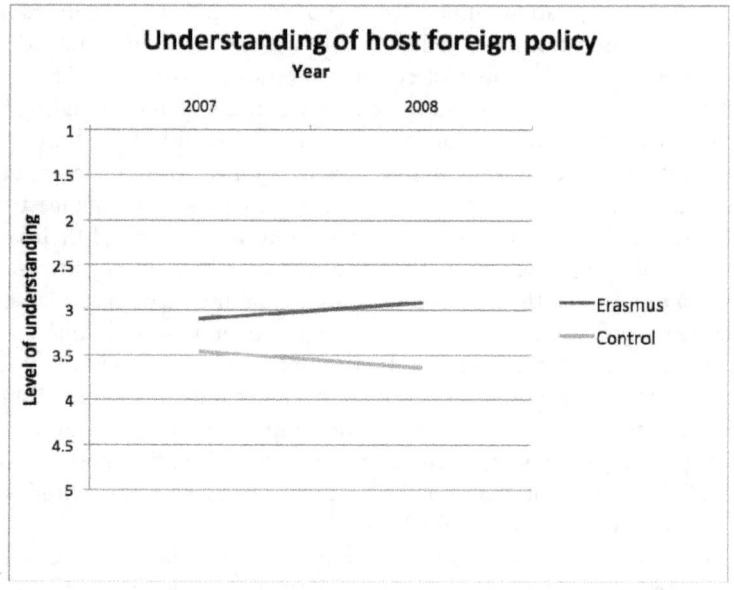

Figure 5.7 Divergence in understanding of the host's foreign policy

The highly significant interaction makes the main effect for time hard to interpret, as the statistic implies that time has no discernable main effect, with $F(1, 218) = .000$, $p = .997$. The main effect of group is still highly significant, with $F(1,218) = 19.2$, $p < .001$. Figure 5.7 shows what is actually going on much more clearly: the changes in the two groups' means are almost exactly equal in magnitude but opposite in direction. The changes in the two groups cancel each other out so that the average response stayed the same over time, leading to the insignificant main effect for time—but Erasmus students believed their understanding increased while control students felt they understood host nationals even less in 2008 than they had in 2007.[21]

The reason for the change in the control group is not instantly obvious. It is possible that students who did not go abroad became more conscious of their relative ignorance due to their increasing education and exposure to experts, or simply because they were conscious that they had been asked the same question a year earlier and had not learned anything. The pattern might reflect a change in the broader student population's sense of understanding over the year, with the general level of awareness of other countries' foreign policies falling as the Iraq war controversy receded into history. Regardless of this speculation, it seems that the experience of going abroad not only protected Erasmus students from the trend but actually moved them in the opposite direction.

Understanding of Host Nationals

> How well would you say you understand French people?
>
> o I do not understand them at all
> o Very little
> o A Little
> o Well
> o Very well

There was also a highly significant divergence between the groups in how well they claimed to understand nationals of the host country, $F(1, 221) = 20.1$, $p < .001$. The substantive effect size, $Eta^2 = .083$, implies that the interaction accounts for a little over 8 percent of variance in the students' scores, which Cohen (1988: 22) classifies as a more than medium effect. The main effects appear to be $F(1,221) = 20.1$, $p < .001$ for time and $F(1,221) = 40.2$, also $p < .001$ for group, suggesting that the groups differed in both 2007 and 2008 and that the average score changed over the year, but these are difficult to interpret accurately with such a strong interaction effect. Both were substantial effects, with $Eta^2 = .083$ for time and $.154$ for group, which Cohen classifies as a very large effect. Again, the chart shows

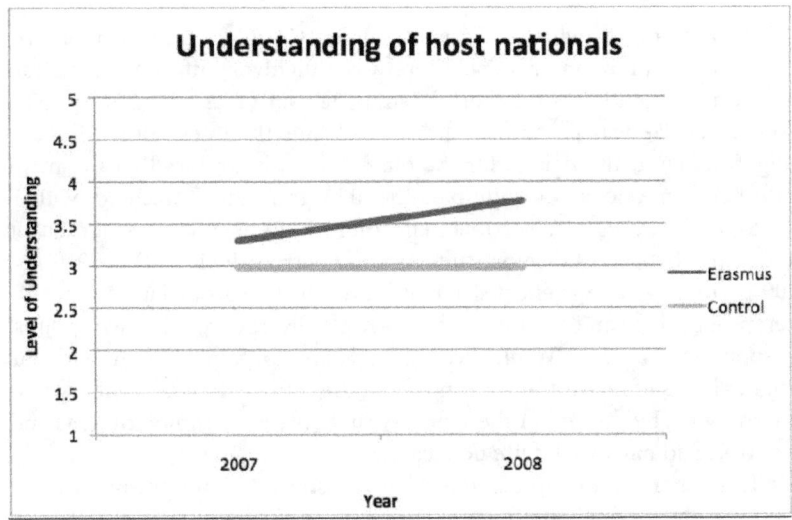

Figure 5.8 Perceived understanding of host nationals diverged

that the interaction is what we would expect: a divergence between the groups over time, with the control group staying more or less constant and Erasmus students' level of understanding increasing.

On both understanding measures, the pattern is highly encouraging. Erasmus students come away feeling that they understand more than they did when they went abroad, and this can clearly be attributed to the Erasmus Program. Of course, this pattern is based on students' perception of their understanding, and it is possible that their confidence is misplaced, but this remains an encouraging finding.

Interest in Learning about Host

How interested are you in learning more about France?

- ○ Very interested
- ○ Interested
- ○ Quite interested
- ○ Neither interested nor uninterested
- ○ Quite uninterested
- ○ Uninterested
- ○ Very uninterested

When it comes to whether Erasmus students would like to learn more, the lesson is more ambivalent. There was a highly significant interaction between time and Erasmus/non-Erasmus status, $F(1,224) = 11.8, p < .001$. The effect size was moderate, $Eta^2 = .05$. While the interaction will have slightly skewed the figures for the main effects, it appears that the main effect for time does not quite pass the .05 significance threshold, with $F(1,224) = 3.2, p = .077$. The main effect for group does show a significant difference between Erasmus students and controls, $F(1, 224) = 99.4, p < .001$, with a very large effect size $Eta^2 = .31$. The two groups were very different, but this time the interaction is not a divergence. The two groups' responses *converged*. While Erasmus students began the year with far higher levels of interest in learning about the country in which they would be studying, by the end of the year the gap between Erasmus students and controls had narrowed quite noticeably.

This pattern is not difficult to explain. Erasmus students, unsurprisingly, began with extremely high levels of interest in the country in which they had volunteered to spend several months of their lives. In 2007, the 'average' response[22] was about halfway between "very interested" and merely

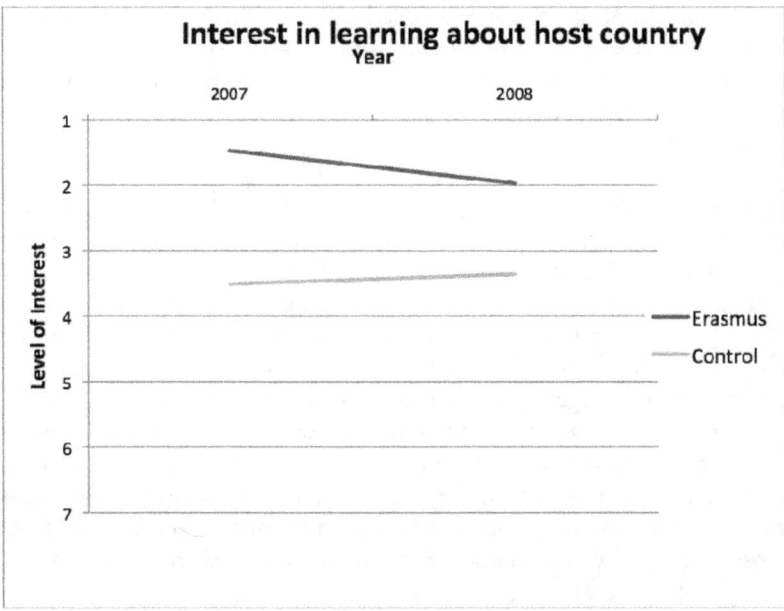

Figure 5.9 Interest in learning more converged

"interested," and by 2008 the average had fallen. The controls lacked this strong interest. It seems that Erasmus students' curiosity was at least partly satisfied by their experience, and so their curiosity fell from its initially extremely high level. However, it is worth noting that even after the Erasmus year, the mean response of Erasmus students was still "interested" (two on a seven-point Likert scale), which was much higher than the controls'. While the Erasmus year satisfied part of their curiosity, it did not extinguish it.[23]

Attitude to the Host Country

How would you sum up your opinions about France?

- Very unfavourable
- Unfavourable
- Slightly unfavourable
- Neutral
- Slightly favourable
- Favourable
- Very favourable

Perhaps the most surprising result of all was that Erasmus students did not become better-disposed toward their host country over the year. This is a very important finding given the political expectations for mobility as a means of changing attitudes, and it was also quite a complex pattern which needs careful analysis.

There was not a significant interaction between group and time on overall attitude to the host country: $F (1,222) = .82, p = .37$. The main effects for both time and group were significant. For time, $F (1,222) = 4.3, p = .039$ with a very small effect size of $Eta^2 = .019$, while for group (Erasmus versus control) $F (1,222) = 36.3, p < .001$ with a more substantial effect size of $Eta^2 = .140$. Erasmus students were different from controls, but it is not at all clear that Erasmus contributed to this difference.[24]

The lack of divergence in overall attitudes is surprising given the change in time for respondents overall, and so I examined the group means to check whether there was some interaction which was not being detected by the analysis. However, this revealed that any pattern which might have existed would have to be almost entirely the opposite of most expectations: most of the change in attitudes over time actually occurred in the *control* group, not among the Erasmus students.

Bearing in mind that this chart is based on the mean responses for the two groups (over time), there are basically two scenarios which might explain the flat line for Erasmus students. There may not have been much

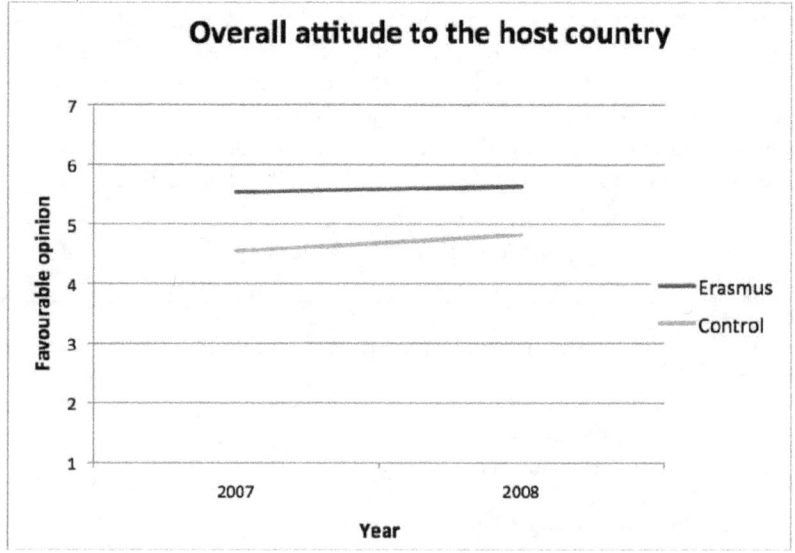

Figure 5.10 Apparent lack of divergence in attitudes to the host

Table 5.19 Differential attrition in attitude to host

		Overall Attitude to Host in 2007						
		Very unfavourable	Unfavourable	Slightly unfavourable	Neutral	Slightly favourable	Favourable	Very Favourable	Total
Attrition Retained	Count	5	8	9	40	27	77	18	184
	%	2.7%	4.3%	4.9%	21.7%	14.7%	41.8%	9.8%	100.0%
Drop-out	Count	5	6	20	88	49	80	26	274
	%	1.8%	2.2%	7.3%	32.1%	17.9%	29.2%	9.5%	100.0%

attitude change, but it is also possible that there were dramatic shifts in attitude among individual Erasmus students which, by some spectacular coincidence, cancelled each other out. The first scenario seems more likely: the standard deviations for the Erasmus group in 2007 and 2008 were virtually identical: 1.179 and 1.171, respectively. It does seem that the experience of living in a country had no significant impact on students' overall rating of it on a favorable/unfavorable scale. While this is a crude measure, the finding is consistent with several others—and contrasts with the political expectations surrounding mobility programs.

The overall rating question was another which was affected by differential attrition, as students who completed both questionnaires tended to give different answers from those who dropped out between 2007 and 2008. Students who had more favorable attitudes to the host country in 2007 seem to have been slightly more likely to complete the 2008 questionnaire. Among the students who dropped out before completing the second questionnaire, a plurality described their attitude as "neutral"; for those who completed both questionnaires, "favorable" was by far the most common response. This is shown graphically in Figure 5.11.

This difference does not seem to be solely due to Erasmus students (who tend to have more favorable attitudes) being more likely to complete

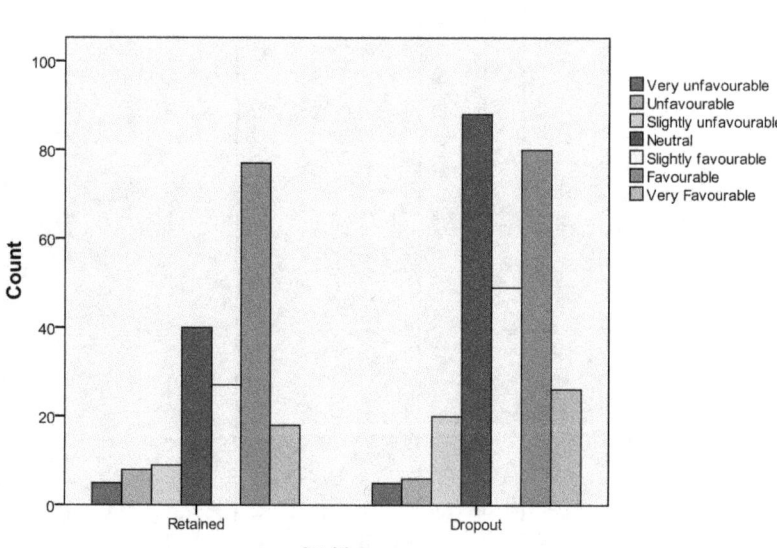

Figure 5.11 Differential attrition on attitude to the host country

both questionnaires, as the attrition rates for Erasmus and control students overall are quite similar. Nor did the groups which had the highest attrition (such as French control students) include greater proportions identifying themselves as neutral on this measure in 2007.

In this case, the findings really may have been influenced by attrition bias, and this is worth bearing in mind. Students who had high opinions of the host country in 2007 were more motivated to complete the 2008 questionnaire. This in turn may have contributed to a "ceiling effect" in which the respondents were disproportionately positive about the host country anyway, and so had less room to improve their attitudes. However, it also seems unlikely that this would make it appear as if there were little or no net attitude change among the Erasmus students if in fact there were a large shift. Even with a slightly odd sample, it is hard to see how I could have obtained these results had there been a dramatic change in reality. A ceiling effect could only account for a small real change in attitudes being missed.

This finding needs to be placed in its political context. In order for the *political* benefits of mobility to justify the costs, they presumably need to be fairly substantial. Even if the attrition pattern has made a difference here, it would be a very minor one. It is unlikely that the Erasmus students became much more positive toward the host country as a result of living there, although they did have more positive attitudes before they left home.

Summary of results

With one slight exception, there was no evidence that Erasmus and non-Erasmus students diverged significantly and controls on any of the attitude measures included in the first page of the survey. Erasmus students were significantly more likely to have developed firm attitudes to the transfer of policy ideas between their home country and the host, and they also became more likely to believe they understood people from the host country and why the host country chose its foreign policies. On the other hand, their desire to learn more about the host country diminished somewhat (while remaining relatively high) and they did not become more favorable toward the host country overall.

My findings on each of the questions are listed in the Table 5.20.

Conclusions

Looking at which dependent variables had significant results, it seems fairly easy to distinguish a pattern. Taken as a whole, this is a picture of mobility increasing knowledge, but not changing *attitudes* very much.

Table 5.20 Summary of changes

Question	Test	Significant interaction?	Direction
How often do you talk about politics with friends and family?	SPANOVA	No	
When you hold a strong opinion, do you ever find yourself persuading your friends, relatives, or fellow-workers to share your views?	SPANOVA	No	
Do you see yourself as (This Nationality and not European / . . . /European and not this Nationality)?	SPANOVA	No	
How attached do you feel to Your city/town/village?	SPANOVA	No	
How attached do you feel to Your region?	SPANOVA	No	
How attached do you feel to Your country?	SPANOVA	No	
How attached do you feel to Europe?	SPANOVA	No	
It would be better for experts, not politicians, to make major decisions according to what they think is best for the country. (Disagree strongly / . . . / Agree strongly)	SPANOVA	No	
People in my country should be more tolerant of unconventional lifestyles. (Agree strongly / . . . / Disagree strongly)	SPANOVA	Yes	Apparent slight convergence
Government should take measures to reduce differences in income levels. (Disagree strongly / . . . / Agree strongly)	SPANOVA	No	
It would be better for my country if more people with strong religious beliefs held public office. (Agree strongly / . . . / Disagree strongly)	SPANOVA	No	
When jobs are scarce, employers should give priority to citizens over immigrants. (Disagree strongly / . . . / Agree strongly)	SPANOVA	No	
Did you vote for [your currently preferred] party (or independent candidate) at the last General Election?	Chi^2	No	
In political matters, people talk of "the left" and "the right." Where would you place [your preferred] party/candidate in comparison to most of the main political parties in your country?	SPANOVA	No	
In terms of political matters people talk of "the left" and "the right." How would you place yourself in comparison to most people in your (home) country?	SPANOVA	No	

(Continued)

Table 5.20 Summary of changes *(Continued)*

Question	Test	Significant interaction?	Direction
Would you say this party or candidate is in favour of or opposed to development toward a European political union?	SPANOVA	No	
Are you in favour of or opposed to development toward a European political union?	SPANOVA	No	
In your opinion, should decisions concerning European defence policy be taken by National Governments, by NATO or by the European Union?	Chi²	No	
On balance, would you say that the United States tends to play a positive or a negative role in preserving peace in the world?	Chi²	No	
Do you tend to agree or disagree that the European Union should develop a common immigration policy toward people from outside the European Union?	Chi²	No	
Of course, we all hope that there will not be another major war in Europe, but if it were to come to that would you be willing to fight to defend your country?	Chi²	No	
Do you think it would be good for your country if some public services were delivered more like they are in [host], rather than as they are now?	Chi²	Yes	Fewer exchangees respond "don't know"
Do you think it would be good for [host] if some public services were delivered more like they are in your country, rather than as they are now?	Chi²	Yes	Fewer exchangees respond "don't know"
Regardless of whether you agree with [host]'s foreign policies, how well would you say you understand why it pursues them?	SPANOVA	Yes	Exchangees' understanding increased
How well would you say you understand [host] people?	SPANOVA	Yes	Exchangees' understanding increased
How interested are you in learning more about [host]?	SPANOVA	Yes	Exchangees' interest decreased
How would you sum up your opinions about [host]?	SPANOVA	No	

There was little sign that Erasmus students' political attitudes were much affected. This meant that, at least on average, exchangees' attitudes could not have converged with those prevalent in the host country, and nor were there many signs that exchangees as a whole were becoming much more liberal, open-minded, or cosmopolitan. Some of the existing literature has championed the argument that going abroad leads to students becoming more globally-minded; my results do not support this. Similarly, there was no significant divergence in any of the measures relating to Europe, suggesting that Erasmus students' perceptions of the institution which sponsored their travels were not affected.

The important exceptions to this pattern were all on the second page of the survey, which dealt with policy ideas and host-country-specific questions.[25]

First, Erasmus students seem to have developed definite attitudes to the transfer of policy ideas between their home countries and those in which they spent time during the 2007–8 year. Students who developed firm attitudes did not necessarily become more favorable, but this is consistent with their having a greater knowledge and awareness of the host country's systems after living there. The fact that they are forming definite opinions could have important implications if they move into policymaking positions in the future, by giving them an expanded range of models from which to draw. The possibility that the development of beliefs about public policies as a student may affect policymaking later in life is explored further in the following chapters.

The second group of changes dealt with issues of understanding. Erasmus students themselves came to believe that they developed a deeper understanding of the host country, on both the personal level of understanding its citizens and the more overtly political level of understanding why the host country's politicians made particular decisions. While it is not possible to judge whether respondents' perception of increased understanding reflected an actual increase in understanding (rather than ignorance of their ignorance) from the survey results alone, it is intuitive that living in a country for a significant period would increase understanding. Their initially very high level of interest in finding out more about the host country was slightly satiated by their time abroad—although they remained, on average, much more curious than the control group.

On the whole, this pattern suggests that Erasmus increases knowledge and (perceived) understanding of other countries, rather than actually changing students' attitudes by converting them to different positions. It had significant educational benefits, but was not an effective tool for shaping political views.

Political Implications

It is worth bearing in mind that diminishing misunderstanding between people from different countries has, historically, been a key objective of international scholarship and exchange programs. The initial mission statement of the Fulbright Program—an inspiration for the British scholarship and exchange schemes considered in Chapter 2—was "to generate a deeper understanding... of the differing cultures and peoples of the world" (Fulbright, quoted by US-UK Fulbright Commission 2008) as much as "the promotion of international good will" (Fulbright, quoted in Woods 1995). Senator Fulbright, its architect, presented the program as part of a means of exerting power over foreigners mainly to secure financial support (Woods 1995: 194). On the other hand, the belief that mobility programs can serve a political agenda has spread.

Considering these programs to be exercises in projecting "soft power" (Nye 2005, see Scott-Smith 2005: 749–50, 769–72) implies a different model of the process in which visiting students go on to become "friends" (e.g. DAAD 2005) of the host country, and ultimately provide it with long-term benefits, such as improved international relations. That relies upon their influencing the world to the benefit of the host country, which relies on changing their behavior. Presumably, this in turn depends on changing attitudes. This model of the impact of exchange programs, while probably very useful in securing the political support which government-funded exchange programs need in order to survive and expand, does not get much support from the findings of this study. If spreading "goodwill" toward, or becoming a "friend" of, the host country implies having a positive attitude toward it, then I have found no evidence that studying abroad leads to noticeably positive attitudes—although sojourners tend to think quite positively about their prospective host country before they arrive. Similarly, there is no sign that it leads students to support existing bonds between the home and host countries, such as participation in the European Union, even when the Union is picking up part of the bill for their travels.

Given the claims which have been made for international student mobility as a tool for improving international relations, the results seem surprisingly modest. Perhaps the pattern should not come as a huge surprise. The historical sketches of the Marshall, Commonwealth and Chevening Scholarships I presented earlier suggest that at least some international scholarships may have been linked to diplomacy not so much by rational calculations as by clever maneuvering within ministries. If the schemes were not really created to serve the function ascribed to them, and most people involved are skeptical that they can detect whether they are doing a good job of it within a reasonable time frame (see Scott-Smith 2008) they might well not be very successful. This would not mean that the programs were not valuable, but rather that expectations of them were misaligned with reality.

However, it would still be premature to dismiss the idea that these students' participation in Erasmus will have a political impact in the future, even though there seems to be little *net* effect. The aggregate results presented in this chapter consider only whether the Erasmus students taken as a whole change relative to the control group. The results do not show whether the limited change occurred because studying in a foreign country *per se* has limited effects, or because the students who were included in this study did not have particular experiences which could have led to more dramatic shifts in attitudes. It is possible that certain experiences make students more likely to change their views, but that the sample drawn here did not have the kinds of experiences which change attitudes. In order to test this possibility, the group of Erasmus students needs to be disaggregated according to the experiences they had while abroad.

6

Varieties of Experience

Surprisingly, there was little evidence of net attitude change among Erasmus students as a group. However, it seems likely that some *individuals'* attitudes do change. If it were possible to identify them in advance, we could retarget our efforts. Are there some subgroups we should expect to be more sensitive, or more profoundly affected, than others?

This is not a new idea. As far back as 1983, Deborah Sell produced one of the most thoughtful literature reviews available on whether exchange students' attitudes toward other countries are improved by the experience. Sell also concluded that, on balance, the evidence then available did not support the assumption that mobility improves the balance of attitudes among groups of exchanges. While she found several studies showing improved attitudes, they were matched by others in which many students actually became alienated from the host country. If all the studies discussed were valid and comparable, this would suggest that while some become more positive a comparable proportion develop more critical (in the negative sense) attitudes. I would treat this conclusion with a degree of caution, given that many of the studies on which the review was based had significant limitations, but the evidence which has emerged in the past 30 years also casts doubt on the "common sense" view. If mobility programs merely redistribute goodwill and hostility chaotically, then it is difficult to see what benefit the sponsor could derive.[i]

Sell's interpretation, however, is more subtle. For her, the interesting question is why *some* students' attitudes do improve—and she finds attempts to provide an answer sadly wanting. Aggregate results do not show whether a lack of net change means mobility *per se* has limited impact, or whether the individual subjects of the research lacked crucial experiences which might have changed their outlook. A lack of aggregate change might conceal changes among subsets of students who share particular experiences. If we could identify individuals whose attitudes would improve as a result of going abroad in advance, then it might be possible to make mobility an effective means of molding desired opinions. We could do so either by carefully selecting participants or else by structuring their experiences while they are abroad. It is worth bearing in mind that political calculations already play into mobility programs' selection processes: administrators are typically looking for some combination of characteristics which will lead to attitude changes in these individuals having a disproportionate effect on others, a strong "multiplier." If governments conceive of mobility as a political tool, then adjusting the selection process to increase the odds of the individuals they choose being influenced in the first place would be no more unethical.

However, in order to make this work governments would need to be able to predict who would be most influenced. They would need to be marked by a predictable set of characteristics beforehand, or share specific experiences during their time abroad. To find out whether this is the case, we need to examine subgroups within the mobile population.

A relatively small number of before-and-after studies have attempted to differentiate in this way. I used their findings to develop a model of Erasmus student socialization, and this model in turn was used to develop a supplement to the post-Erasmus (2008) questionnaire.

Maturity

Participants' level of intellectual and personal development probably affects how far the experience of mobility is likely to influence them. Scott (1955) asserts that established scholars are less malleable than students, an idea which was supported by some of my more mature interviewees (e.g. DAAD Interview One, Marshall Interview One).

As a general rule, it would seem sensible to take account of respondents' maturity when looking for evidence of attitude change. However, this was less of an issue with the Erasmus students, as this was a relatively homogenous group dominated by undergraduate students midway through their first degrees.

Generalization of Affect

Salter and Teger (1975) advance the "generalization of affect" hypothesis, suggesting that students who enjoy their time abroad are likely to develop positive attitudes toward the host country—and perhaps foreigners in general. Students who are miserable are likely to develop negative opinions. Again, this seems intuitive, and the concept is backed by psychological theory (Auster 1965)—although Salter and Teger's findings are based on the reactions of students who were put to work over the summer in conditions which were (hopefully!) more challenging than any of the Erasmus students would have faced. Making mobile students happy probably does have some impact on their attitudes, but of course coming up with a formula to manufacture happiness is a difficult task.

Status

As a general rule, whether sojourners come from similar backgrounds to the bulk of their contacts in the host country seems to affect whether they develop positive attitudes (Stephan 1985). One factor which does seem to undermine contentment is a feeling of not being accorded satisfactory social status by host nationals. Morris' *The Two-Way Mirror* (1960) examines students who came to the United States from foreign countries, many of which were perceived as lower status, and illustrates how this shaped their reactions to the United States. Those who believe host nationals look down on their home countries become resentful and are unlikely to improve their attitudes. While the experiences of non-Caucasian students in the 1950s may make this an unusual case, many other studies have shown that equality of status is one of the conditions for intergroup contact to improve perceptions (see Amir 1969). For example, Matross, Paige, and Hendricks (1982) found that US undergraduates who had contact with foreign undergraduates reported improved feelings toward foreign countries, but those who had contact with foreign postgraduates acting as their instructors showed noticeably increased hostility.

Marion

Paul Marion's (1974) work on student attitudes covered a very wide range of hypotheses. Marion has gone on to become a senior administrator in a range of US colleges, and has been President of Tiffin University in Ohio for more than a decade. In the early 1970s, however, he was a PhD student using panel surveys to track participants in study abroad programs. His thesis, reinterpreted for publication in 1980, explored the possibility that particular groups of students might be more susceptible to changing their attitudes than others. The investigation considered an enormous number of possibilities, and several relationships seem to meet his criteria for statistical significance. The number of hypotheses under consideration hugely exceeds the number of subjects, which complicates causal inference (see e.g. Landman 2003: Ch. 3). It is very important to remember that when a relationship is reported as "significant," this means there is less than a fixed probability of the test showing a relationship when in fact there is none (a type II error). This probability is generally set at one-in-twenty ($p = .05$), although Marion reports as "significant" relationships with a probability as high as one-in-ten. The problem is that with so many variables included (he posed over 200 questions) many more than twenty relationships are possible. Marion does not use a statistical correction to control this family-wise error, so we need to apply some theoretical judgment.

Marion's 90 (no doubt very patient) respondents completed questionnaires which produced scores on 174 attitudes and behaviors, before and after their time abroad. They were also asked 16 questions about previous experiences, 9 about their activities while abroad, and rated their own perceptions of their personal characteristics on 31 dimensions. This produced a vast corpus of data, which suggests a slightly bewildering array of hypotheses. Many relationships between variables seem highly significant. Focusing on perceptions of the host country, improvements were observed among students who had sociable hobbies and who chose to study in multiple foreign countries; for some unknown reason Protestants became favorable more than Catholics. Foreign students from other countries, who were going to visit third countries (for example, Chinese students who were studying for American degrees but chose to spend time in Germany), tended to develop positive attitudes toward the third countries. One clear trend was that students who had more host-national friends and fewer friends of their own nationality (American) tended to become more positive.

Selltiz et al. and Foreign Friends

The importance of friendship patterns is echoed by another omnibus study by Selltiz and Cook (1961). Synthesizing the results of a large series of before-and-after interviews, they suggest that there is no consistent pattern of change in visitors' attitudes toward the United States (pp. 10–11). How attitudes change varies too much depending on students' experiences, and there was an element of unpredictability to this. The amount of interaction foreign students had with US nationals did affect how much they approved of American social habits and relationship patterns (which is perhaps not surprising) but contact alone did not affect their views on broader social issues. One factor which *was* consistently associated with approval of virtually everything, including "public institutions," was having at least one close host-national friend (p. 18). There was a clear link between having American friends and forming positive opinions about the country.

It is worth giving some thought to what this means. This relationship may mean that making American friends *caused* positive views of the

United States. However, this relationship might also be a circular one, with approval of the country leading students to make host-national friends, or open-mindedness leading them both to make friends and to see the country in a positive light during their experiences, or approval might be related to how tight the students' definition of a "friend" was. Nonetheless, this finding is intriguing.

Following the 1961 review, Selltiz et al. produced probably the most ambitious attempt to model the manifold influences on foreign students' socialization, their 1963 volume *Attitudes and Social Relations of Foreign Students in the United States*. Using a very large number of structured interviews the authors set out to test whether the type of university attended was a significant determinant of the amount of contact foreign students had with US nationals, and whether this, in turn, determined their eventual attitude toward the United States. The team questioned students first in October, a few weeks after their arrival, and again the following April, but the study did not follow them up on their return home. The eventual questionnaire ran to around 120 items[2] (1963: 307–13), and many elements of students' lives appeared to be significantly related to attitude change insofar as they passed the 0.05 probability threshold. Again, there may have been some familywise errors.

Of Selltiz et al.'s hypotheses, the most relevant to this study was that foreign students who befriend US nationals develop favorable attitudes toward the United States. Befriending Americans was related to opportunities to interact with them, which in turn was a consequence of personal circumstances. The team observed "significant" relationships between

- attending small universities outside major cities and interacting with Americans
- "housing interaction potential" (an index including, for example, having American roommates) and actual interaction
- housing interaction potential and friendships in April
- "other" interaction potential (for example, taking part in extracurricular activities with Americans) and actual interaction
- actual interaction with Americans and having close American friends by April

Students' initial expectation of, and interest in, getting to know US nationals seemed to predict their interaction with them in April. Visitors who expected they would get to know Americans and who rated their English proficiency highly in October seemed to interact more and make more friends. However, interest in getting to know US nationals correlated significantly only with having American friends in October, not in April. Again, having US friends was related to improved attitudes toward the United

States over the year. This relationship only held for generalized approval of the United States, not more specific characteristics, such as feelings about US foreign policy, level of democracy, or freedom of speech.

A Model

In short, Selltiz *et al.* present a bewildering number of hypotheses about international students' attitudes. We need some kind of theory to explain how the many factors that have been labeled "significant" causes of improved attitudes relate to each other. Fortunately, friendships with host nationals are clearly very important—and this makes it easy to see possible theoretical links.

Out of this rather convoluted—and occasionally inconsistent (Selltiz *et al.* 1963: 217)—set of relationships, the central message seems to be that students who interacted more with US nationals were significantly more likely to have close US friends by the end of the year. There were predictable factors which increased this interaction. And again, having US friends seemed to improve students' attitude toward the United States over the year.

Heider's Balance Theory (1958) offers one of several possible links between friendship and attitude change. Heider's central message is that people strive to reach "balanced states," in which they associate positive things with people they have positive attitudes toward. One strategy they can (perhaps subconsciously) use to reach a balanced state is to adopt the attitudes of people they like. Simply put, it is uncomfortable to have a positive relationship with someone while having negative views of things associated with that person. People by definition have positive attitudes to their friends, and host national students who have been socialized into a country since childhood are likely to give relatively positive messages about it. In this context, Balance Theory has similar implications to cognitive dissonance and self-perception theories, which claim that it is uncomfortable to hold contradictory ideas or behave in ways which contradict self-image (Fazio et al. 1977, Wood 1999: 552–4). Visitors who like people they associate with the host country are more likely to develop positive attitudes toward that country.

Balance Theory is useful here because it suggests how the many factors known to affect attitudes may fit together. The theory implies that friendship with host nationals can be *approximate* cause of attitude change. In other words, many other variables influence attitudes indirectly by influencing the likelihood of friendships developing. Other factors influence attitudes, but do so only indirectly through the intervening variable of friendship.

Combining Balance Theory, and several others which suggest similar predictions, with the previous studies allowed me to produce a simple model. First, we need to determine whether befriending host nationals leads to developing positive attitudes, and second whether there are particular circumstances which make friendships more likely to form. If these circumstances are consistent and predictable, it may be possible to replicate them. If so, then mobility could be made into an effective instrument for shaping political attitudes.

I added a page of supplementary questions to the end of Erasmus students' second (2008) questionnaires, and also asked control students a few of the questions about friendships.

Friendship Related to Attitude Change

I asked all respondents whether they had made close friends in the past year, whether any of the friends were host nationals, and whether any were foreigners other than host nationals. The precise wording was taken from Selltiz et al.'s 1963 study, and it is always worth treating 50-year-old questions with some caution. My biggest concern here was that semantic shift might have taken place since 1963 leading modern students to define "close friends" much more loosely than their (probably now long-retired) counterparts from the 1960s. Obviously, to make the data useful I needed some students to admit to not having made friends. To minimize the risk I also asked another version of the question, which used a more rigorous standard—whether respondents had made a friend, host friend, or other foreign friend who now ranked among their five closest friends.

Would you say you made any **close** friends during your time in France?

When we say a **close** friend, the kind of person we have in mind is someone you trust a great deal, who you enjoy spending time with and you would feel comfortable sharing your thoughts with, rather than simply someone you see regularly and are on good terms with.

  o Yes
  o No

If so, were any of these close friends French?

  o Yes
  o **No**

> Are any of these *close* friends from countries other than France and the UK?
>
> ○ Yes
> ○ No
>
> If you made any *close* friends, how much difference would you say there is between your political views and their views?
>
> ○ Their views tend to be almost identical to mine.
> ○ Their views tend to be similar to mine.
> ○ Their views tend to be quite different from mine.
> ○ Their views tend to be very different from mine.
> ○ Other *(please specify)*.
>
> Please think of your five closest friends. Are any of them people you met during your time in France?
>
> ○ Yes
> ○ No
>
> If yes, are any of those friends French?
>
> ○ Yes
> ○ No
>
> Are any of those friends from countries other than Britain and France?
>
> ○ Yes
> ○ No

Unsurprisingly, Erasmus students were dramatically more likely to have made close host and foreign friends in the past year than the controls (Chi^2 test = 42.4 at 1df, $p < .001$). While nearly identical proportions of Erasmus and non-Erasmus students reported having made a close friend in the past year (85.9 percent of Erasmus students, 85.4 percent of control students), 37 out of 73 Erasmus students who answered this question had befriended a host national (51 percent) and 57 of 77 had befriended someone from another foreign country (74 percent). By contrast, only 7 out of 126 control students had made a close friend from the country where the corresponding group of Erasmus students studied (6 percent) and only 43 of 125 had made a close friend from another foreign country (34 percent). These figures cannot "prove" that Erasmus caused students to befriend foreigners, as the kinds of students who go abroad might have been more likely to do so had they stayed at home, but the idea that someone living abroad is more likely to befriend foreigners than someone who stays at home seems rather uncontroversial. What is important is whether this made them more likely to change their views.

I divided the Erasmus students who had made host-national friends from the other respondents, and then repeated the SPANOVA analysis to find out whether they diverged significantly from the others. On most questions, this produced roughly the same results as when the respondents were divided into Erasmus and control groups; excluding Erasmus students who did not befriend host nationals made little difference. For example, Erasmus students who made close friends do not seem to have become more pro-European. But there were two important exceptions to this pattern, both of which related specifically to the host country.

First, having made host national friends was associated with becoming more positive toward the host country. While the interaction between time and group was not significant when the respondents were split up based on their Erasmus/control status (F [1, 221] = 4.3, p = .37), there *was* a significant interaction when the split is between students who did and did not report having made a close friend (F [1, 221] = 5.5, p = .019). The effect size for this relationship was modest (partial Eta^2 = .024), but that level of significance means the results very probably reflected real divergence between the groups. Furthermore, when I split off those students who ranked a host-national friend they had made among their five closest and those who did not, the interaction was both more significant (F [1, 165] = 8.1, p = .005) and had a larger effect size (partial Eta^2 = .047). Students who made friends with host nationals were much more likely to become more positive about the host country, and this was even more obvious when a more rigorous definition of friendship was used.

Second, having host friends seemed to influence Erasmus students' desire to learn more about the host country. When I compared Erasmus and control students there had been a significant interaction between time and group (F [1, 223] = 11.9, p = .001), which indicated that Erasmus students became less interested in learning about their host country. But when I isolated only the students who befriended students from the host country, the interaction term lost its significance (F [1, 223] = 1.9, p = .17). Erasmus students who simply made a close host-national friend still seemed to be moving in the same direction as the Erasmus group as a whole: with the average interest score for them fell from 1.7 to 2.07—as opposed to 1.47 to 1.98 for all Erasmus students. This meant the average level of interest still fell, although not as sharply or enough to show up as a statistically significant convergence with the controls. The picture became more encouraging when I considered only students who counted a host national among their five closest friends. For this group, the trend might actually have reversed. Again, the interaction was insignificant (F (1, 167) = 1.4, p = .25) but the average disinterest score fell from 2.26 to 2. Making very close host friends may have preserved Erasmus students' existing levels of interest in the host country, which would otherwise have eroded. This could potentially be the foundation of a longer-term relationship. One caveat is that the group which went on to form close friendships, oddly, expressed lower-than-average interest in the host country before arriving there. This was not a situation where Erasmus students with foreign friends became unusually interested in learning about their friends' countries, but rather those were students who were less interested than the others and moved toward the norm.

Looking only at students who made close host-national friends gives a much more positive impression than considering the Erasmus students *en bloc*. This may not be definitive proof that going abroad and befriending host nationals improves attitudes, because students who formed positive views might be more liberal in their definition of "friend." However, it is a reasonable basis for (tentatively) suggesting that mobile students' attitudes might improve if they were to befriend host nationals. If administrators could orchestrate this, it might generate the kind of political influence envisioned in the opinion-leader model.

Unfortunately, I was unable to explain *why* some students made friends with host nationals while others did not.

Contact

In 1963, Selltiz et al.'s work on international students' experiences identified factors which could predict whether or not they were likely to befriend host nationals. I asked my sample of Erasmus students a series of questions about the lifestyles they had chosen while they were abroad, based on lifestyles which had been found to increase contact with host nationals in the past. These questions were presented in a supplement to the second-round questionnaire—reproduced in Appendix Two. I tried to use the Erasmus students' responses to these questions as the independent variables for a logistic regression in which the dependent variable was probability of having made a host-national friend counted among their five closest friends. In this regression, none of these proved a good predictor of friendship—in fact, Table 6.1 shows that they were very far from showing meaningful relationships.[3]

Table 6.1 Logistic regression model, probability of making host-national friends

Variable	Wald	d.f.	Sig
Where did you eat most of your evening meals? [In a shared kitchen or dining room/ In a communal dining hall / In a restaurant/ In my bedroom/ Other:]	.004	3	1.000
If you ate most of your meals in a shared kitchen or dining room . . . how many of the people sharing your kitchen were [French]?	.078	1	.780
Where did you live while in [France]? [A house or flat of my own / University halls of residence / A shared house or flat / Other:]	.405	3	.939
Thinking back to the time when you arrived in [France] last year, how interested were you in meeting specifically [French] people? [I did not want to meet French people / I was not particularly interested in meeting French people / I was quite interested in meeting French people / I was very interested in meeting French people / Meeting French people was my top priority]	1.996	1	.158
Did you volunteer (work without pay) while you were studying in [France]? [Yes/No]	.000	1	1.000
Did you work for money while you were studying in [France]? [Yes/No]	2.322	1	.128

I should stress that this inconclusive analysis absolutely does not show that these aspects of students' lifestyles are not important, only that my work cannot predict how they influence international friendship patterns. The fact that no coefficients reached significance was a consequence of the high, often extremely high, standard errors in the regression (Table 6.2). This is consistent with the analysis being woefully underpowered, regardless of whether or not the model was valid. It is not, therefore, evidence that friendship patterns *cannot* be modeled given more data. Only 54 Erasmus students answered these questions, and this might have been too small a number for data-hungry logistic regression. The research, of course, had to be designed several years before the final numbers were known, and the rate of non-completion and attrition could not have been predicted in advance. More specialized research on international students' socialization may well provide some means of predicting which kinds of students are likely to befriend host nationals (see for example Bochner, McLeod and Lin 1977, Marginson and Sawir 2011, Montgomery 2010, Murphy-Lejeune 2002, Selltiz et al. 1963). My findings do provide further evidence that friendship with host nationals has a significant positive impact on views of the host country, and also helps maintain interest in learning more about that country. Encouraging visitors to befriend host nationals might have

Table 6.2 Logistic Regression Standard Errors

Variable	Standard Error
Where did you eat most of your evening meals?	
1) In a shared kitchen or dining room.	5.68×10^4
2) In a communal dining hall.	6.962×10^4
3) In my bedroom.	5.684×10^4
If you ate most of your meals in a shared kitchen or dining room . . . how many of the people sharing your kitchen were [French]?	.245
Where did you live while in [France]?	
A house or flat of my own	5.684×10^4
University halls of residence	4.019×10^4
A shared house or flat	4.019×10^4
Thinking back to the time when you arrived in [France] last year, how interested were you in meeting specifically [French] people? [I did not want to meet French people/ I was not particularly interested in meeting French people / I was quite interested in meeting French people/ I was very interested in meeting French people/ Meeting French people was my top priority]	1.073
Did you volunteer (work without pay) while you were studying in [France]? [Yes/No]	4.019×10^4
Did you work for money while you were studying in [France]? [Yes/No]	1.220

political consequences, as well as being worthy for its own sake, if we knew how to make it happen.

However, we cannot be absolutely certain that living abroad would consistently generate positive attitudes, even if all visitors made close friends. It is possible that a positive attitude toward the country affected students' perception of how close their friends were. While the case looks promising, it is not definitively proven, and of course we still do not have a formula for generating friendships. I did not gather enough information to show what kinds of contact with foreigners would produce enduring social bonds.

While the results from this attempt to generate a statistical model were disappointing, these questions proved very helpful in the follow-up interviews. The interviews deepened my understanding of the interviewees' experiences abroad. An important trade-off for this depth of understanding was, of course, that it is much more difficult to generalize from qualitative investigation, and that these interviews are all retrospective (not before-and-after). As I have stressed throughout, this means we should be very cautious about inferring cause and effect.

7

Individual Perspectives

I interviewed seven of the Erasmus students who completed online surveys. Only Erasmus students (not controls) were included in these post-panel interviews, which took place in the summer following their return home.

Which Respondents Consented to Interview?

As the respondents had only consented to online data collection with the initial questionnaire, I needed further consent before I could contact them to arrange interviews. The supplementary questionnaire sent to Erasmus students asked them to opt in to the interview group, and not all of them consented. The fact that they had to choose to join the interview group in this way suggests that they may not have been representative of the Erasmus group, and the interview findings should not be considered statistically generalizable. It was possible that the students who chose to consent to this relatively intrusive follow-up research might have done so because of characteristics which also made their experiences atypical.

Fortunately, tests revealed that the students who consented to an interview did not seem to have had dramatically different profiles from the others. For example, a Chi^2 test of whether consent to interview is independent of rating of the host country, a variable which might be expected to affect willingness to discuss the subject, returned a value of 1.08 (at 2 df, $p = .58$) indicating no significant association between the two (Table 7.1). The fact that the students who consented to interview do not seem to have done so because they had developed particularly pro-host views was reassuring, as partisan interviewees could have given a misleading impression.

Fifteen British Erasmus students initially consented to interviews, but not all responded when I contacted them again several months later to arrange interviews. Of the original fifteen, I interviewed six in person and

Table 7.1 Consent to interview and change in view of host country, no significant correlation

			Change in Overall Rating of Host			
			Negative	None	Positive	Total
Consented to interview?	No	Count	16	37	16	69
		%	23.2%	53.6%	23.2%	100.0%
	Yes	Count	3	8	6	17
		%	17.6%	47.1%	35.3%	100.0%

one by phone. I strongly preferred in-person interviews and the telephone interview was rescheduled only because my interviewee was unable to get to our original meeting.

The seven interviewees were all British students who went to France. They therefore represent a narrower range of experiences than the panel as a whole. At this point I was depending on the extended cooperation of a group who had already made substantial contributions to the research, and an aggressive recruitment effort seemed inappropriate. The aim of these interviews was to provide qualitative depth to the study, rather than necessarily to provide a representative view, but some recurring themes in the interview may well be peculiar to British students in France. In particular, some of the practical problems in making social contact with French students, and the interest aroused by a wave of strikes on university campuses during the 2007–8 academic year, may be specific to France.

Rather than repeat the survey strategy of directly seeking evidence of changing attitudes, the interviews focused on students' experiences while they were abroad. I was interested in "softer" elements of the stay which would be much harder to quantify in a survey, such as how happy respondents felt and how they thought host nationals reacted to them. I paid particular attention to the kinds of people with whom interviewees formed personal relationships. As the results of the panel survey had already been partly analyzed before these interviews, I could probe further into areas which had proven particularly interesting in the survey results. The results had provided surprisingly strong evidence for policy learning, and I aimed to gather information on why this was the case. Beyond this, in keeping with the logic of a semi-structured interview I encouraged interviewees to emphasize whichever aspects of their experience they believed were most important.

The interviewees were promised anonymity and are identified by pseudonyms. They were

"Sarah," an English female student who spent an undergraduate Erasmus year at Sciences-Po, Paris;

"Deirdre," a female Northern Irish Erasmus student who spent an Erasmus year as an undergraduate in Dijon;

"Ruth," an English female student who spent an undergraduate year in Nice;

"Karen," a female Scottish student who spent an Erasmus year as an undergraduate in Grenoble;

"Stephanie," a female German undergraduate at a British university who spent an Erasmus year in Lyons;

"James," a male Scottish undergraduate who spent an Erasmus year as an undergraduate in Nice;

"Sophie," a female English undergraduate who spent a year working in a research laboratory in Lyons.

Support for Mobility

The political agenda behind Erasmus is distinct from support for the Erasmus *Program* itself. Several interviewees were eager to express their positive views of Erasmus, and there was a sense of their having developed a "loyalty to the program" (Deirdre, echoing my phrase). Their views of Erasmus, as opposed to the experiences of Europe or France that Erasmus made possible, were strongly positive. In some cases interviewees were preparing to go out of their way to help other students to take part, either as a future career (Stephanie and James) or by making an effort to support foreign students visiting Britain (Karen). The support of enthusiastic alumni may well help the *program* to develop—but it does not necessarily show that it fulfills a political purpose.

"Soft" Factors: Status and Happiness

Past work on international students' socialization suggested two hypotheses that I had trouble testing through the survey, so I waited to discuss them in the interviews. It seemed theoretically plausible that students who were happy and felt they were accorded high social status while abroad might be more likely to develop positive attitudes.

Status

Following Morris' (1960) finding that perceptions of their social status within the campus community greatly influenced how visitors perceived their host country, and the importance of social status in revisions of the contact hypothesis (see Amir 1969), I was curious about how my respondents placed themselves. I gave some thought to including a measure of how respondents perceived their social status in the questionnaire supplement. Unfortunately, framing a good survey question about status would be difficult, and I was worried that respondents would find any questions I tried off-putting. Social status is both an abstract concept and can be quite a sensitive subject, and an online survey does not lend itself to sensitive, abstract questions. The survey was not set up to let me clarify terms or probe into answers interactively, and of course it is difficult for any respondent to build up a rapport with a website.

These fears were justified by the interviews. When pressed on how they would have estimated their own social status in France, Deirdre, Karen, and Sophie found the question obscure and, judging from non-verbal cues—such as tone and expression—they may have found being asked about this uncomfortable. James' response was far more nuanced than a simple placement on a scale:

> Q: Do you think you were treated with more or less respect in France or Britain—or did it not make a difference?
>
> A: I think it's a different culture and you get respect in different *ways*. I think the French have a much higher opinion of intellectualism, and people are a lot less afraid of being, of voicing their opinions, which I found quite refreshing. People would ask you for your opinions, which was quite good. However, I think in higher education scenarios, I think you get the opposite effect, where like I said you get much more treated in a kind of formal academic environment like you're just a kind of a schoolchild, that you're just there to learn by rote ... So it's a bit of a kind of contrast there, a bit paradoxical [. . .]
>
> I don't really think about my personal social status, I'm not really sure what that means.

While there may be theoretical grounds to believe that this is an important factor, broaching it in the survey would not have been wise and could well have deterred respondents. There are less direct means of tapping this concept, but of course they would have added many more questions to an already long questionnaire. I was cautious about social status in the interviews as well, but questions on the concept of happiness gave some important clues.

Happiness

Another hypothesis left out of the survey, largely because it was difficult to frame questions in straightforward ways and not deter respondents, was that students' levels of happiness while abroad could affect how their political attitudes developed. This may be significant because happiness will almost certainly interact with other aspects of their experience, particularly friendships with the people around them. Having host-national friends might even be symptomatic of being happy and open. The interviews gave me a chance to test whether respondents could relate to the concept, and how it would fit into the overall pattern.

Interviewees seemed to have no problem in estimating their level of happiness, either absolutely or relative to other points in their lives. Furthermore, the interviews suggested at least a tentative hypothesis. Some of the respondents who agreed to be interviewed had fairly traumatic experiences in their personal lives in the year before they went abroad.[1] By comparison, their lives in France seemed pleasant (e.g. Sarah, Sophie). These were also interviewees who seemed to be atypical of the sample as a whole, in that they reported several positive attitude changes. It is at least possible that their relative contentment made them develop more positive opinions of things they associated with a happy time in their lives. Salter and Teger (1975) offer a similar "generalization of affect" explanation for why some foreign visitors—but not all—develop positive attitudes to their host country. Foreign students who are happy might tend (perhaps irrationally) to develop a more positive attitude to the host country overall. Again, this fits with much of the psychological literature on attitude formation. The predictions we would get from Heider's (1958) Balance Theory are consistent with dissonance and self-perception theories (Fazio et al. 1977, Wood 1999: 552-4)—people tend to develop positive attitudes to things they associate with positive experiences.

Of course, these few interviews cannot prove that happiness levels are a factor more generally. With such small numbers the apparent relationship could be purely coincidental, and since my estimates of the respondents' levels of happiness are based solely on retrospective statements they may not be wholly reliable. They certainly could not tell us whether attitude changes linked to temporary happiness will prove enduring. Nonetheless, the link between happiness and attitude change among overseas students warrants some further exploration in the future.

Prior Experience

While it was unsurprising to find that all the students interviewed (like most other British undergraduates) had experience of traveling abroad, I was struck by their very extensive experience of foreign travel. They had visited France before, and their experiences ranged from short holidays in France (Karen) to having worked there for several weeks (Sophie) to previous exchanges which involved living with French families (Deirdre, Stephanie and James). More generally, most of the interviewees had lived abroad for extended periods, often working in other foreign countries for several months on gap years (Sarah, Ruth and Stephanie). Several mentioned having families with long-standing French connections: Sarah and James in particular emphasized the important part Francophile relatives played in their lives.

It is perhaps not surprising that the interviewees were so accustomed to traveling abroad, and to France in particular. Not only were they willing to embark on this adventure in France, but all bar one of them (Sarah, who took her classes in English while abroad) mentioned having pre-university qualifications in French. This may be particularly pronounced among British students going to France. French is a very commonly taught language in British schools, and five of the seven interviewees were taking a course which included a major French language component and for which going to France was compulsory. Their choices of course were generally motivated by a strong existing interest in the country: only Karen was willing to say that she had chosen to study French largely because she wanted to get a degree in "something" and had enjoyed French at school. This may not be typical of Erasmus students generally. Many exchanges within Erasmus can be done while taking classes through the medium of English, and thus do not require such advanced prior knowledge of the host country and its language, with related acculturation. France is somewhat unusual in providing almost all university courses in French. For my interviewees, however, existing familiarity with France clearly influenced their experiences there in 2007–8.

The impact of the interviewees' prior experience was complex. It would be fair to say that their experiences tended to have been positive, given that the interviewees had chosen to return. On the other hand, the experience of actually living in the country for an extended period as a student can be very different from shorter and perhaps more superficial exposure. As Stephanie remarked, trivial aspects of life—such as having to deal with French bureaucracy—do not really affect tourists, but become unavoidable as an Erasmus student.

> Obviously when you're a tourist you perceive the country completely differently [. . .] when I was studying I realized France is a bureaucratic country and everything's really difficult—like in the university there's so many different layers of bureaucracy. And as a tourist you don't really experience it that way, it's really simple and straightforward.

Nonetheless, interviewees seemed to believe that they would have been more susceptible to major changes in their attitudes if they had not previously traveled abroad: two of them (Sarah and Deirdre) independently brought up examples of American friends they had met in France who had never previously traveled abroad and whose experiences, they believed, had made more of an impact on them as a result. The interviewees' previous experience of traveling abroad also led to the related idea that students might experience more dramatic changes in their attitudes if they went to countries which were less familiar and more dramatically different from their home countries. For example, Ruth reported that friends who had gone to South America had changed their political attitudes significantly because of the political differences between the countries they had visited and the UK.

> Q: Do you think the *average* Erasmus student has a big change in their political views or attitudes to the country they're in while they're away?
>
> A: Yeah, I think it depends where you go, I have friends who were in Chile and Venezuela and I think for them it was a huge part, I mean Cuba, I think it was a big—because it's so, so different. But I think—for friends of mine who've been in Italy and Spain and France, it was more the education—that was the thing, the thing we noticed that was different. That was what we sort of—"oh, you know, can you believe this;" "oh, it's the same in this country;" "oh it must be a Europe-"—you know, it was more about the education, the culture rather than the politics. As I say, I think that would have been different if you were in South America or somewhere.

These ideas may suggest a reason for the relative lack of change in the panel: perhaps I might have found more changes in students who had never gone abroad before, or for that matter less change in students who had lived abroad for years. Furthermore, this research does not allow us to generalize about the impact of moving between countries which are at greater cultural and political distances from each other than is normal in Western Europe. In order to establish this, the study would need to be repeated with students moving between more distinctive countries. This is of course a limitation of the scope of my conclusions, rather than a challenge to their validity.

Contact with the French

Given that Erasmus places students in a foreign country, it might seem obvious that they will socialize with citizens of that country. This is not always the case.

Social Interaction within the University

One striking finding from the interviews was that the students I spoke to had oddly restricted social lives. Interviewees reported relatively limited interaction with French students. This may be a feature specific to French universities: as was pointed out repeatedly (by Deirdre, Ruth, Karen and James) there is a significant cultural difference between Britain and France with respect to the social dimension of university life. French universities tend to have extremely limited social facilities and to be completely quiet outside of class times because most students continue to live with their families and socialize with their school friends. As a consequence, there was a strong feeling that most French students were not interested in befriending Erasmus students. As Ruth put it, Erasmus students at her institution felt "a bit shunned." Interviewees claimed to have made significant effort to meet local people but found it extremely difficult. Those who did include French students in their social circles either considered them "very superficial" (Stephanie), "not integral to our group" (Sarah) or else realized on reflection that they were attracting existing anglophiles ("the French friends I did have were bilingual," Ruth noted). One exception was Sophie, who actually spent the period working in a laboratory rather than attending classes, but she was socializing with her colleagues from work rather than fellow students and the laboratory in question was dominated by foreigners.

On the other hand, most interviewees formed much closer relationships with other Erasmus students. In most cases co-nationals were well-represented in their social circles, but most also had significant relationships with students who were neither French nor British. When interviewees were asked for the nationalities of their five closest friends, they tended to describe cosmopolitan groups: Ruth included a group of Irish girls, a Spaniard and an Italian (who communicated through French as a second language) with a French-Canadian closest, while Sarah included a Russian, Canadian, American, Australian and a German. This association with third-country students, as opposed to host nationals, is a common theme in the Erasmus program. The survey results showed this was common, with 77 percent (65) of the Erasmus students saying they made at least one close friend from a third country—as opposed to 49 percent (39) who befriended host nationals!

These third-country friendships may well be compatible with the aims of the Erasmus program, and perhaps even more welcome than relationships with French students. The program was not conceived as a means of building bilateral relationships between European countries, but as a means of fostering a general European consciousness. In this sense, while students spending all their time with co-nationals may not be a desirable outcome, it is immaterial which European nationalities they come into contact with.

In this respect, however, Erasmus is somewhat atypical. Most mobility programs and scholarships which have a political aim are very much tied to the host country's diplomatic agenda, not a supranational Union's. This research was designed to test how far mobile students absorb norms of the host country: a proposition which the panel results did not support. If students in the sample had limited contact with host nationals, this may offer a partial explanation. And if this is common, it does not bode well for the opinion-leader model more broadly. Is it common? The interviews following my pilot found a similar isolation from host nationals, and I chose to focus on Erasmus students in the hope that they might have more chances to socialize than elite scholarship holders.

Interaction with the Broader Community

Further to their lack of contact with French students, and consistent with the findings of the post-pilot interviews, students tended to have fairly limited contact with French people outside the campus community. Some causes of this isolation were practical and peculiar to France. For example, Stephanie reported being effectively forced into housing away from locals because most French tenancies required a French national to act as guarantor, and only certain areas were available to foreigners who could not find a French citizen to vouch for them, with the result that the only neighbor she ever met was another Erasmus student. There were, of course, idiosyncratic relationships formed with host nationals: Karen seemed to have developed a surprisingly close relationship with the woman who sold her fruit and vegetables.

Q: Apart from people who were students or lecturers in the university, who do you think was the French person you had the closest relationship with while you were away?

A: Em... Apart from students? [laughs] The lady, there was a little organic fruit and vegetable shop on my street, em and I used to get all my fruit and veg there and I had great chats with the lady that owned the shop, she was so, so friendly. And that's probably, bizarrely enough, the person I had the closest relationship with.

Q: [...] What kind of discussions would you have with the lady who owned the organic fruit and veg shop?

A: Em all sorts, discussing, we had discussions about the strikes, Sarkozy em she recommended me places to visit when I was traveling, Eh we had conversations about fruit and veg as well. Like, here, I'd never really thought about it but you can get just about any kind of fruit and veg at just about any time of year, whereas in her shop they sold what was in season...

They appear to have had meaningful political discussions and Karen showed an unusual knowledge of French agriculture. In general, however, interviewees seem to have become acquainted with non-student French nationals through working or volunteering off campus (Deirdre, Ruth and James), and there was no sense of their becoming particularly intimate. The general impression was that the interviewees had fairly limited contact with French people outside the campus community, as well as inside.

Why are the Erasmus students' cloistered lifestyles important? The opinion-leader model implies that visiting a country shapes views of the host, perhaps even producing warm feelings about it that make people want to share their experience. The reason for underwriting a whole year there is to produce an intense familiarity, perhaps even a change of perspective from seeing that country through the eyes of its citizens (Snow 2009: 235–9). Living in a group of foreign sojourners implies seeing the country from these outsiders' perspective. That may go some way toward explaining the muted changes in attitude the survey uncovered.

Political Attitudes

As part of the interview I asked each respondent whether they thought the panel study would have shown that Erasmus students, as a group, changed their political attitudes because they went abroad. I chose interviewees who were willing to talk and who had interesting response patterns, so they were in no way representative. I also included some whose survey results suggested that their views had changed and others whose results suggested that theirs had not. This question was important because I invited them to rationalize *why* they thought this would be the case and *how* the exchange experience might affect people.

Surprisingly, interviewees came up with a range of different answers to the question—and these were not always in keeping with the development of their own attitudes as revealed by the surveys. Some generalized that exchangees' views would have changed significantly, others that the impact would be modest or negligible.

Of the interviewees whose survey responses showed the most obvious changes in their own views, Sarah was surprised because she generalized from her own case but she was also aware of friends from France who had quickly settled back into their previous behavior. By contrast, James was not at all surprised that there had been little change, even though he himself had been politically active while in France, would frequently discuss political issues with a French friend, and had shown a few modest changes in his own political views. He believed it was impossible to know whether those changes could have occurred had he remained in Britain.[2] While going abroad had increased his self-confidence, it had not necessarily moved his attitudes in a direction they would not have taken otherwise. Interestingly Sophie, who had worked closely with foreigners in a lab and showed a penetrating interest in French policies, echoed this lack of surprise. She was aware of people's feelings about the host country influencing their views, and these in turn being influenced by their feelings about the time they spent there (a restatement of Salter and Teger's "generalization of affect"). Personal unhappiness could influence attitudes:

> I suppose it would depend on what your experience was whilst you were out there. If someone's had a bad experience, you may come away a lot less pro-the-country-you-were-in than if you'd had a really good experience [. . .] If you'd had really good feelings toward the country and you haven't had a great time there I can see why you'd come down the other way. [. . .] I had a really good time, I know one other friend who just – I don't know how they managed it, several people went out with boyfriends left in the UK, or girlfriends left in the UK, and they were doing return trips to the UK every three weeks and I think they felt split between the two countries and I think that as a result they didn't settle in in the country and they'd have come back with a less positive feeling.

Her own thinking had mainly developed in a way she thought could not be picked up by the survey instruments: the experience had generally "enhanced" rather than changed her existing attitudes, with one exception: she was increasingly willing to express pride in a British identity which she had previously felt guilty about expressing publicly in the way in which she saw French people celebrating being French. She was already pro-European before going abroad but, as a result of her Erasmus experience, she did feel better-informed about the European Union and therefore more confident in presenting her case. There is of course a converse possibility, that exchangees who begin with a skeptical attitude also gather evidence to back this up in future arguments. While it may seem plausible that Erasmus would strengthen the argumentative power of already pro-European Erasmus students, the interviews do not provide enough information to consider this more than a speculative hypothesis, and the surveys did not show respondents becoming more convinced of their own persuasiveness.

The themes of generalized affect and enhancement of existing attitudes were echoed by other interviewees, although none raised the possibility of improving their ability to act as advocates in quite the same way. Karen was also aware of a temporary increase in nationalistic feelings as a result of being Scottish but constantly identified as English by the French, although she suspected this had subsided before she took the second survey (it did not show up in the survey results). Stephanie, who expressed a desire to work in facilitating international exchange, perhaps unsurprisingly believed that Erasmus would have increased support for European integration. Her thinking was again based on increased knowledge, although unlike Sophie (and indeed several sponsors within the Commission—see Corbett 2005) she seemed to be working on an assumption that knowing more about the reality of European integration would increase support for it. Her thinking was modified, however, by a belief that if students had social problems while abroad these were likely to affect the development of their attitudes. Ruth's expectation that changes were common seemed to be based on the behavior of a few of her friends who were particularly politically-aware, and who may simply have been very unrepresentative.

Even if Erasmus students' attitudes had changed, the impact of short-term changes in individuals' could only be modest unless it spread within their home communities. I asked interviewees if they had done anything that might affect their acquaintances' views of France or Europe. It would be fair to generalize that, at the time of these interviews, spreading the impact of their Erasmus experiences did not seem to be foremost in the interviewees' minds. They made few suggestions of things they had done which might affect the attitudes of their associates to the host country, but those examples seemed fairly trivial in terms of transmitting attitudes to the host country.

> Q: Since you've got back, have you been aware of influencing anybody's attitude to France?
>
> A: Not really influencing attitudes, but I think I'm able to give a bit more in-depth, when—especially when my family are discussing news stories and stuff, I'm in a position to explain more of the background behind things to do with France. But I'm not sure that I'd really influence their opinion.

Understandably, the students were not filled with missionary zeal.

As my interviewees were not a probability sample, it would not be safe to conclude that former exchangees in general do not behave in ways which spread the impact of their experience. However, these interviews did not provide many examples either.

While expectations varied, the explanations these interviews seemed to offer for *why* Erasmus students might (or might not) change were surprisingly consistent with theoretical expectations outlined in the literature. First, most stressed that they thought the extraneous experiences exchangees had while abroad would significantly influence the development of their attitudes. Problems fitting into the host country socially were expected to encourage negative attitudes toward the country as a whole and its values (see Sell 1983). They also laid particular stress on the increased *knowledge* students gained about the world outside their home country.

Career Plans

When I discussed mobility programs with the officials who run them, they repeatedly stressed that their aim was not simply to change the individuals who received grants, but to multiply the impact into their home communities. One possible multiplier of changes in the individual students involved is through their influence in subsequent careers. Does living abroad lead students toward the kinds of careers where they can lead public opinion or directly affect international relations?

Understandably, the interviewees tended to have fairly vague ideas of what career they would end up pursuing. Only Deirdre, who was going on to train as a lawyer, was willing to commit herself with certainty. However, many of them had ambitions which were very internationally-oriented. Deirdre had deliberately chosen a legal training contract which could lead to a placement abroad; James intended to work as a teaching assistant for the British Council. Sophie, who worked in the laboratory, committed herself to a research career in the knowledge that it would entail almost compulsory international mobility, while Stephanie went even further and expressed a wish to organize international exchange programs for a living. These aspirations are consistent with Wiers-Jenssen's (2008) finding that internationally-mobile students, including those involved in relatively short exchanges, are much more likely to find employment which involves either physically relocating to another country or using intercultural and language skills on a regular basis. Teichler and Maiworm (1997: 147–56) come to a similar conclusion specifically about Erasmus students.[3]

This finding cannot be taken completely at face value. Because students were not asked about their career aspirations prior to going abroad, I cannot prove a cause-and-effect relationship. All the problems with imputing cause and effect based on retrospective accounts apply to this observation: for example, interviewees may not accurately recall their pre-Erasmus career aspirations. Given that they were unusually well-traveled before going abroad, it may be that they were predisposed to seek internationally-oriented careers anyway.

If it is truly caused by Erasmus, this diversion of former Erasmus students into internationally-focused careers might point to a longer-term impact independent of attitude change. The opinion-leader model is not the only way of understanding how student mobility could affect the politics of the future. Mobility could also move students into positions where they will support the Union out of blunt self-interest. As Hix (1999: 146–7) shows, graduates—and especially mobile graduates—are much more likely to support European integration than the rest of the population. This is presented by some more thoughtful advocates of Erasmus as a means of building European consciousness.

The reasoning here is that Europeans who become mobile develop interests in the continuation of transborder mobility. The EU maintains ease of movement between member states, which has significant benefits to such mobile, educated workers. Graduates who may have families in one country, work in another, and professional aspirations in still another are likely to see the benefits of being able to move easily between countries. Mobile graduates should, therefore, be expected to support the European Union, but this support may only develop many years after graduation, once they have developed the habit of crossing borders which Murphy-Lejeune (2002) conceptualizes as "mobility capital." According to this logic, the full effects of Erasmus will not be felt in the short-term. Instead, studying abroad once can be expected, in some cases, to generate a kind of mobility addiction. Being mobile builds support for the institutions which enable mobility over the long term.

Alternatively, a willingness to cross borders in their future careers might make former Erasmus students more influential than they otherwise would have been. Bear in mind that I found Erasmus students had very positive attitudes toward host countries and the EU, even though Erasmus did not cause these attitudes. If Erasmus makes them mobile or influential, it probably increases the average level of approval among mobile and influential workers. A student who goes on to a diplomatic career is likely to have a disproportionate impact on international relations compared to one who stays at home. It would be at least logically possible for Erasmus to have a long-term impact without changing attitudes, despite the academic literature's focus on attitude change.

My work on Erasmus students, based on a panel study a little over a year long, cannot by its nature test whether such long-term impact actually occurs. There is no way to know whether the students will actually end up following these ambitious career paths, whether they would have done so without Erasmus, or whether their doing so will have a broader impact. Instead, I examine this hypothesis in the next chapter, which specifically considers long-term impacts of exchange programs.

Policy Ideas

Interviewees affirmed that they really had become aware of the comparative merits of the British and French policy systems, particularly education and health care. Only Sophie conceded that the pre-test survey might have sensitized her to the possibility, and she was able to point to a range of genuine experiences she had while abroad which were linked to the development of her attitudes. The stories interviewees told about why they developed policy interests seemed very plausible. They can be broadly categorized as changes which resulted from personal exposure to French governance, changes brought about by information interviewees acquired from social acquaintances, and ideas they picked up through their academic studies. The most powerful examples came from personal or second-hand experience rather than things they had learned in the classroom, which strongly suggests they would not have picked up these ideas had they stayed in their home countries.

Personal Experience

The interviewees placed great emphasis on their personal experience of how the health and education systems in France affected them. With regard to education, Sarah had a distinctive experience insofar as she had studied at an elite Grande Ecole (the Institute of Political Sciences—"Sciences Po"—in Paris). She was impressed by the institution's emphasis on providing skills for the workplace with the expectation that all its students would go on to senior managerial careers. Other interviewees emphasized negatives, such as the bureaucracy involved in life in a French university (Deirdre, Ruth, Karen, Stephanie and James were all critical of this) and the lack of opportunities for social interaction between students (Deirdre, Ruth and Stephanie had particularly strong views here). Perhaps unsurprisingly, there was some approval of the lack of tuition fees in French universities (Deirdre) but on the other hand, several interviewees perceived the French system as being under-resourced (Ruth, James and Sophie had developed clear views on this trade-off). Their direct personal experiences of French universities, perhaps unsurprisingly, gave them information they would not otherwise have possessed—but they also used these to form firm opinions on the relative merits of the systems.

Two respondents had direct experience of the French health system. Ruth compared the French system favorably to the British due to having received fast and effective care on an occasion when it was needed.

> That's the one thing I thought "France was brilliant!" I—one of my friends got quite ill, we were able to just walk into a hospital, we were seen within about ten minutes, and they were arranging X-rays and blood tests and she had them all done within the space of about three days and, you know, it was actually relatively cheap. [. . .] Myself—I actually had to go in an ambulance one day. [. . .] I was really impressed with that.

James, however, offered a more complex response. His admiration of the French system was slightly reduced, but this was largely a reaction to the realities of the system not meeting high expectations he had developed of French health care while studying the country in the UK. His French tutors had often drawn comparisons between the two which left an impression that the French system was far superior, which did not accord with the personal experience.

> [A friend] had to go to hospital to get her eye checked ... And it was very good actually, it was a very good service but em you had to pay on the point of service and the waiting time was as long as it would be in Britain, which I was kind of surprised at.
>
> Q: How did that impact on your judgment about the health-care system in general?
>
> A: I think it made me a bit more realistic. I don't think it made me have a big negative impression of it. I actually think—although I'm completely for universal health care—there's an argument to be made for making people pay on the point of service, so people don't waste time. [...]
>
> Q: What was your attitude to it before you went to France?
>
> A: Em I think that it was kind of, that it would be marked, a lot more efficient than it was in Britain. Again I can only go on my personal experience [...] Maybe I thought it was more efficient than it was before I went.
>
> Q: Why did you have that impression?
>
> A: I think you often just, there's a lot of news reports and stuff that consistently say that France has very good healthcare. The World Health Organization rate it - again if you're - the top healthcare system in the world. If you're studying French and talk about the country they talk about the healthcare system quite a lot.

Education and health were by far the most common policy areas in which interviewees mentioned changes in attitude (possibly because these appeared in the questionnaire). The only other policy areas mentioned were public transport (Ruth heartily approved of the cheap fares in France) and the French post office, which James used as an example of excessive bureaucracy. The other policy comparison which was probed in the survey, between the British and French legal systems, was not something of which any interviewee had personal experience.

All of these observations fed into students' relative evaluations of the British and French higher education systems, and personal experience was a major contributor to developing a clear personal opinion.

Although this did not always result in ideas for change, there were a few cases in which interviewees could point to the experience changing their beliefs about how their home country should be run. For example, seeing the consequences of a university system which admitted any school-leaver with a Baccalaureate strengthened James' views on the consequences of expanding university intake in Britain. Stephanie thought British universities should be more tolerant of late work, as her French university had been with few negative consequences for the students.

Second-Hand Experience

As well as direct personal experience, interviewees were influenced by second-hand experience, relayed from friends and acquaintances and occasionally the mass media. This would have been limited by their relative isolation from French students and locals, but nonetheless there were many intriguing examples. Sarah's skepticism of the French legal system would fall into this category, as she attributed it to being surrounded by fellow students who held the system "in contempt," or through reading about scandals in newspapers, rather than personal contact. It is a good example of attitudes sometimes being contagious. However, more often such changed attitudes were due to increased knowledge or having factual misunderstandings corrected. For example, Deirdre, who developed a more positive attitude to the French school system, remembered having been under the impression that the French Baccalaureate (school leaving examination) compelled all students to study an inflexible set of subjects.

> Probably from talking to French people, being like "Ew, that's really horrible, if you really hated math, having to do it until you're 18." They're like "well, no because you can reduce it, it's not like having to do an A level in maths, you can adjust the Bac to what your preferences are . . ." I can't really think of anything else that changed my opinion. [. . .] Probably just having more information about it.

She had developed this impression from studying the system in high school and considered the Baccalaureate undesirable as a result. Learning from French students that they had been able to specialize in their curriculum changed this attitude. Similarly, Stephanie, who worked part-time looking after children, was able to learn about the school system from those children and their parents ("I was working in a daycare center [and the children] were telling me about school"). James' high expectations of the French health system after studying it in Britain were dampened partly by direct experience of the system but also through discussions with his landlord, who happened to be a medical doctor.

> I think I got a kind of insight into the way the French system works . . . the way that doctors are more like private doctors. In Nice, there's a lot more private doctors and private specialists, not that they don't take state patients but in the sense that they take private patients as well and instead of having a health clinic they'll just work out of an apartment. And I found that a bit haphazard [laughs].

Possibly the most colorful examples came from my final interviewee, Sophie, who was sure that Erasmus had made her think about international comparisons. Her opinion of the French health system was heavily influenced by the fact that several of her colleagues became pregnant during her stay: other women in the laboratory took a keen interest in their progress and consequently in their experiences of maternity care in France. From these discussions she developed a positive impression of several elements of the French system, which she saw as emphasizing preventive healthcare more than its British equivalent.

> When you get a group of women together and there are babies that's one of the more popular topics of conversation: when you have a bump everyone wants to know how the bump's doing. And so as a result, we ended up discussing I think the differences in the French healthcare system [a long, involved discussion of the details of the French health system follows]. . .
> Once the baby's born, the women get I think it's six sessions of physiotherapy to help them sort of regain control of all the muscles which they lose control of during childbirth. Someone was discussing this with an English woman who'd given birth and they kind of laughed about this and they're like—well, of course we have that done. Because I mean you'd kind of have bladder problems basically later on. I suppose it's a difference in culture. And then children will have their own pediatrician who they'll go to regularly during the year. Visits to doctors are more like a regular—just health care to check everything's ticking over. Whereas in the UK it's always "once something is wrong, then you go to the doctor."

This interviewee also had extended contact with her laboratory supervisor, who was a lecturer in the university. From casual discussions she was able to learn about the realities of teaching in a French university: for example the implications of central political control of universities. In her fast-moving field this meant that lecturers with specialist knowledge could not respond to new developments in the same way as their British counterparts.

> It's like having a national curriculum at university [...] in the UK the curriculum is set by the university dependent on the specialism of the lecturer [...] Whereas in France the lecturers are teaching you from sometimes textbooks which they *know* are out of date. But they have to teach you that textbook because that's what's set and that's what you're going to be marked on, even if they know it's out of date.

One national difference which dominated several interviewees' thoughts on higher education was industrial action, which they "homed in on" (Ruth) because of a wave of strikes in French universities while they were abroad. In several cases these directly affected them, and even those who were not studying on affected campuses were aware of the situation. As none of the interviewees were personally involved in the strike action their understanding of the situation came from other students; personal experience revealed only that campuses were closed and this by itself contributed very little to their understanding. For some students, a combination of the strikes and the new French government was important in stimulating more general discussion about politics.

> In November, there was loads of strikes in France and our university was blockaded for a week, we had no lectures or anything. We just couldn't get our heads round it. Something like that would just not happen in Manchester, students would not mobilize themselves. Our neighbors were quite active in that way, like 'yeah, yeah we need to take a stance get government, it's the only way we can get change. So we would discuss that [...] if their demands were unreasonable (Deirdre).

> Because the French students were all striking when we were there it was a very topical subject. And Sarkozy hadn't been in power very long, so yeah there was quite a lot of political discussion going on, especially between the Erasmus people and the French students, they would explain a lot of what was going on to us, cause we were kind of on the outside and didn't really understand at the beginning why the students were even striking (Karen).

The strikes themselves, and the perceived propensity of French people to take direct action, obviously had an impact on the interviewees' opinions of the French systems. Karen was critical of the whole process, because she was under the impression that only a small number of students in a large university were "actively striking," and they used administrative control of the students' union to close the campus when the vast majority of students were willing to return. This seemed unfair. It was a detail of the process which she became aware of through personal contact with the individuals involved, as was the fact that the situation was, eventually, quietly resolved by the university organizing a secret ballot of all its students.

It was estimated that [. . .] there was about a hundred students that were actively striking. For the rest, the university was shut down so they couldn't go to class. So if about a hundred students managed to keep the entire university shut for six weeks that doesn't seem very fair on the rest of the students. [. . .] They had meetings once a week to discuss the strike, run by the strikers, and at each meeting they had a vote, whether to keep the strike, but it was a show of hands. There were easily 1,000–1,500 people in a lecture hall and it was done by show of hands so basically it's whoever's standing on the stage who gets to say who won the vote and surprise, surprise it was always the strikers who wanted to continue who won the vote, and when the university eventually got around to organizing an anonymous online ballot it was ridiculous, like 80 percent wanted to end the strike.

She was unimpressed with the authorities' willingness to contemplate allowing students unable to attend to pass their year automatically, at the cost of "devaluing" qualifications. This situation seemed highly unlikely within the British system, and probably not desirable. However, the positive result of this experience was an increase in her understanding of why strikes happen, rather than a stereotype that the French are simply innately prone to take direct action. James, at another university which experienced major strikes, formed a similarly negative view of the students organizing strikes, suggesting that they were somewhat unrepresentative and had a limited understanding of the broader political context. On the other hand, Ruth reported taking an interest in the strikes but simply remained confused by what was going on.

In each of these cases, interviewees apparently believed that they were influenced by acquiring new information, rather than necessarily by the opinions of the people with whom they were discussing the systems. In practice, the distinction may be a fuzzy one on any given occasion—but the pattern is interesting.

Study

While changes in the content of courses may also have played a part in students' policy learning, this was less dramatic. The curricula in French universities would have been different from those of interviewees' home institutions, and slanted toward the French context. I did not actively seek evidence that changes in courses caused changes in attitude, and the impact of courses taken in France only arose spontaneously in the course of discussion twice. In the first case, Sarah became interested in the oil industry following a class on its political role (which could conceivably have happened if she had taken a class on oil in Britain). In the second, an interviewee who was studying French law during her time abroad changed her views of how it compared to English law quite considerably.

The fact that courses were mentioned so rarely suggests that these particular students were less aware of changes in course content affecting their views than they were of either direct personal exposure to French governance or hearing about experiences second-hand.

Patterns of Policy Learning

It was less clear that interviewees' attitudes to the French legal system changed than their attitudes to health or education, which accorded with the findings of the surveys. Only two interviewees changed their positions on the French legal system. One was the law student, Deirdre, whose opinion was influenced by having studied French legal principles in class, while Sarah was influenced by French classmates who seemed to hold the system "in contempt. The difference between the legal system and health or education seems to be lack of exposure, either through personal experience or acquaintances who had direct experience of the French system. This familiarity with health and education seems reasonable: all interviewees were university students, while they and most of the French students they would encounter would have recently spent many years of their lives in the school system. The health system would not dominate their daily lives in the same way, but most exchangees would have some exposure through routine healthcare and, as the interviews showed, it is very possible to be influenced by stories of more serious medical issues without actually experiencing them in person. By contrast, neither interviewees nor acquaintances had personal experience of the legal system. Reassuringly, interviewees did not seem to be associating with criminals, or for that matter lawyers, probation officers and police, or any of the other professionals involved in the legal system.

Students who stayed in their home countries would presumably have much more limited exposure, and hence would be much less likely to develop firm attitudes. However, it is worth remembering that the panel results did not show that respondents' views of how things were done in France became more favorable or unfavorable. Many respondents who did not express an opinion before going abroad were willing to express one afterwards, but those of them who became more positive or favored policy transfer were outweighed by others who developed negative attitudes and opposed transfer. There was not a pattern of net change in the ratio of positives to negatives.

These findings suggest that exposure solidifies respondents' views on policy matters, and that actually being in the country is a big part of this.

Being abroad led to direct exposure but also made indirect exposure much more likely. However, their having firm views does not point to a simple, straightforward political impact. Educating foreigners about a country's governance may be a worthy goal, but these interviews by themselves do not show how countries can benefit from causing foreigners to develop favorable views and welcome policy transfer, so long as they are balanced by equal numbers who develop unfavorable views and oppose such transfers.

However, these interviewees were not alone in taking an interest in the governance of the host country. The interviewees I encounter in the next chapter, which considers the long-term impact of exchange programs, will also mention such ideas—and give an indication of how they might relate to political objectives.

Conclusions

My analysis of the survey supplement suggested that friendship with host nationals was a significant factor in the development of Erasmus students' attitudes toward the host country.[4] It also seemed to preserve curiosity about the host country. However, the reality of the experience of studying in France for my interviewees was that they tended not to befriend as many French people as they expected. Instead, the interviewees tended to form bonds with other foreign students, either from Britain or a third country. This may have been exaggerated because of the countries involved: the interviewees were all traveling to France from Britain. In Britain, an active social life for students tends to grow up around universities (particularly the relatively prestigious institutions which generate large numbers of Erasmus students). In France, students tend to socialize with each other much less. We would need interviews with Erasmus students moving between different combinations of countries to know how far this is typical, but other sources have also turned up evidence of international students finding it much easier to socialize with each other than within the host society (e.g. Murphy-Lejeune 2002, Selltiz et al. 1963). The interviews provided clues as to what encouraged and inhibited social interaction, but it was not possible to produce a generalizable model.

There was, of course, variation in interviewees' experiences. However, the interviews were consistent with the panel results in two important respects. There was no clear pattern of change in political attitudes, but interviewees did develop a clearer understanding of host country policies. This emphasis on learning is consistent with the findings of the panel and supports the idea that students increase their knowledge and understanding of the host country. There was much less evidence that attitudes change as a result of any emotional attachment or process of acculturation. Where there was evidence of attitude change it was often due to factual misconceptions being corrected.

Interviewees did express a preference for internationally-oriented careers which might in the long run promote some aims of the scheme. Other studies indicate that studying abroad is associated with pursuing international careers (Wiers-Jenssen 2008). But we cannot conclude much from the uncertain career plans of undergraduate Erasmus students.

The evidence presented here is necessarily limited to the relatively short term. It is conceivable that the full effects might only be seen over the very long term about which interviews with students who went abroad in the previous year will reveal very little. The next chapter engages with the experiences of alumni who are able to look back over decades of post-mobility experience.

8

Impact over Decades

Studying how the Erasmus, Marshall, and DAAD grantees changed over a year abroad gave some indication of whether we can expect net change among international students in the short term. That research considered only the difference between the participants' attitudes a few months before they went abroad and a few months after. Clearly, this does not encapsulate the impact of youthful mobility over the whole course of someone's life.

This chapter traces scholars who went abroad many years ago. Nearly forty years ago, Karl Deutsch's observed that there is a "critical need for more post-sojourn research" (1970: 91): this still holds true today. Although obviously the two are likely to be related, the long-term impact of mobility is not necessarily a continuation of its short-term impact. As the experience fades into the past the impact may be attenuated, even if participants' attitudes and behaviors change significantly in the short term. More recent experiences may seem relatively so much more relevant that ten or twenty years after studying abroad the difference between former exchange students and their non-mobile peers is negligible. Alternatively, there may be little tangible evidence of change immediately after returning from abroad when in fact the experience has had some latent impact. Mobility could change people in ways that cannot be detected at the time, but which lie dormant until activated by some other experience later in life. Hypothetically, a former participant might be posted to a position which involves dealing with some intercultural trouble and might call on the experience of being immersed in a foreign culture to solve the problem. Auster (1965: 405) provides an introduction to the controversy within the psychological literature about the possibility of such "sleeper effects," but it is important to recognize the *possibility* that they arise.

Observing the behavior of students or early-career professionals is also a very unreliable guide to how the same people might behave if they were in positions which allowed them direct influence over policy. The cultural relations specialists responsible for organizing mobility programs express hopes that their alumni will go on to become not only respectable members of the general public in their home countries with favorable attitudes to the sponsor, but potentially "future decision-makers," or at least people with influence over decision makers. As British Council Interviewee Two put it, "our ultimate aim is not to work with individuals, it's to use those individuals as . . . multipliers into a wider community."

Some students will go on to positions of influence. There are plenty of examples of powerful people who have received government funding to study abroad—for many of them that is part of their allure. Once they become influential, are some of their decisions influenced by mobility much earlier in their lives?

To answer we need evidence which cannot be gathered from students who have only recently returned. Given the enormous complexity of people's careers, and even greater complexity of their lives, we cannot reliably predict which students those will be.

Retrospective Views

This approach needs to accept all the problems of retrospective research alluded to in previous chapters. I need to look at long-term impact retrospectively because it is practically impossible to track a sample of participants for long enough to allow some of them to reach positions of influence. Respondents would need to mature after taking part in the program for much longer than the few years available for this research. Despite the best efforts of selection panels, it is impossible for administrators (and certainly academic researchers) to predict reliably whether individual participants are likely to go on to positions of influence in the distant future. The chances of anyone reaching such a position are small, so I would need an enormous sample of contemporary participants to have favorable odds of generating any influential alumni. Finally, tracking alumni could in itself influence their behavior. To overcome the inevitable recall problems built up over a long career they would need to be interviewed regularly about their decision-making, and this might well sensitize them to how their experience could be influencing them. This would exaggerate the impact on the sample, making them unrepresentative.

Using a before-and-after survey design including the period spent abroad is obviously completely impractical. Instead, I contacted a select group of alumni long after they had returned home and become established in their careers (Bamberger, Rugh and Mabry 2006: 270–1, 326–7 discuss comparable "purposive sampling"). I asked about the impact their experiences had on them *in retrospect*. While the great strength of surveys is that they can gather large, representative samples, these interviewees are far from a probability sample. Alumni who gain positions where they can influence important decisions are not likely to be representative.

The claims made for this chapter are different from those made earlier. It aims to cover the longer-term consequences of youthful mobility for a particularly important subset of alumni.

Reservations

While a retrospective approach is necessary, its methodological disadvantages remain. The possibility of faulty recall is significant. It is very unlikely that interviewees remember the details of most instances when they exercised influence, and almost certain that they cannot remember all the occasions on which they might have. More seriously, when respondents' recall is imperfect they often make their experiences appear more ordered and logical, make their motives seem more socially desirable, and so on. It is difficult to establish a link between receiving a scholarship up to forty years previously and later decision-making without a lot of prompting. I did try to focus parts of the interviews on specific incidents within the past few months, but there is no all-purpose solution to these problems. And of course, it is possible that the interviewees who were easy to trace were unusual. These interviews can only show that exchange programs *can* cause certain chains of events. If I did not detect other causal pathways, that does not mean those pathways are never followed.

Commonwealth Scholars and Fellows

I located one former Erasmus student, but the rest of the interviewees for this chapter were influential former Commonwealth Scholars. The Commonwealth Scholarships have a diplomatic agenda,[1] originally framed in terms of strengthening links between Commonwealth countries but increasingly understood in terms of securing influential allies for the sponsor country (Perraton 2009). Usually it is very difficult to contact alumni who went abroad over a decade earlier. It would have given the research a pleasing symmetry if I had been able to interview members of the first classes of Erasmus students who have gone on to prominence, but there is no open database of Erasmus alumni. CSFP administrators, on the other hand, have shown an unusual and impressive interest in keeping track of their alumni,[2] and several officials in the British and Canadian administrations were assigned to compile a catalogue of alumni years before I started interviewing (Kirkland et al. 2003). The preface to this catalogue makes clear that one motive for the creation of the catalogue was to provide tangible evidence that alumni were going on to positions of influence.

> ... publication is timely because in recent years governments have taken a welcome interest in the extent to which scholarships can be measured against their objectives, and to which their impact can be enhanced by follow-up activity. To justify investment in scholarship schemes by 'anecdote'—in other words reciting details of alumni who have risen to particular prominence—is no longer sufficient. We need to know more about the career progression of much wider numbers of award holders, and find ways of engaging with them on a more regular basis. (Kirkland et al. 2003: vii)

The catalogue comes in two parts, a register of 20,000 names of recipients by country and profiles of 1,800 providing details of their subsequent careers and in many cases current contact details. With over 20,000 grantees since the Plan's inception and 1,800 profiles, at least 18,200 were not profiled. The 1,800 alumni profiled are not a perfect sample. The more prominent alumni, and those with more favorable attitudes to the CSFP, were easier to track and more likely to consents and, because the British and Canadian administrations were responsible for producing the document, alumni who were included were disproportionately those who had studied in either Britain or Canada. The Canadians in particular had more complete records for alumni who had received awards relatively recently (Kirkland et al. 2003: viii). In practice, all the Commonwealth Scholars who consented to interview had studied in the UK.

The alumni interviewed here were selected from the register of CSFP alumni for very specific reasons: their occupational profiles in the register showed they had gone on to positions where they could potentially exert influence on behalf of the country which sponsored them as scholars, or on behalf of the Commonwealth more generally. Obviously not all of the alumni who met this description were willing or able to grant an interview. They have been interviewed only once, about all their experiences since they completed their scholarship program—in some cases a period of up to forty years.

All but one of these scholars came from a developed country,[3] funded by the British Foreign Office in the hope that they might be diplomatic assets in the future. Although the Commonwealth Scholarship and Fellowship Plan's success in producing alumni who go on to influential positions in government is often mentioned as evidence of its political importance (Kirkland 2003, Perraton 2009), breaking down the scholars by nationality reveals that this is slightly misleading with regard to the British political objective. While large numbers of scholars who studied in the UK have gone on to senior positions in their home countries' governments, most of these are actually citizens of developing countries whose participation was funded through DfID, officially as a form of development aid, rather than by the FCO. Developing countries that received British scholarships as a form of international aid were often small, and alternative sources of support for advanced education were hard to come by, so the odds of selecting a future national leader for a scholarship were much better. Put simply, a Canadian who received a Commonwealth Scholarship was much less likely to become Prime Minister or Chief Justice in the future than a scholarship holder from a small Caribbean island, simply because the Canadian would have to defeat a larger number of qualified applicants for the top jobs. I tried to select interviewees from developed countries.

To protect the interviewees' anonymity I am identifying them with pseudonyms. Some details have been left deliberately vague. These interviewees are important figures in their communities and they occasionally discussed sensitive subjects during the interviews.

"Paul," the only former Erasmus student who was interviewed for the study, was a lecturer at a British university. He had received an Erasmus grant to study in Germany in the mid-1990s while he was an undergraduate at a university in another European country. There is no database of Erasmus alumni, and he was discovered by chance during the research process. He had since worked only in academia.

"Alexander" was an Australian who received a Commonwealth Scholarship to study in Britain in the 1970s. He went on to hold an elected position in the Australian federal government.

"John," who received a Commonwealth Scholarship to study in the UK in the 1970s, was a civil servant in a small British dependency. He was a manager of a key natural resource for that dependency.

"Anne" was a senior Australian academic who received a Commonwealth Scholarship to study in London in the 1970s. She had spent her career in Australian academia, which sometimes included lobbying the national government.

"Peter" was an Australian who received a Commonwealth Scholarship in the UK in the 1960s. He had spent much of his career as a policy advisor to his state government, as well as working in journalism and academia.

"Matthew" was a Canadian who received a Commonwealth Scholarship to the UK in the 1980s. He subsequently worked as a diplomat for the Canadian Government.

"Mark" was a Canadian who received a Commonwealth Scholarship to the UK in the 1990s. He went on to become a federal civil servant.

Personal Development

Although I was mainly interested in the diplomatic impact of scholarship programs, the interviews revealed important influences on the scholars' own lives. It would be difficult not to notice the important benefits to the interviewees personally, in terms of education, career progression and development of their personalities.

Purely intellectual benefits seem to have been particularly important to interviewees who became professional academics, who had ongoing research agendas related to their interests (Paul) or had formed networks with overseas scholars which helped them advance their research and careers (Anne). The educational benefits of the scheme were a constant background in the interviews. The scholarships enabled some interviewees to develop interests in disciplines which simply did not exist in their home countries (Alexander, John), while others cited less tangible benefits of education in developing their problem-solving skills (Peter, Anne) and cultural awareness (Alexander, Matthew). The educational and personal development associated with scholarships fed into respondents' careers, not least because they usually attended elite institutions and gained more prestigious qualifications than they could have in their home countries (Anne, Peter). Several interviewees independently raised the increased self-confidence they gained from living abroad, which helped them follow a demanding career. Paul ascribed his ability to pursue an academic career to a mixture of good undergraduate performance and increased confidence, both derived from Erasmus.

> I thought that the final year—in which I did my Erasmus exchange—was very liberating and I all of a sudden started to perform much better than I had been doing until then. Because it gave me some degree of confidence I think which perhaps wasn't there [before] . . . Had I stayed I am not sure that I would have performed as well as I did, and had that been the case . . . I might not actually have considered the possibility of applying abroad for a PhD scholarship and so forth.

Similarly, Alexander claimed his success at an elite institution increased his confidence: "when you emerge victorious, you feel absolutely confident that you can tackle any project that anyone asks you to undertake." Anne, who found living abroad while she completed her PhD to be a "very lonely" experience, also considered that the "basic training on which I've built the rest of my career."

The career benefits associated with the scholarship were particularly pronounced for John, who came from a small Commonwealth country which was unable to provide adequate higher education opportunities. John had since reached an important managerial position, but would probably have been unable to obtain an undergraduate education without the scholarship as the dependency could not afford to subsidize it. He was unusual, however, in that his grant from the British government came as part of the aid component of the scheme, intended primarily to contribute to the economic development of his home country rather than to secure influence. In this case, the economic benefit of providing a Commonwealth territory with a skilled worker largely fulfilled the scheme's objectives. However, many of the important political figures among the alumni of the scheme who are used to illustrate its success (Kirkland et al. 2003) are actually recipients of aid, rather than diplomatic, scholarships.

For the interviewees who came from developed Commonwealth countries, whose own higher education systems could provide almost all the skills required for their economies to function, simply benefiting the individual grantees would not fulfill the scheme's objectives. It would be difficult to deny that scholarships brought significant benefits to all of the interviewees themselves. This basic finding would probably not have changed if I had interviewed hundreds of alumni. However, this is distinct from promoting the sponsor's national interest or Commonwealth solidarity—important goals of FCO funding (Perraton 2009: Ch. 5).

Individual Experiences and Individual Change

The interviews illustrate several examples of individuals' idiosyncrasies interacting with their experiences abroad. The long-term impact of scholarships was heavily influenced by the idiosyncrasies of the scholars' personal biographies for years after the initial award. For example, Anne's desire to leave her hometown for personal reasons led her to choose a research agenda focusing on the UK and that then interacted with her social and family lives as they developed.

> There's a sort of life story that goes along next to it. I remained very engaged in British academic life even after I returned to Australia. Partly [because her discipline was centered on British universities] but on my scholarship I ... had a family in Britain so I was very regularly going back for sabbaticals and summer/winter research periods. So I remained very engaged until [the family situation changed].

In a slightly different version of this relationship, Alexander's perceptions of British governance were largely shaped by his health. He had ongoing health problems, which he happened to experience in both home and host countries, giving him a chance to compare two health systems and develop a view of their strengths and weaknesses. His view of the National Health Service did not change just because he was physically in the country, but also because he had direct experience of the system. The scholarship and his health problems interacted. Fairly obviously, the chances of grantees going on to become influential alumni are also dependent on the vagaries of economic and political circumstances. John is a good example. He used his scholarship to pursue a degree in the management of a natural resource which, coincidentally, was to become vital to the territory many years later. This allowed him to move more easily into a senior position.

This interaction underlines the uncertainty of trying to select scholars based on apparent potential in their youth. The impact of future family commitments on career progression, for example, might be positive or negative in terms of ongoing relationship with the host country, and it would be difficult to predict grantees' future personal lives. It also suggests that "sleeper effects," in which the true long-term effect of an experience lies dormant until an event in the future activates it (Auster 1965: 405), are a real possibility. These unpredictable interactions between exchange experience and apparently unrelated personal circumstances seemed to be particularly significant in determining interviewees' longer-term contact with the host country after their awards ended.

Ongoing Relations with the Host Country

If grantees retained contact with the host country after the end of their awards, then this could greatly influence the impact it had on them. Accordingly, I asked all interviewees directly about ongoing contact with the host country.

All interviewees mentioned having ongoing contact with individuals they met during their studies, but how much contact they had varied dramatically. For Mark, contact was limited to roughly annual correspondence with a former flatmate, but Anne and Matthew had met their current partners while studying and had close family ties as a result. They saw ongoing relationships as magnifying the initial impact of their time abroad.

One diplomatic benefit that did emerge was quite direct, as Matthew went to work as a professional diplomat after graduation. In his view, meeting and marrying a foreign woman he met in Britain ultimately increased his effectiveness at his job.

Increased fluency in the host culture is a more subtle explanation for ongoing relationships with the host country than simply retaining the same personal contacts. Alumni might have increased contact with other host nationals later in life because they felt comfortable dealing with them. With Matthew this was the central theme.

Matthew had worked closely with British counterparts throughout his career, apparently with considerable success, on issues of major importance to both countries. Subtle advantages in communicating across cultures could be very helpful in his career. In his view, his success was due—at least partly—to an "intuitive understanding" of British people, which increased his "comfort level" when dealing with British diplomats. Their shared cultural experiences, he claimed, enabled him to develop cooperative working relationships with British diplomats he did not already know. The experience of living in the UK (and subsequently marrying into a British family) gave him an "ability to relate to British colleagues and understand precisely where British colleagues are coming from." The understanding element is key: familiarity made him able to interpret subtle elements of communication, which in turn led to many examples of successful collaboration. None of his examples were of promoting the British national interest, but he could point to situations where there was conflict between the two countries' interests. He believed this understanding also helped him deal with those conflicts constructively, rather than leading him to take a pro-British line. Familiarity helped lubricate the diplomatic process.

It is worth being aware that Matthew had an unusually cosmopolitan background before he gained the scholarship, which could have enabled this cultural fluency. He had lived in Britain before as a teenager. He was also educated at both levels in a socially elite setting, noting that he became aware of British diplomatic practice because so many of his friends had parents working in the FCO. His "familiarity" with the UK might, in fact, be familiarity with an elite social stratum which tends to dominate professional diplomacy—and it is not obvious that this would have brought similar benefits had he followed a different career path.

To a lesser extent Anne echoed this point. Although she went into less detail on how this might come about, she claimed that

> self-evidently these kinds of schemes, that enable people to live in another country, to understand the culture, must generally have a beneficial effect. I mean there are times that they don't [. . . but generally they] do have the desired impact of doing up elites and leadership networks that know each other or at least are familiar with the other culture."

For her, this led to intangible connections to nationals of her former host country.

These reports echo the academic literature on the concept of cultural fluency and mediation (e.g. Bochner 1981, Snow 1992: esp. 28–37), which is based on a model of individuals who have been immersed in a foreign culture becoming more comfortable operating within it, and in some cases acting as interpreters for their home culture. Cultural fluency, whose effects could only be meaningfully explored over a long time period, seems to be a complex phenomenon. I am not in a position to argue that the "comfort level" reported by my interviewees is politically significant based on a small number of interviews. I can say that a cultural fluency model of how mobility affects international relations would be consistent with the Erasmus students' belief that they increased their understanding of the host country and its people, which would be an essential condition for cultural familiarity (Snow 1992: 36–7). This does not rely on scholars' attitudes changing (for which there was little evidence from the panel studies overall). While the panel results do not actually show whether exchangees' *perception* that their understanding increased is accurate, this is not necessarily an essential condition either. It is possible that alumni who believe they understand the host culture may be more confident operating with host nationals, even if they are in fact often *mis*understanding them. The important point is that these accounts point to a mechanism by which exchange programs *might* lead to improved international relations. It is revealing that the interviewees who raised this kind of influence were quite open about the fact that they were talking about relations with British elites. Given the limited contact both they and the Erasmus students reported with the rest of British society, this seems realistic. We are not seeing evidence of scholars becoming comfortable with a whole society, but instead with a relatively narrow slice of it.

If cultural fluency is the significant outcome, then there may be a mismatch between the actual outcomes of mobility and the expectations some officials have for it. There was not nearly such strong support for the suggestion that mobility molded attitudes in a predictable pattern.

Attitudes toward the UK

There was little sense of interviewees becoming more supportive of the Commonwealth as a transnational community—which probably should not be a big surprise given its changing role (see Perraton 2009). The Commonwealth has become a slightly abstract idea. The experience of being in Britain, on the other hand, must have dominated their everyday lives for years. The impact on these interviewees' views of the UK is not clear-cut—certainly not every scholar fell in love with their host country. Mark was willing to say that

> I would say that it affected my attitude toward the UK in a very positive way. I learned quite a bit more about the UK culture . . . I have very fond memories.

Before leaving Canada he had a "fairly neutral" view of the country and "I don't think I would have distinguished the UK from any other country in . . . Europe." Other interviewees doubted that their overall views shifted. Peter was fairly adamant that "there wasn't really a change in my political views," at least as far as partisan allegiance was concerned.

As both Perraton (2009) and I have argued, the Commonwealth Scholarships—at least the crucial British contribution to them—did not begin as a calculated means to generate political sympathy among alumni. By 2008 they were clearly being touted as a means of strengthening Britain's relationship with other Commonwealth countries (Kirkland 2003), but at the time many of these alumni were studying that shift was a long way in the future.[4] Perhaps it would not be surprising if their memories were not dominated by considerations of Britain's future relationship with their countries, with which the CSFP would become entangled decades later. Of course, a handful of interviews with former Commonwealth Scholars chosen in this way does not give me a secure basis for generalizing about attitude change. That said, it is useful to see diversity among them. The examples they brought up of how their experiences had changed their behavior tended not to be about advocating for Britain, but instead about giving more thought to specific British ideas that they thought might be useful to their home countries (and vice versa). They preferred to focus on more specific comparisons with their home countries.

Policy Learning

These conversations continued the theme of increased knowledge and understanding of the host country, often at quite a detailed level. Going abroad inspired comparisons between the policies of home and host countries that stayed in scholars' minds decades later. In some cases, this led them to develop clear preferences for one system or the other, and to see potential for policy transfer. The conversations also revealed that interviewees did not automatically become advocates of copying ideas from the host country, but instead reflected on the institutional context within which they found themselves. However, following their decades of experience interviewees could point to tangible consequences of this increased familiarity with how things were done in another country.

Again, interviewees had greatest exposure to the higher education system, and this was a popular subject for comparison. Paul, who went on to work as a lecturer, clearly took most interest in higher education in his host country for precisely this reason. One aspect of this was his approval of the Erasmus program itself, which he often found himself defending to colleagues. However, his approval of many aspects of the host university system did not often lead him to copy them. He considered himself constrained from doing so by the institutions of the British system within which he found himself operating, and with which he did not believe many foreign practices to be compatible.

> Q: Has it affected how you do your current job—having experience of another system?
>
> A: Um . . . Well, there's limits to the degree in which it can, because I find the British system is very strongly institutionalized. So if I were to say I'd rather not do a course this semester, and take all my students for a compact seminar . . . and we'll do 3 days of full-time presentations . . . and that will be the mark for your degree, then obviously I'm going to run into trouble because we have this problem here of external adjudication. . . . I recognize the strength of the other systems, but I cannot organize them because they would be incompatible with the degree requirements and the teaching requirements that we put forward in our university system here.

Peter offered a broader view. He had written several papers comparing British practices with Australia's on a wide range of subjects, building from an example which received considerable media attention while he was in the UK.

> Things that struck me as interesting and important would have been conditioned by things I came to regard as interesting and important. Some of those things I was less aware of before I went to the UK. For example, I found myself writing quite a bit about [a particular technical area] . . . looking at things that had been done in Australia, thinking more in an international environment.

However, he viewed the change as more subtle than simply copying specific examples. Rather, mobility affected his perspective on how Australia's system was seen by outsiders.

> It's not so much a matter of 'oh wow when I was in London I came across this and therefore we ought to do it,' more—one of the biggest values of the

Commonwealth Scholarship was getting me outside of my own country and looking back in and seeing how other people looked at issues and talked about issues.

This led to an enduring habit of looking abroad for solutions to Australian problems, and suggesting Australian solutions to foreigners. He offered several examples of searches for possible policy transfers, but also noted that many of these were rejected after it became clear they were unlikely to succeed.

[With British counterparts I would] argue it through—not argue it through, talk it through—and say 'oh, well I can see how that might be of value to you but for us it wouldn't be as good *because*' or whatever. And with a lot of issues that was the way I approached things throughout my professional life.

Again, with the virtue of experience opportunities for successful policy transfer perhaps seemed less commonplace than they did to students who had recently returned from France, but learning about foreign experience was still important.

While policy learning is clearly a significant and enduring consequence of international mobility, its political usefulness to the sponsor is not self-evident. There may be plausible routes by which it might influence international relations, but they have not been elaborated fully by academic researchers and, judging from my interviews, are not foremost in policy-makers' minds when they think about the costs and benefits of funding international students. Changing attitudes toward discrete policies, but not toward the country as a whole, does not seem to fit easily into models of influence usually applied to mobility programs. The division between policy learning and attitude change is not always clear-cut, however. A story Alexander chose to illustrate the impact studying in the UK had on him offers a good example of this distinction.

Policy Ideas and Political Action

Alexander made a particularly interesting observation on the political consequences of his time abroad. He was clearly a politically-engaged personality whose career involved positions of authority in national politics. While his general attitude to the UK seemed temperate he was definitely not uncritical, particularly on the British class system and Britain's shift in trading preferences away from the Commonwealth toward the EU (which harmed Australian farmers). Nonetheless, he articulated a plausible causal pathway in which the increased knowledge about host country policies acted as an antidote to propagandistic ideas he had encountered in his home country. As a teenager in postwar Australia he had suffered serious health problems which put severe strain on his family's finances, adding considerably to the stress of the experience. His health problems in Australia

> virtually bankrupted my parents because I was in hospital for so many months. The private health scheme ceased paying benefits after 13 weeks and it was all pretty drastic financially for the family.

By coincidence he also had to seek treatment through the British NHS, at the time when there was a widespread skepticism of tax-funded health care in Australia. His personal experience of the two systems within a short time convinced him that such fears were erroneous, partly motivating his entry into professional politics.

> When I arrived in England four or five years later I was still having problems [when] there was a recurrence of the problem ... I was immediately whisked off [to hospital]. I was able to tell my parents that this was all on the National Health scheme, it had been the most wonderful surgery, excellent nursing care, good rehabilitation, and it didn't cost them a cent. So all the propaganda I'd swallowed over the years about the National Health scheme, as opposed to private cover, evaporated and I was determined on coming back to Australia to join any political or social process which made the provision of medical and hospital care more accessible for more people without having to pay private insurance premiums.

Given that this interviewee's involvement in party politics eventually led him to high office, the coincidence probably had quite a significant impact on Australia and Australians. Learning from abroad played a small part in the reform of Australia's public services. But, again, Alexander was acting for himself and for Australians. There was no sense of any overriding loyalty to Britain, despite the quite considerable financial investment made by the British Government. In terms of narrow national interest, it is difficult to see a return on investment in this compelling story about learning—which may have benefited many people in Australia.

On the other hand, by providing a particularly clear link between knowledge, policy, and Alexander's subsequent career this story ties together several strands of argument. First, it reinforces the impression from the panel results that personal experience can change visitors' perceptions of specific policies—about which they might not have had much information in their home country—rather than their overall feelings toward the host country. Alexander may have engaged more with left-wing ideas, but the evidence from my panel studies suggests that we cannot expect this to be a pattern. If increased knowledge of how things are done in other countries is translated into changes in exchangees' ideological positions, then it does so rather chaotically and the impacts on different students tend to cancel each other out. Hypothetically, there might well have been another Australian scholar who visited the UK, encountered the NHS, and became vehemently opposed to public health care. However, a significant element in Alexander's story is that his exposure to the system was part of a process which led him to his future position of influence. Going abroad not only changed his attitude, but quite probably also increased his future influence. In retrospect, the experience affected *multiplication* as well as changing his opinion.

The Erasmus students' reports suggested that *on average* exchangees' attitudes were unaffected by their experience, but it is difficult to deny that some people who have gone on to be politically influential claim their experiences of living and studying abroad shaped their attitudes. One or two of them showed up in my study, although there were others who said the opposite. Anecdotally, many of the positive stories came from alumni who were well-placed in foreign ministries and international organizations. There are two possible explanations for individuals showing positive effects while groups of exchangees tend to show little change.

First, individuals' recollections of their attitudes are not usually very reliable (Bochner 1981: 18, Lamare 1975). It may be that these people overestimate the impact of mobility, and that they were brought up with positive attitudes to foreign countries (or the preconditions for developing such attitudes) and simply do not remember this. That might explain why they sought such opportunities in the first place.

However, it is also possible that these enthusiastic and well-placed alumni may represent the large minority of mobile students whose attitudes do improve. Alexander changed his attitude to an element of British society, and that was part of what pushed him into politics. This career led him to relative prominence, and also led him to be included in my interviews. It also increased the impact of his experiences abroad on his home country. It seems self-evident that an important official has greater influence than an ordinary member of the public. In this case, multiplication is not independent of short-term change. A visitor who gained nothing from the experience besides a formal education might not have sought out high-profile opportunities, and would have remained obscure.

It is clear that some sojourners do become more positive about the host country, more cosmopolitan, and more liberal,[5] just as some become hostile, nationalistic and conservative. Some of those sojourners do seem to become particularly influential in later life. Students who have positive views of foreign countries by the time they graduate may seek opportunities to deal with foreign countries in the future, and these positions will give some of them influence. Those who are alienated by the experience may simply select themselves out of positions which would otherwise give them influence over international relations, and remain quiet. In other words, the "multiplier" effect may be more pronounced for visitors whose attitudes to foreign countries improve than for those who move in the other direction.

The panel studies tried to draw representative samples, and they show what large groups of exchangees' initial attitudes were and how those developed. The interviews following on from those were informed by those initial attitudes, and I can trace which of the interviewees accurately recalled the change in their positions. The interviews with older alumni are not accompanied by any information about their initial position, and they have been selected *post hoc* on the basis of being influential. Particular changes in understanding and attitude may make alumni more likely to become influential in the first place. Research which could track such differential multiplication would be extremely expensive, in both time and money. The possibility was not suggested in my interviews with policy makers responsible for mobility programs (e.g. British Council Interview One, Two, Chevening Interview One, Two, Three; Entente Cordiale Interview Three, Four; Marshall Interview Two) and the academic literature remains dominated by the opinion leader model (Scott-Smith 2008), anecdotes and the search for a net attitude change. Of course, my research—while an advance on previous work—does not provide solid evidence on the question either. Differential multiplication might, hypothetically, explain why policy makers tend to believe mobility has a greater impact on attitudes than the empirical evidence suggests. Existing studies, including this one, cannot provide much indication either way. Alexander's story suggests an as-yet-unanswered question.

Interviews with influential alumni can show only that giving scholarships to foreigners *can* have certain effects over the long term. They provide little insight into how frequent these effects may be. However, they have produced some insights into how mobility affected past generations of internationally-mobile students.

In many ways, the findings from older alumni are consistent with what much more recent Erasmus, DAAD and Marshall students told me. They continued to stress the role of mobility in promoting knowledge of the host country, and were divided on whether and how the experience affected their political attitudes and views on the host country.

Alumni interviews show that the long-term consequences of studying abroad for individuals cannot simply be extrapolated from the changes which occur in the short term. Individuals' complex personal and professional development interacts with their experience abroad, and this complex interaction determines their longer-term relationship with their former host. Sometimes a scholarship will push a life in a direction it would not otherwise have taken, and this might push some scholars to prominence within their home society.

Like the earlier interviews, speaking to alumni gave mixed evidence on whether exchanges cause significant attitude change. I showed that the net effect of going abroad on attitudes is likely to be fairly negligible under many circumstances. If the degree of multiplication is independent of the direction of attitude change, then the overall effect should also be negligible. Different attitude changes might be differentially multiplied, so that international students who develop passionate beliefs about particular issues have a disproportionate impact in the future. Unfortunately, there is little evidence to test this idea.

Acquiring knowledge—perhaps very subtle, tacit knowledge—about the host country might have significant implications. If this leads to incorrect beliefs being rejected, and provides a model for political change, then it may lead to political activity (very broadly understood). I did not come across examples which clearly served the national interest of the host country in my interviews with long-established alumni, but this learning clearly did benefit the scholars themselves and many people around them. Learning tends to be a fairly linear process. As a rule people become better-informed, rather than more ignorant, as a result of exposure. This seems to have been true for my panels. Attitude change, on the other hand, can occur in either direction—so we have to wonder if one participant's changes are cancelled out by another's. In the panel studies that was often the case.

These interviews show a *prima facie* case that certain interviewees' increased understanding of their former host had political outcomes. Alexander became an advocate for a particular domestic policy within his country as a result of exposure to the British system; Matthew claimed that his increased knowledge facilitated diplomatic cooperation. It was not clear that these tied into the host country's perceived national interest, or that the alumni provided levers for influence.

Conclusion

I began by asking what political benefits governments may gain by sponsoring foreign students to visit their countries. Governments have encouraged scholarly mobility for a long time, and for a constellation of different reasons. Among all of these possible rationalizations for the practice, a strong current of thinking has developed around the opinion-leader model of elite mobility shaping foreign policy. This reflects a belief that, over the long term, these programs shape international relations to the benefit of the sponsoring country. As a result, many prestigious scholarship programs are actually funded by foreign ministries seeking to support conventional diplomacy. Increasingly, this is tied into a "public diplomacy" agenda in which public opinion in foreign countries is seen as something which can be manipulated in order to influence their behavior. Funding carefully-selected foreign visitors is one technique of public diplomacy (Snow 2009). But does this tactic actually work?

We have seen various assumptions about the eventual political impact of mobility from academics, diplomats, administrators and, especially, governments. Although there is an obvious case that the act of *creating* scholarships for foreigners sends useful signals about how governments see their relationships with target countries developing in the future, most long-established programs do not claim that they serve a diplomatic function solely because of their symbolic power. Typically, their supporters claim that the students and scholars who benefit from mobility grants serve a para-diplomatic role.

I have examined several ways in which alumni might potentially be useful to their sponsors. No list of these can hope to be exhaustive: it is always possible to come up with new hypotheses. But by far the most common suggestions were that former international students go on to positions of power where they can directly shape foreign policy to the benefit of their sponsor, that they lead public opinion in their home countries, that they form elite networks with host nationals, or that their experience makes them better-informed about the host and allows them to educate others.

Of these four possibilities for influence (direct influence, opinion leadership, networking and educating), two seem to rest on an expectation that spending a prolonged period in a foreign country will affect students and that this impact on individuals is "multiplied" (e.g. Mitchell 1986) in some way to affect international relations. These are direct influence and opinion leadership. The possibility that former visitors are directly shaping their home country's behavior to the benefit of their former sponsors need not imply disloyalty. It is possible that sympathetic people in positions of power (such as government ministers or civil servants) find common interests with a friendly country, or at least opportunities to help without cost to the home country which has put them in that position of influence. On the other hand, alumni might go on to positions where they themselves do not influence outcomes directly, but they can help shape public opinion and encourage sympathy for a country they themselves have come to respect (for example, as newspaper columnists). These are, of course, not mutually exclusive. While the kind of multiplication may be different (in one scenario alumni work their way into positions where they themselves influence how a country behaves, in the other they have disproportionate influence on public opinion), both of these seem to require more visitors to come away with positive views of their host country than negative views. Otherwise, alumni acting in a way that benefits the former host will be counterbalanced by others pulling in the opposite direction.

Academic analyses of the supposed political impact of exchange programs have tended to focus on these possibilities, particularly the opinion-leader model, and the personnel who actually run the programs have adopted the kind of rhetoric it implies (Scott-Smith 2008), speaking of winning "friends" and promoting "sympathy" abroad. How visitors are socialized during their time in the country is crucial to both the opinion-leader and direct-influence models. The opinion-leader model is intimately tied to the idea that exchanges and scholarships secure soft power and contribute to public diplomacy, increasingly popular slogans within many foreign ministries, and this makes it doubly important to understand whether the model corresponds to social reality.

I found surprising weaknesses in the empirical evidence available when I began this study, so I devoted a great deal of my effort to examining the assumptions underpinning it. I used a set of panel surveys to find out whether going abroad actually changed contemporary international students' attitudes. Despite a careful design, these studies did not support the idea that going abroad causes net change in the political attitudes of large groups of exchangees. Changes in one visitor's attitudes were generally cancelled out by other visitors' moving in the opposite direction. Not only were students' broader political views apparently unaffected but, surprisingly, they did not seem to become more positive toward the host country. The students who went abroad did have more positive attitudes to the host country after going abroad, but only because they were more positive before they left home. They tended to be more left-wing, but this was because they were more left-wing before they left home. They were more in favor of international cooperation, but that was also true before they went abroad. The students were a self-selecting group who had an unusual profile before they received any funding.

This finding contradicts those of other authors who claim to have found that students who go abroad tend to become more favorably disposed toward European integration, more open relations with foreign countries, and so on (e.g. King and Ruiz-Gelices 2003, Carlson and Widaman 1988). I have argued that the findings reported here are based on a more rigorous methodology, and as such are more likely to accurately reflect the real impact of mobility.

There are three important caveats to this rather negative interpretation.

The first is that the students included in this study were all moving between developed, liberal-democratic Western countries, mainly in Europe. There is still a possibility that significant changes in attitudes might be seen among more adventurous students who moved to countries further removed from their own, culturally and politically as well as geographically. It is important to recognize that enormous resources are channeled into moving people between Western countries, often with a diplomatic agenda, but we need more research to find out whether movement outside this cultural sphere makes more of an impact.

The second caveat is that the students seemed to have formed relatively few close friendships with host nationals, and there is some evidence that this is an important factor in developing positive attitudes toward the host country. It is at least theoretically possible that more active management of their time abroad could encourage mobile students to make friends with host nationals. The exchangees' failure to bond with host nationals hardly seems to be unique to my sample. It was a common theme in other studies of international students. Aside from any qualms about manipulating students' social lives, there are two reasons not to be too excited by this idea. First, we do not have a ready-made formula for generating international friendships, and second, it has not been definitively shown that friendship *causes* improved views of the host country. I found that students who had close friends by the end of their stay tended to develop positive attitudes to the host country, but this is not quite conclusive evidence of a causal relationship. Even if friendship causes warm feelings toward the country, we do not know whether this is a short-lived "feelgood" factor or if it has long-term consequences.

The full effects of studying abroad may not become apparent within a few months of students' return home, so I combined the panel studies with a program of interviews with longstanding alumni of the Commonwealth Scholarship and Fellowship Plan. These suggested another unexamined possibility. As far as I know no-one has systematically tracked how international students develop politically in the many decades after they return home—which is when their sponsors expect them to actually deliver the hypothesized benefits. Like everyone else who has analyzed the *net* effect of studying abroad, I was forced to assume that positive and negative attitude changes are going to be multiplied equally by respondents' future careers. It is possible to imagine that positive and negative attitude changes might be differentially multiplied. For example, developing positive views of the host country while abroad might propel someone to seek a career in international relations, as a result of which they might exercise disproportionate influence. That one influential enthusiast would more than cancel out the impact of a corresponding alumnus who became disillusioned. Differential multiplication is a logical possibility, although there is little by way of solid evidence to support it. As a result, the possibility of differential multiplication remains nothing more than speculation and will do so without further investigation. However, the fact that they never floated this idea suggests this is not how administrators believe their scholarships secure influence.

Despite these caveats, there is no denying that these findings are a blow to some of the assumptions about international mobility programs which are being used to justify government funding. Given the tenuous evidence that giving awards to study abroad influences attitudes, it is perplexing that so many programs rely upon this assumption in their mission statements.

Drifting Objectives

This conception of student mobility as something governments can encourage in order to make friends and influence foreigners was not always as prevalent as it has become. It is an idea which may well have been applied retrospectively to scholarships and mobility programs that were actually set up to achieve other ends. The histories of some long-established British Government-sponsored programs provided some examples. Historically, these programs began as symbolic ventures signaling cooperation, or else as convenient distractions from embarrassing diplomatic problems. Their missions shifted toward influencing the students who accepted scholarships once they had already been operating for many years. A belief that overseas students should come away with positive attitudes toward Britain crept in over time.

Although these scholarship programs now make their case for continued or expanded funding primarily on the basis that they are winning friends and influence for Britain, the case for funding them has evolved. The coalitions of bureaucratic actors who supported the creation of scholarship programs were dominated by those who sought other ends. A few supporters may always have considered the possibility of political advantage, but they were a weak minority. Over time, the activities of these programs have changed relatively little. Yet they are presented rhetorically as diplomatic tools, which create sympathy for Britain among soon-to-be influential alumni by exposing them to British way of life. This rhetoric is far from unique to the British government, and similar shifts may well have taken place in other countries as well. In these cases, officials converged on the assumption that mobility programs manufacture sympathetic alumni in other countries. The idea clearly had some appeal within government.

It is difficult to know for sure why this shift has taken place because different ideas about what the programs were supposed to achieve probably crept in slowly over an extended period of time, as one generation of officials succeeded another. I suggested that the opinion-leader/influential-alumni models of influence, both of which imply that visitors come away with positive views of the host country, may actually be popular because they are useful to defend public funding of mobility programs. There are several good reasons for the personnel who have devoted their careers to mobility to hope those programs will survive. If the models were correct, that would point to a clear benefit to the sponsoring government for supporting these programs. Hence it could have spread even without strong evidence that it accurately reflected social reality. Taking into account this historical perspective, the weakness of the empirical evidence is less surprising—and shows we need to be even more careful not to assume that mobility is an effective tool for changing attitudes just because it is being treated as such.

Political Influence by Other Means

I mentioned two other possible routes by which mobility could influence international relations—elite networking and education. There are conceptual links between them. These routes to influence do not necessarily require net attitude change and could conceivably benefit the sponsoring country even if alumni retained quite negative attitudes toward it. I did find some circumstantial support for both networking and education, although any political impact was much less straightforward than, say, an opinion-leader model might suggest.

Networking and Cultural Fluency

One way of thinking about how international mobility promotes networking seems to rest on alumni having formed links with host-country nationals. Those links would need to exert some kind of influence over international relations. While there may be some examples of this kind of influential enduring relationship, the evidence I came across in the course of my research was far from overwhelming. Visitors tended to interact with rather narrow segments of the host population, typically other students and academics in the case of visiting students, but this elitism would not necessarily be a problem for the idea that networks lead to political influence. More concerning was that many of the contemporary exchangees had surprisingly superficial connections to local students, while the alumni had either lost touch with old acquaintances over the years or struggled to point to political consequences from their social relationships. It is worth bearing in mind that this research was not ideally designed to capture network effects like this, because realistically I could only have observed influential networks in the interviews with long-standing alumni and it was not practical to contact large numbers of them. Relying on longstanding alumni is also problematic because different generations may have different experiences. Scholarship holders who visited Britain from overseas in the 1960s and 1970s, when travel and communications were much more time-consuming and expensive, would have found it much more difficult to retain social ties to people they met as visitors.

In any event, looking for ongoing links to specific host nationals might well obscure a more interesting possibility. Living in a foreign country for an extended period might also help international students to communicate with strangers they meet in the future who share that cultural background.

Several interviewees felt their intercultural fluency or competence increased as a result of their experiences. In other words, they did not maintain relations with specific host nationals, but they felt better prepared to deal with other host nationals they met in the future. This did increase their confidence and may have helped them to come to constructive agreements which in some cases benefited both countries. There is quite an extensive literature on this idea, to which Deardorff (2009) provides a good introduction. More detailed debates on how intercultural fluency can be promoted are playing out in the pages of academic journals such as *Intercultural Relations*. Even though they were unusual alumni in very politically-oriented jobs, it was sometimes difficult for my interviewees to specify instances where this affected a specific outcome—but the idea has been explored by others and is consistent with other findings I have discussed. In particular, the concept of intercultural fluency is closely tied to enhanced understanding of other countries and cultures. I did indeed find extensive evidence that supporting foreign citizens to visit a country for an extended period does make them (feel as if they) understand the country and its people better.

Mobility and Learning

While this study uncovered very limited evidence that going abroad systematically shapes students' attitudes, my research did reveal abundant evidence of the educational impact of living and studying in a foreign country. Most of this learning came from the experience of being immersed in another country in everyday life, not from what the visitors learned in their classrooms and lecture halls. There was considerable evidence that sojourners increased their knowledge of the host country, and at least believed they had increased their understanding of its people.

This educational benefit extended to understanding surprisingly technical dimensions of the host country. Visitors returned home with clear ideas about whether public policies were superior in the host country or at home, and why, leading to the possibility that they could become agents of policy transfer in the future. Contemporary students displayed impressive knowledge of aspects of life in the host country as diverse as university funding, maternity care, industrial relations and organic vegetable markets, which they would have been highly unlikely to acquire if they had not lived abroad for several months. These served as models for commending or criticizing the policies of their home countries. While my evidence about contemporary students showed that there was real change, interviews with scholars who had returned home many years earlier showed that this could have long-term ramifications. Established professionals who had received awards to study abroad were still able to point to ideas they had encountered in their former host country decades later, and could tell plausible stories about how these had an impact on their subsequent careers. They provided examples of having sponsored policy ideas they had seen working in the host country, although they were often constrained from adopting host-country policies because these were not compatible with the institutions in which they worked. The policy learning which occurred tended to be a reflective process, rather than simply a case of former Commonwealth Scholars copying ideas from a country they admired. At the very least, they gave me evidence that they contributed to more informed debate about how their countries should go about achieving their objectives. Mobility programs have considerable educational potential, and they can improve the formulation of public policy.

Improved policymaking benefits taxpayers. However, it is harder to see the direct benefit to the country that sponsored the visit. It is possible to imagine ways in which helping to develop more effective policy in foreign countries could bring indirect benefits to the host, particularly if its nationals were in turn able to learn from foreigners as part of a genuine process of mutual learning—but the causal pathway would need to be much more complex than the projection of "soft power" implied by an opinion-leader model in most public diplomacy literature (see Scott-Smith 2008).

While my evidence for this conclusion is new, I am hardly the first to argue that exchange programs are effective means of informing students about foreign countries (see e.g. Snow 1992, 2009). The evidence that they are effective at increasing understanding is much stronger than the evidence that they "win friends" for the sponsoring country. The fact that this is not presented as their primary objective, while another objective based on a faulty assumption is, seems to be driven by tactical maneuvering. An ill-defined promise that alumni will one day bring political influence seems to have been effective as a means of securing funding from foreign service bureaucracies. However, there are risks to conceptualizing mobility programs primarily as a means of securing diplomatic influence.

The Problem of Unsustainable Assumptions

If mobility seems to be "a good thing" from an educational perspective, why does it matter if it is being underwritten for diplomatic reasons? Although there is no simple framework within which to conduct a cost-benefit analysis, this study has shown some potentially very valuable results from mobility. Why does it matter if scholarships are offered in the hope of securing one kind of benefit, but they in fact bring another?

Unfortunately, there is a risk that tying funding to political objectives may distort the whole process. If we think of mobility funding as an investment in the sponsor's diplomatic influence, then there is a risk that a political agenda scholarship programs cannot realistically hope to fulfill eclipses the real benefits. It emerged in several interviews (e.g. British Council Interview One, Marshall Interview Two) that grants are often awarded, at least partly, on criteria that make most sense if their function is to secure political influence by changing grantees' future behavior. In this age of targets and accountability, there are already signs that governments are seeking to maximize the influence that their scholarships secure for them. Evaluation procedures are being put in place which could potentially result in resources being reallocated away from programs which cannot show that they bring long-term political outcomes (e.g. British Council Interview

Two). Diplomats are being ordered to ensure that awards are given only to those candidates who seem most likely to bring political influence in the future (Miliband 2008). Demand for scholarships will always outstrip supply, and governments have to choose who receives their money. If they make these decisions according to what they perceive to be the national interest, aiming to maximize their influence over the influential, then there is a danger of a pressure to deliver results distorting the whole process. It would be a sad irony if the pursuit of political influence, in the service of the sponsor's national interest—which the evidence thus far suggests they do not reliably deliver—distorted the real benefits of academic mobility.

If mobility is not effective in changing political behavior then potential grantees who could bring other substantial benefits are being erroneously selected out. A great deal of effort clearly goes into selecting from among all the thousands of potential grantees those who will bring the greatest benefits to the sponsoring country. The individuals who are believed to bring the greatest political benefit will not necessarily be those who would benefit most from the educational opportunity.

Helping a group of largely young and impressionable students to live abroad does not seem to be a particularly effective way of shaping the political opinions of future elites in another country. This emphatically does not mean that scholarship programs are a waste of money. However, it does suggest that we would do better if we thought of their objectives differently. It is important that we have an accurate understanding of what supporting international mobility can achieve. It is important intellectually, because much sociological thinking is based on the assumption that international contact changes attitudes. It is important practically, because the assumptions on which funding is distributed determine which applicants receive the opportunities which are available. It is important politically, because if the hopes invested in these programs as a means of achieving political objectives, such as international harmony, are misplaced then other strategies should receive greater attention. This book has called into question widespread assumptions about what governments can expect to gain from their investments in international mobility programs; it has also pointed to other benefits that investment in them may bring.

Appendices

The research on which this book is based produced a large amount of data which is not strictly necessary to support the central argument of the book but that may be of some interest to investigators who want to know more about exactly how I conducted the analysis. Rather than print the material, with the kind assistance of the team at Palgrave, I have put it online.

I conducted a pilot panel study of DAAD and Marshall Scholars in the 2006–7 academic year. Although the results were not conclusive, I have presented a summary of them—and the questionnaires respondents were asked to complete—as Appendix One. Appendix One can be found at:

http://us.macmillan.com/uploadedFiles/internationaleducation_Appendix%20One1.doc

Please keep in mind that the sample size may have been too small to allow for generalization.

Appendix Two includes a supplement to the main questionnaire. Although an analysis of response patterns is included in the main text, the online version should give a much clearer idea of how the questions would have appeared to respondents. Appendix Two can be found at:

http://us.macmillan.com/uploadedFiles/internationaleducation_Appendix%20Two2.doc

Notes

Introduction

1. Arndt (2005) and Cull (2006) link the changing usage of these terms to bureaucratic manoeuvring within the US State Department and foreign relations agencies. In their view, the semantics shifted partly to reflect tensions between personnel who emphasized the need to disseminate an American perspective, and their counterparts committed to more of a two-way engagement, with the currently very fashionable "public diplomacy" convenient because it united the two agendas (Cull 2006: 6). This suggests that the academic discourse may be led by the internal politics of the organizations it scrutinizes at least as much as vice versa.
2. These are not mutually exclusive. In Chapter Two, I will show that there is a recurring pattern of scholarships being created to send signals but then coming to be seen as tools for shaping public opinion over time.
3. The word "sympathy" cropped up repeatedly in interviews, but seemed to have very different connotations for different interviewees.

Chapter 1

1. The particular program being described is slightly different from the typical Fulbright grant, in that it is intended to bring citizens of former Soviet countries to Poland where they will be taught the lessons of Poland's post-Communist transformation by American academics.

Chapter 2

1. Perraton's (2009) major study was written simultaneously.
2. This worry, in fact, proved to be justified (Entente Cordiale Interview Four).
3. One of the less-desirable copies of the Magna Carta was eventually moved to Washington in the 1980s thanks to the significant financial inducements of private billionaire Ross Perot; it became a successful attraction at the National Archives (Reynolds 2007).
4. The original plan was to award scholarships at Cambridge University, on the grounds that Oxbridge would naturally make a greater impression than other universities and because Oxford already had Rhodes. A large chunk of

the filing involves disagreements over whether other universities should be included, before it was decided to leave choice of institution open. Ironically, a plurality of the awards are now held by postgraduate students at Oxford (Marshall Interview Two).

5. The first reference of this term on file is actually a handwritten correction in which "leaven" replaces the original typing of "lever" (Foreign Office 1951d). It is difficult to be certain of whether the original typing was simply a clerical error, and this could greatly change the meaning of the whole passage. However, subsequent correspondence adopts the term "leaven," which seems to have become accepted. Incidentally, the scheme has since become dominated by research postgraduates instead.
6. This figure probably exaggerates British dominance because other contributors tended to support full-year awards, while Britain inflated its numbers by counting students on shorter courses and even distance-learning. Even if these were excluded, however, Britain would remain the largest donor, with Canada a distant second.
7. Exceptions are usually for small and/or developing Commonwealth countries whose citizens cannot access suitable undergraduate courses in their home countries.
8. As Perraton (2009: 8) puts it, "at least four Canadian academics [lay] claim to its paternity." There are two interesting links with the Marshall story. As with Marshall, existing international scholarships may well have been models, as these academics had received such scholarships to study abroad themselves. Intriguingly, one key player in the British delegation which agreed the CSFP was senior diplomat Sir Roger Makins, aka Lord Sherfield, who was also responsible for creating the Marshall Scholarships (Perraton 2009: 6 n4).
9. The CSFP, like many other international scholarship programs (see Saunders 2000) was seen as a means of retaining the allegiance of elites in undeveloped countries, who might otherwise send their children to the USSR (Perraton 2009: 27). This seems to have been less of a worry with the developed Commonwealth countries whose nationals were funded by the Foreign Office. The chances of, say, New Zealand being drawn into the USSR's orbit were obviously much lower than the risk to some of the less-developed Commonwealth states.
10. A much smaller set of "Commonwealth Scholarships" aimed at the developed Commonwealth has been resurrected, but they differ radically from their namesakes. These scholarships are funded by the department responsible for higher education and the universities themselves, and have educational rather than diplomatic objectives.
11. This interviewee was in a key position on the Cultural Relations side of the Foreign Office. He was identified both in private correspondence with a former civil servant and by another interviewee (Chevening Interviewee Three) as the key decision-maker.
12. How the FCO could assign responsibility, if the benefits might not be seen within those officials' careers, remained unclear.
13. "Bijou" is a French term meaning a jewel, which used as an adjective, can also mean "small and elegant, luxurious (applied esp to houses)" (Oxford English

Dictionary 1989) or "something small, delicate, and exquisitely wrought" (Random House Dictionary 1966: sense 2).
14. One interviewee who was included as an eyewitness to the program's early history took a different view on the diplomatic potential of scholarships in general, claiming that "if you spend a year in a country, then you probably fall in love with it and you will never forget it" (Entente Cordiale Interview One). This interviewee had moved away from France after witnessing the Scholarships' creation in the mid-1990s, and was speaking partly from experience of administering Chevening Scholarships.
15. The relationship would probably not be completely linear, as the most promising grantees would be recruited first.
16. It might be possible to justify their continued existence on the basis that terminating the programs would carry heavy costs, but this would be risky and would only justify stagnating support, not expansion.
17. Here I mean "bureaucracy" in the sense of a large, complex group of officials, rather than in the pejorative sense.

Chapter 3

1. In a multivariate world, the absence of actual, observable change could represent *ceteris paribus* change, if without that stimulus other forces would have led to change. For example, traveling abroad might stop a student from becoming xenophobic by insulating that student from a wave of xenophobia sweeping across his or her home country. Without the grant that student would have stayed at home and been exposed with the rest of the population.
2. "After an event, therefore because of that event."
3. Richmond's work focused on the use of exchanges as a weapon against the Soviet Union: *U.S.-Soviet Cultural Exchanges, 1958–1986: Who Wins?* is most revealingly titled.
4. The Soviet Union was a largely closed society, which may have made this more likely; travel simply allowed people to learn what life was like outside the Warsaw Pact.
5. Structured interviews are essentially surveys.
6. The authors note that the 17 students in this control group may not have been enough to make a reliable comparison.
7. Researchers cannot force some students who would otherwise go abroad to stay at home, although this might be methodologically more satisfactory. Instead, they need to rely on self-selecting participants, which makes statistical control even more crucial.
8. This included measures of self-identification as a European citizen, pride in Europe, attachment to Europe, trust in other Europeans, closeness to Europeans, whether the respondent believed the current level of European integration was appropriate, and feelings of having "things in common with other Europeans."

9. It is difficult to know if some of these were familywise errors. Each statistical test conducted has a fixed probability of generating a type I error, or suggesting there is a significant relationship when in reality there is not. Setting $p = .05$ as the significance threshold, for example, means there is a one-in-twenty chance of a type I error for every test. If the analyst then runs more than twenty tests, the odds are that at least one significant result will be incorrectly detected. Reporting this result as evidence of an overall change would be a familywise error.

Chapter 4

1. Roommates.
2. Erasmus is open to some students from the European Free Trade Area and candidates for EU membership, such as Turkey.
3. The exploitation of other agendas to advance the use of education in socializing citizens into a European identity can also be seen in the creation of the European University Institute in Florence. While this was initially seen as an adjunct to European cooperation in nuclear energy (and, therefore, expected to specialize in engineering), well-placed officials were to ensure it focused on social sciences, which were believed to be more likely to produce future leaders in political integration (Corbett 2003: 160).
4. These samples probably also included much smaller numbers of students on the Leonardo program, which facilitates work placements in other European countries. The political agenda behind Leonardo is analogous.
5. Strictly speaking these figures do not actually reflect the number of students, but the number of "study periods." An Erasmus study period is one semester for one student, but many stay abroad for two semesters, so they may have been counted twice. This does not change the fundamental point that Britain and France were exchanging very large numbers of students.
6. Neither Reading nor Leeds had a convenient central email list for first-year students, and so the emails had to be passed to individual departments for distribution. The secretaries of those departments that were willing to cooperate then forwarded the emails to their students much as the Erasmus coordinators did for students in the treatment group.
7. French undergraduate degrees at the time were significantly longer than their British equivalents, although this is changing as a result of the Bologna Process.
8. Not all social networking sites are so restrictive in their membership conditions, but in 2006 several sites targeting students admitted only students and alumni of fairly exclusive groups of universities and colleges.
9. The tiny number of British students who went to Spain was not included in this analysis.
10. A standard reaction to the problem of family-wise errors is to apply a Bonferroni correction, which means increasing the threshold for statistical significance in proportion to the number of variables tested. In this case, however, a

Bonferroni correction would mean setting a very high threshold, equivalent to a one-in-several hundred chance of a type I error (Field 2005: 339–40). This would be extremely conservative, as even relationships which are really very strong rarely meet such a demanding test.

11. Technically, SPANOVA requires parametric data and interval-level measurement, which means that we can say, for example, that a respondent giving an answer valued at "3" is twice as far from "1" as a respondent answering "2." In practice, many of the measurements were actually collected on Likert-type scales in which an assumption that the intervals are regular is tenuous (it is not obvious that "neutral" is twice as far from "strongly agree" as "agree"). There is, however, ample precedent for treating them as such in the political science literature, and it seems to make little difference to the results (Garson 2009). Jaccard and Wan (1996: 2–4) provide part of the rationale for using ANOVA in such circumstances.

12. The approach is slightly different from regression analysis using a dummy independent variable, which may be more familiar to political scientists. Both are implementations of the General Linear Model, and as such there are close conceptual links (see Cohen 1968, Field 2005: 311–2). This form of ANOVA is particularly suitable for a quasi-experimental scenario because it requires only categorical independent variables; in this case which questionnaire the responses come from (2007 or 2008) and whether the respondents are Erasmus students or not.

13. If only the respondents who completed both surveys are included in the analysis, this means that 100 percent of the responses to the first survey will be matched up with responses to the second, and so respondents in 2008 were a perfect "sample" of the 2007 respondents. Of course, this is just a semantic distinction—respondents to the first survey who did not complete the second were simply not included in the analysis. As noted earlier, that was not a major concern so long as the drop-outs were reasonably similar to the students who eventually completed both.

14. Bausell and Li (2002: esp. 7–9) provide a technical discussion of circumstances under which this is inappropriate. Thomas (1997: 278) suggests that complex ANOVAs of the kind used in this study are among the tests for which retrospective power calculations of this kind can be useful, although it is best to allow for a certain level of statistical uncertainty around the precise figure calculated for the effect size.

15. The figures given here are intentionally imprecise partly because r is unknown but also because, as Thomas (1997) points out, analyzing power retrospectively involves a degree of statistical uncertainty.

Chapter 5

1. "Student" is recorded as an employment status by World Values, with a value of 6 on variable X028. This excludes apprentices but does not distinguish, for example, between students at universities and colleges.

2. A major difference between this study and World Values is that World Values questionnaires form the basis for highly structured interviews in which a member of the survey team can guide respondents through the more complicated questions. My study was a self-completion design in which complex questions are far more problematic. This also meant, of course, that any comparisons between the two would be vulnerable to method effects, and so judgments about convergence could only be approximations.
3. A "Moreno question," named for the technique's pioneer Luis Moreno, asks respondents to describe themselves as exclusively one nationality or another, or to choose from a limited number of intermediate positions expressing mixed loyalties (Kiely, McCrone and Bechhofer 2005: 66, 81n4)
4. Partial Eta Squared is known to overestimate the effect size in the population slightly (Field 2005:357, 384–5). In this case, slight overestimates are unlikely to affect any of the conclusions drawn, and this measure of effect size is convenient when dealing with unequal sample sizes.
5. Questions explicitly about attitudes to the host countries were kept on a second page, as respondents could not change their answers for the first page once they had moved on.
6. I generated thirty codes to give a unique number to every party preference expressed by a respondent. The codes in 2007 were subtracted from those in 2008, and all non-zero scores were converted to one.
7. Yates' continuity correction, which is designed to reduce Chi^2 overestimation where two dummy variables are cross-tabulated, gives a Chi^2 value of .98, $p = .26$. There is some controversy about the continuity correction (see Field 2005: 685–6), and in this case it does not affect the substantive finding.
8. The continuity correction value was .75, $p = .39$.
9. This interpretation should be treated carefully because the data from the second questionnaire have unequal error variances. Levene's Test for Equality of Error Variances passes the significance threshold for the 2008 data, $F (1, 196) = 5.53, p = .020$. Equal error variance is one of the key assumptions on which SPANOVA analysis is based; if the variances are unequal this can distort findings. However, Levene's Test can show significant results without seriously compromising the analysis if the sample sizes are reasonably similar or if the error variances are comparable—typically, if the ratio of one variance to the other is less than roughly 1:2 (Field 2005: 98). In this case, the variances are 1.760 for the sample of 86 Erasmus students and 2.327 for the 125 controls; these are comfortably within a 1:2 ratio, so it should be safe to treat the analysis as reliable.
10. On this dependent variable, there was a notable violation of the assumption that the error variances of the two groups were equal, and Levene's Test consequently returned highly significant results for both the first and second waves of the survey ($p < .001$ and $p < .01$, respectively). Equality of error variances is an important assumption of Split-Plot ANOVA. However, ANOVA can generally tolerate violations of this assumption provided that the sample sizes for the two groups are similar or that the ratio of error variances is no greater

than roughly 1:2 (Field 2005: 98). In this case, the sample sizes are reasonably comparable and the variance ratio is well below 1:2, with a variance of 1.84 for 86 exchange students and 3.13 for 134 controls. Given that the p (significance) values for this analysis are all very far from the .05 threshold, it seems safe to accept the general pattern of results reported above, that there was no significant change overall or divergence between the groups, although the F values may be slightly inaccurate.
11. The continuity correction was .642, $p = .423$.
12. In this case, the analysis included the direction of change (from agree to disagree or vice versa), so there was an extra column in the table and no need to calculate a continuity correction.
13. Levene's Test did return a significant result for the 2008 data. This was not problematic because the sample sizes were relatively similar and the variance ratio was not excessive. Eighty-one Erasmus students and hundred and nineteen controls from Britain and France were included, with variances of .407 and .855 respectively.
14. Both Box's Test and Levene's Test (in both 2007 and 2008) registered significant results on this variable. It was considered safe to ignore Box's Test given the similar sample sizes in the two groups (81 Erasmus students, 120 controls), but the ratios of variance between Erasmus students' scores and controls' were slightly larger than would normally be considered acceptable. In 2007, the variance for Erasmus students was 1.109 to the controls' .476, while in 2008 the figures were 1.377 to .580. Given that the average scores of the control group were close to the bottom of the scale, this difference was not hugely surprising. As the interaction did not approach statistical significance, the issue was not pursued any further although it may have slightly distorted the results.
15. Translated literally, the Japanese term for overseas student can mean "bearer of enlightenment from beyond the sea" (McConnell 2000: 10).
16. With so many relationships, identifying family-wise errors with a sample of this size would be difficult.
17. Again, the "not applicable" response was intended to highlight students who were answering the wrong survey. Fortunately, only one respondent chose this option, and the pattern of responses indicates that it was simply a mistake.
18. In this case the continuity correction put the result just beyond the probability threshold, at 3.779, $p = .052$. Given that it was only very slightly beyond the $p = .05$ threshold and there are some questions about the reliability of the correction (Field 2005: 685–6), this finding was still considered to be a "significant" association.
19. Yates' continuity correction was .694, $p = .405$.
20. Unlike the other figures reported here, this is not a measure of change over time, but the response pattern in 2008 *after* the Erasmus students had returned home.
21. Again, this data gives a significant result on Levene's Test for the 2008 data. This should not have seriously distorted the findings as the sample sizes and variance ratios were again roughly similar. The analysis included 87 Erasmus

students with a variance of .879 and 136 controls with a variance of 1.108, a ratio of much less than 1:2.
22. I mean "average" in an almost figurative sense here. Strictly speaking, these responses are not arranged on a scale which can have an average, but it is a convenient way to express the situation.
23. Several violations of SPANOVA assumptions were recorded in this analysis. First, Box's Test for Equality of Error Variances gave a highly significant result, with $p < .001$. There are several issues surrounding the interpretation of Box's Test, but it is generally safe to ignore significant results if the sample sizes for the treatment and control groups are similar (Field 2009: 604). In this analysis, the sample sizes were roughly similar (88 Erasmus students, 138 controls, a ratio of less than 2:3), so the violation could be safely ignored. Levene's Test also returned significant results for both the 2007 (F [1, 224] = 44.5, $p <.001$) and 2008 data (F [1, 224] = 11.6, $p < .001$). This is not a critical problem in itself, because the sample sizes were fairly similar, but the variance ratios are also very different. The variances in 2007 were .711 for Erasmus students and 2.675 for controls, while in 2008 they were 1.813 for Erasmus students and 2.566 for controls. This should not be entirely surprising: the Erasmus students were clustered at the top of the scale, particularly in 2007, and so there was simply little room for their responses to vary above the group mean. If anything, this is likely to have led to a mild underestimate of the interaction, since the Erasmus students who were most interested could not be distinguished from the others by the scale that was used.
24. Again, Box's Test returned a significant result, $p = .001$, but the sample sizes (87 Erasmus, 137 controls) were similar enough that this was not a major concern. Levene's Test returned significant results in both 2007 and 2008 ($p = .004$ and $p = .02$ respectively), but again the variance ratios were similar enough to safely ignore this. For the 2007 data, the Erasmus students had a variance of 1.369 and the controls a variance of 1.899, while for the 2008 data the Erasmus variance was 1.352 and the controls' 1.621, all comfortably within a 1:2 ratio (see Field 2005: 98).
25. One possible interpretation of this would be that mentioning the name of the host country triggered reactions in students who had recently returned from that country, influencing their responses. However, the semi-structured interviews with members of the panel did not suggest that these findings resulted from the design of the survey.

Chapter 6

1. Assuming, of course, that the students who become more positive and those who become more negative go on to become equally politically influential.
2. Selltiz *et al*'s report is based on a combination of two studies, so some students were asked more.

3. Perhaps surprisingly, the overall model predicted 38 percent of variance in the dependent variable (Nagelkerke R^2 = .38) even when none of the independent variables approached the .05 significance threshold.

Chapter 7

1. The details are too sensitive to discuss here.
2. His scepticism is in keeping with the logic of this study.
3. However, their research design cannot demonstrate that this was caused by Erasmus.
4. The survey could not directly rule out causality running in the opposite direction.

Chapter 8

1. As I showed in my discussion of the Marshall, Commonwealth, and Chevening Scholarships, this agenda emerged over time to justify scholarships which were endorsed for rather different reasons.
2. Given the political agendas for mobility programs and scholarships, it is slightly odd that many did not keep central databases of alumni until relatively recently. This accords with the idea that their creation was a more complex process than simple means-ends calculation.
3. "Developed" Commonwealth countries were Australia, the Bahamas, Brunei, Canada, Cyprus, Malta, New Zealand and Singapore (CSFP 2006: 6). These are relatively wealthy countries whose citizens have access to postsecondary facilities.
4. I have not attempted to fit a timetable to this evolution of the Scholarships' *raison d'etre*.
5. In the European or classical sense of the term.

References

Interviews

British Council Interview One—An official responsible for organizing a range of British Council activities, including many scholarship programs, during a long career

British Council Interview Two—An official responsible for evaluating British Council performance of its quasi-diplomatic objectives

Chevening Interview One—A British Council official administering the Chevening Program

Chevening Interview Two—A diplomat responsible for creating the Foreign and Commonwealth Office Scholarships and Awards Scheme (FCOSAS)

Chevening Interview Three—A very senior British Council in the early 1980s who was involved in the Council's reaction to the creation of the Foreign and Commonwealth Office Scholarships and Awards Scheme (FCOSAS)

Commonwealth Scholarship and Fellowship Plan (CSFP) Interviews:

"Alexander"—An Australian politician who received a Commonwealth Scholarship to the UK in the 1970s

"John"—A civil servant in a small British dependency who received a Commonwealth Scholarship to study in the UK in the late 1970s

"Anne"—A senior Australian academic who received a Commonwealth Scholarship to study in London in the early 1970s

"Peter"—An Australian policy advisor and journalist who received a Commonwealth Scholarship to study in the UK in the mid-1960s

"Matthew"—A Canadian diplomat who received a Commonwealth Scholarship to study in the UK in the 1980s

"Mark"—A Canadian civil servant who received a Commonwealth Scholarship to study in the UK in the 1990s

DAAD Interview One—A student who received a DAAD grant to study in the UK in the 2006–7 academic year

DAAD Interview Two—A student who received a DAAD grant to study in the Republic of Ireland during the 2006–7 academic year

Entente Cordiale Interview One—A diplomat who was working at the British Embassy in Paris when the Entente Cordiale Scheme was being established

Entente Cordiale Interview Two—A French administrator with responsibility for the Entente Cordiale Scholarships

Entente Cordiale Interview Three—A source with past experience of managing exchange schemes sponsored by the French government, including the Entente Cordiale Scheme

Entente Cordiale Interview Four—A British Council official responsible for administering the Entente Cordiale Scheme

Erasmus Interview:
"Paul"—A lecturer at a British university, who received an Erasmus grant to study in Germany in the 1990s while an undergraduate at a university in another European country

ESN Interview—An interview with a student in a position of responsibility in the European Student Network, a voluntary organization lobbying on behalf of Erasmus student interests in Brussels

Mallaby Interview—An interview with Sir Christopher Mallaby, the senior British official responsible for creating the Entente Cordiale Scholarships

Marshall Interview One—A student who received a Marshall Scholarship to study in the UK in the 2006–7 academic year

Marshall Interview Two—An administrator responsible for organizing the Marshall Program during the 2006–7 academic year

Post-panel Interviews:
"Sarah"—An English female student who spent an undergraduate Erasmus year at Sciences-Po, Paris

"Deirdre"—A female Northern Irish Erasmus student who spent an Erasmus year as an undergraduate in Dijon

"Ruth"—An English female student who spent an undergraduate year in Nice

"Karen"—A female Scottish student who spent an Erasmus year as an undergraduate in Grenoble

"Stephanie"—A female German undergraduate at a British university who spent an Erasmus year in Lyons

"James"—A male Scottish undergraduate who spent an Erasmus year as an undergraduate in Nice

"Sophie"—A female English undergraduate who spent a year working in a research laboratory in Lyons

Publications

Abrams, I., and W. Hatch. 1960. *Study Abroad*. Cited in Sell, D. "Research on US Students who participate in Foreign Study [CE1] Experiences." *International Journal of Intercultural Relations* 7, pp. 131–47.

Adia, E. 1998. *Student Mobility Policy in the European Union 1946–1996*. Unpublished PhD thesis, Leicester University.

Allport, G. 1958. *The Nature of Prejudice*. Garden City, NY: Doubleday.

American Field Service. 2007. *Welcome to Our 90 Year History*, downloaded from http://www.afs.org/AFSI/content/page.php?uid=12 on February 9, 2007.

Amir, Y. 1969. "The Contact Hypothesis in Ethnic Relations." *Psychological Bulletin* 71 (5), pp. 319–42.
Anderson, B. 2006. *Imagined Commuities*. New York: Verso.
Arndt, R. 2005. *The First Resort of Kings*. Dulles, VA: Potomac.
Arndt, R., and D. Rubin. 1993. *The Fulbright Difference*. New York: Transaction.
Aspden, P. 2004. *Selling Democracy?* Downloaded from http://www.counterpoint-online.org/download/216/Selling-Democracy-report-FINAL.pdf on 4/11/07.
Atkinson, C. 2010. "Does Soft Power Matter?" *Foreign Policy Analysis* 6, pp. 1–22.
Auster, D. 1965. "Attitude Change and Cognitive Dissonance." *Journal of Marketing Research* 2 (4), pp. 401–5.
Ayabe, T. 1977. "Foreign Students as an important channel for cultural change." Cited in Mitchell, J. 1986. *International Cultural Relations*. London: Allen and Unwin.
Bausell, R., and Y. Li. 2002. *Power Analysis for Experimental Research*. Cambridge: Cambridge University Press.
BBC. 2007. "Muslim focus for British Council," downloaded from http://news.bbc.co.uk/hi/uk/6396413.stm on November 11, 2007.
BBC. 2008. "Fears over foreign students cuts," downloaded from http://news.bbc.co.uk/1/hi/education/7306689.stm on 17/8/08.
Bochner, S. 1973. *The Mediating Man*. Honolulu: East-West Centre.
Bochner, S. 1981. "The Social Psychology of Cultural Mediation". In Bochner, S. (ed.) *The Mediating Person*. Cambridge, MA: Schenkman.
Bochner, S., B. McLeod, and A. Lin. 1977. "Friendship Patterns of Overseas Students." *International Journal of Psychology*, 12(4), pp. 277–94.
Boomans, V., E. Krzaklewska, S. Krupnik, and S. Lanzilotta. 2008. *Generation Mobility*. Brussels: European Student Network.
Bristol Online Surveys. 2013. *Bristol Online Surveys*. Downloaded from http://www.survey.bris.ac.uk/ on 12/6/13.
British Council France. 2008. *Entente Cordiale Scholarships*, Downloaded from http://www.britishcouncil.org/france-education-scholarships-entente-cordiale.htm on 26/9/08.
British Council. 2013. *Erasmus Operational Handbook for UK Higher Educational Institutions Annex VI, 2013-14v1*, downloaded from http://www.britishcouncil.org/erasmus-institution-funding.htm on 29/5/13.
Bryman, A. 2004. *Social Research Methods*. Oxford: Oxford University Press.
Bu, L. 1999. "Educational Exchange and Cultural Diplomacy in the Cold War." *Journal of American Studies* 33, pp. 393–416.
Carlson, J., and K. Widaman. 1988. "The Effects of Study Abroad during College on Attitudes to Other Cultures." *International Journal of Intercultural Relations* 12, pp. 1–17.
Cheiladaki-Liarokapi, M. 2007. "The Model of Path-Dependency and the Comparative Analysis of the EU Policy-Process." *Political Perspectives* 2 (6). Downloaded from http://www.politicalperspectives.org.uk/General/Issues/EPRU-2007-1/EPRU-2007-S1-06.pdf on 18/4/08.

Chevening. 2002. *What does "Chevening" mean?* Downloaded from http://www.chevening.com/cgi-bin/item.cgi?id=57&d=11&h=24&f=46&dateformat=%o%20%B%20%Y on 17/8/08.

Chevening. 2006. *Annual Report 2005–06*, downloaded from http://www.chevening.com/about/reports/chev0506.pdf on 1/9/08.

Chevening. 2013. *Guidance for Applicants*, downloaded from http://www.chevening.org/apply/guidance on 7/5/13.

Cohen, J. 1968. "Multiple Regression as a General Data-Analytic System." *Psychological Bulletin* 70 (6), pp. 426–43.

Cohen, J. 1977. *Statistical Power Analysis for the Behavioural Sciences, First Edition*. New York: Academic Press.

Committee on a People's Europe. 1985. "'Adonnino' Report to the Milan European Council," downloaded from http://www.ena.lu/ on 15/2/08.

Commonwealth Secretariat. 1989. *Commonwealth Scholarship and Fellowship Plan: Tracer Study Final Report*. London: Commonwealth Secretariat.

Converse, P. 1964. "The Nature of Belief Systems in Mass Publics" in Apter, D. (ed.) *Ideology and Discontent*. New York: Free Press of Glencoe.

Corbett, A. 2003. "Ideas, Institutions and Policy Entrepreneurs." *European Journal of Education* 33, pp. 315–30.

Corbett, A. 2005. *Universities and the Europe of Knowledge*. Basingstoke: Palgrave.

Corbett, A., and H. Footitt. 2001. *Why Cross the Channel?* Downloaded from http://www.francobritishcouncil.org.uk/reports/crosschann.pdf on 11/4/08.

Council of the European Union. 2004. "Council Decision of 26 January 2004." *Official Journal of the European Union*, downloaded from http://eacea.ec.europa.eu/citizenship/documents/legalbasis/legalbasis_en.pdf on January 24, 2008.

CSFP. 2006. *47th Annual Report to the Secretary of State for International Development*, downloaded from http://www.cscuk.org.uk/docs/cscannrep2005-06_000.pdf on August 19, 2008.

Cull, N. 1995. *Selling War*. Oxford: Oxford University Press.

Cull, N. 2006. *Public Diplomacy Before Gullion*, downloaded from http://uscpublicdiplomacy.org/pdfs/gullion.pdf on 30/8/13.

DAAD. 2005. *The German Academic Exchange Service*, downloaded from http://www.daad.org?p=46391 on 12/11/07.

DAAD. 2007a. *FAQs – Study, Research and Life in Germany*, downloaded from http://www.daad.org/?p=faq1 on 29/7/07.

DAAD. 2007b. *Stipendiendatenbank*, downloaded from http://www.daad.de/ausland/foerderungsmoeglichkeiten/stipendiendatenbank/00658.de.html?land=42&overview=1&daad=1 on 29/7/07.

Dahl, R. 1969[1961]. *Who Governs?* New Haven: Yale.

Deardorff, D. (ed.) 2009. *The Sage Handbook of Intercultural Competence*. Thousand Oaks CA: Sage.

Dekker, H., M. Oostindie, and D. Hester. 1993. *International Political Socialization Through an International Joint Study Program*, downloaded from http://docserver.bis.uni-oldenburg.de/publikationen/bisverlag/rusrec93/kap15.pdf on 25/3/08.

Demetry, C., and R. Vaz. 2002. *Assessing Impact on Students' Educational and Personal Development,* downloaded from http://fie.engrng.pitt.edu/fie2002/papers/1511.pdf on 12/11/07.

Deutsch, S. 1970. *International Education and Exchange.* Cleveland: Cape Western University.

DeVaus, D. 2002. *Surveys in Social Research (5th Edition).* London: Routledge.

Dizard, W. 2004. *Inventing Public Diplomacy.* Boulder, CO: Lynne Reiner.

Dolan, C. 2002. *Public Diplomacy, Exchanges and the War on Terror,* downloaded from http://www.state.gov/r/adcompd/rls/15805.htm on 11/11/07.

Dolowitz, D., and D. Marsh. 2000. "Learning from Abroad." *Governance* 13(1), pp. 5–24.

Dudden, A., and R. Dynes. 1987. *The Fulbright Experience.* New York: Transaction.

EACEA. 2008. *Education, Audiovisual & Culture Executive Agency,* downloaded from http://eacea.ec.europa.eu/index.htm on 6/2/08.

Eide, I (ed.). 1970. *Students as Links Between Cultures.* Oslo: Universitetsforlaget.

ESN—The European Student Network. 2007. *Project Description: ESN Survey 2006,* downloaded from http://www.esn.org/survey/?s=project on 15/3/07.

ESN. 2007. *ESN Survey 2007: Generation Mobility,* downloaded from http://www.esn.org/survey2007/ on 6/2/08.

Espinoza, M. 1976. *Inter-American Beginnings of U.S. Cultural Diplomacy,* Washington, DC: State Department.

ESS—The European Social Survey. 2007. *Data Archive,* downloaded from http://www.europeansocialsurvey.org/index.php?option=com_content&task=view&id=78&Itemid=190 on 3/2/2008.

Eurobarometer. 2008. *Standard Eurobarometer Archives,* downloaded from http://ec.europa.eu/public_opinion/archives/eb_arch_en.htm on 6/2/08.

European Commission. 2001. *How Europeans See Themselves,* downloaded from http://ec.europa.eu/publications/booklets/eu_documentation/05/txt_en.pdf on 6/2/08.

European Commission. 2008. *Directorate-General for Education and Culture,* downloaded from http://ec.europa.eu/dgs/education_culture/index_en.html on 6/2/08.

European Commission. 2013. *The Erasmus Programme,* downloaded from http://ec.europa.eu/education/lifelong-learning-programme/erasmus_en.htm on 27/5/13.

European Court of Justice. 1985. *Case 293/83 Gravier – v – City of Liège [1985] ECR593.*

Fairbank, W. 1976. *America's Cultural Experiment in China.* Washington, DC: State Department.

FCO. 2002. "How to apply for a Chevening scholarship," downloaded from http://www.chevening.com/cgi-bin/item.cgi?id=461 on 11/11/07.

FCO. 2005. *CheveningProgramme Annual Report 2004-5,* downloaded from http://www.chevening.com/about/reports/che0405.pdf on 8/12/06.

FCO. 2006. *About Us: Public Diplomacy Board,* downloaded from http://www.fco.gov.uk/servlet/Front?pagename=OpenMarket/Xcelerate/ShowPage&c=Page&cid=1035898725758 on 23/11/2006.

Field, A. 2005. *Discovering Statistics Using SPSS, Second Edition.* London: Sage.
Field, A. 2009. *Discovering Statistics Using SPSS, Third Edition.* London: Sage.
Fisher, A., and A. Bröckerhoff. 2008. *Options for Influence.* London: Counterpoint.
Fiske de Gouveia, P., and H. Plumridge. 2005. *European Infopolitik.* London: FPC.
Foreign and Commonwealth Office. 1985. *Review of British government and British Council funded award schemes.* Stored at the UK National Archives at Kew, reference FO972/144.
Foreign Office. 1952. *General Correspondence from Political and Other Departments.* (Internal code FCOAU 1952). Stored at the UK National Archives at Kew, reference FO371/91013.
Foreign Office. 1951a. *"Question of presenting a copy of Magna Carta to the United States in gratitude for Marshall Aid, memo from J. N. O. Curle."* (Internal code FCOAU 1952/1). Stored at the UK National Archives at Kew, reference FO371/91013.
Foreign Office. 1951b. *"Extract of personal letter from Minister of Labour to Secretary of State, dated October 1951."* (Internal code FO AU 1952/20). Stored at the UK National Archives at Kew, reference FO371/91013.
Foreign Office. 1951c. *Memos on question of presenting copy of Magna Carta to US, March.* (Internal codes FCOAU 1952/2 and FCOAU 1952/8). Stored at the UK National Archives at Kew, reference FO371/91013.
Foreign Office. 1951d. *"Minute of meeting between J. N. O. Curle and Mr. Roberts of Pembroke College Cambridge, 4 October."* (Internal code FO AU 1952/17). Stored at the UK National Archives at Kew, reference FO371/91013.
Foreign Office. 1951e. *"Memo on 'Question of presenting copy of Magna Carta to US (George Marshall Scholarships),' 25 March"* with comments on 4 and 5 April. (Internal code FO AU 1952/14). Stored at the UK National Archives at Kew, reference FO371/91013.
Foreign Office. 1951f. *"Memo from J. N. O. Curle, 16 March"* (Internal code FO AU 1952/3). Stored at the UK National Archives at Kew, reference FO371/91013.
Foreign Office. 1951g. *"Letter from E. W. Playfair, 4 June"* (Internal code FO AU 1952/9). Stored at the UK National Archives at Kew, reference FO371/91013.
Foreign Office. 1951h. *"Letter from J. N. O. Curle, 25th July"* (FO AU 1952/10). Stored at the UK National Archives at Kew, reference FO371/91013.
French Embassy London. 2008. *Entente Cordiale Scholarships,* downloaded from http://www.ambascience.co.uk/article.php3?id_article=1283 on 1/9/08.
Fulbright. 2007. *"The Fulbright Program . . ."* (page header, quoting J. William Fulbright), downloaded from http://exchanges.state.gov/education/fulbright/ on 9/2/07.
Fulbright Association. 2007. *Legislative Alerts and Updates,* downloaded from http://capwiz.com/fulbright/issues/ on 11/11/07.
Fulbright Poland. 2007. *Commission's Objectives,* downloaded from http://www.fulbright.edu.pl/index.php?strona=73&wiecej=157 on 11/11/07.
Garson, G. 2009. *Data Levels and Measurement,* downloaded from http://faculty.chass.ncsu.edu/garson/PA765/datalevl.htm on 29/5/09.

Golay, P. 2006. *The Effects of Study Abroad on the Development of Global-Mindedness*, unpublished EdD thesis, downloaded from http://etd.lib.fsu.edu/theses/available/etd-06292006-231440/unrestricted/DissertationforPatriciaGolay.pdf on 23/4/08.
Gould, M. 1989. "Equality of Access to Education?" *The Modern Law Review* 52 (4), pp. 540–50.
Gudykunst, W. 1977. "International Contact and Attitude Change." In Jain, N. (ed.) *The International and Intercultural Communication Annual, Volume 4*, Annandale, VA: Speech Communication Association.
Hayden, C. 2011. *The Rhetoric of Soft Power*. Lanham, MD: Lexington.
Heider, F. 1958. *The Psychology of Interpersonal Relations*. London: Wiley.
Henderson, G. 1973. *"Guinea."* In Henderson, G. (ed.) *Public Diplomacy and Political Change: Four Case Studies*. New York: Praeger.
Henrikson, A. 2006. *What Can Public Diplomacy Achieve?* Downloaded from http://www.clingendael.nl/publications/2006/20060900_cdsp_paper_dip_c.pdf on 15/8/07.
Hensley, T., and D. Sell. 1979. "A Study-Abroad Program." *Teaching Political Science* 6 (4), pp. 387–412.
Hewson, C. et al. 2003. *Internet Research Methods*. London: Sage.
Hix, S. 1999. *The Political System of the European Union*. Basingstoke: MacMillan.
Hogwood, B., and L. Gunn,. 1984. *Policymaking for the Real World*. Oxford: Oxford University Press.
Hogwood, B., and B. Peters,. 1983. *Policy Dynamics*. Brighton: Wheatsheaf.
House of Commons Foreign Affairs Committee. 2006. *Third Report of Session 2005–6*. London: Stationery Office.
IIE—Institute of International Education. 2006. *International Visitor Leadership Program*, downloaded from http://www.iie.org/Template.cfm?Section=Programs_Portal&Template=/Activity/ActivityDisplay.cfm&activityid=440 on 12/11/07.
IIE—Institute of International Education, 2007. *About the NSEP David L. Boren Undergraduate Scholarships*, downloaded from http://www.iie.org/programs/nsep/undergraduate/default.htm on 12/11/07.
Inglehart, R. 1990. *Culture Shift in Advanced Industrial Societies*. Princeton: Princeton University Press.
Jaccard, J., and C. Wan. 1994. *LISREL Approaches to Interaction Effects in Multiple Regression (Quantitative Applications in the Social Sciences 07–114)*. Thousand Oaks, CA: Sage.
Jacobsen, D. 2001. "Higher Education as an Arena for Political Socialization." *Scandinavian Political Studies* 24 (4), pp. 351–68.
Jennings, M., and Markus, G. 1977. "The Effect of Military Service on Political Attitudes." *American Journal of Political Science* 71, pp. 131–47.
Kharmalova, E. 2005. *The US Government-Sponsored Graduate-Level Exchange Programs*, unpublished MA Thesis, Duquesne University.
Kiely, R., D. McCrone, and F. Bechhofer. 2005. "Whither Britishness? English and Scottish People in Scotland." *Nations and Nationalism* 11(1), pp. 65–82.

King, R., and E. Ruiz-Gelices. 2003. "International Student Migration and the European 'Year Abroad'." *International Journal of Population Geography* 9, pp. 229–252.

Kingdon, J. 1984. *Agendas, Alternatives, and Public Policies*. Boston: Little, Brown and Co.

Kirkland, J., et al. 2003. *Commonwealth Scholarship and Fellowship Plan Alumni Directory 2003*, downloaded from http://www.cscuk.org/docs/profile.pdf on 7/8/08.

Klineberg, O. 1981. "The Role of International University Exchanges." In Bochner, S. (ed.) *The Mediating Person*. Cambridge, MA: Schenkman.

Kubler, J. 2008. "Marshall Scholarships—A Long-Term Investment in a Special Relationship." *Bulletin of the Association of Commonwealth Universities*, number 164, pp. 12–13.

Lamare, J. 1975. "Using Political Science Courses to Inculcate Political Orientations." *Teaching Political Science* 2 (4), pp. 409–32.

Landman, T. 2003. *Issues and Methods in Comparative Politics*. London: Routledge.

Lazenby-Taylor, A. 2005. *The Student as National Ambassador*, Unpublished MA Dissertation, University of Edinburgh.

Lennon, A. (ed.). 2003. *The Battle for Hearts and Minds*. Cambridge, MA: MIT.

Leonard, M., and V. Alakeson. 2000. *Going Public*. London: FPC.

Leonard, M., A. Small, and R. Rose. 2005. *British Public Diplomacy in the 'Age of Schisms.'* London: FPC.

Leonard, M., C. Stead, and C. Smewing. 2002. *Public Diplomacy*. London: FPC.

Lincoln Study Abroad Fellowship Program Commission. 2007. *Global Competence and National Needs*, downloaded from http://www.alliance-exchange.org/Lincoln%20Commission%20Report.pdf on 23/4/08.

Mallaby, C. 2004. "Entente Cordiale Scholarships." In Mayne, R., D. Johnson, and R. Tombs, (eds.). *Cross-Channel Currents*. London: Routledge.

Marginson, S., and E. Sawir. 2011. *Ideas for Intercultural Education*. New York: Palgrave Macmillan.

Mariani, M., and G. Hewitt. 2008. "Indoctrination U?" *Political Science* 41(4), pp. 773–83.

Marion, P. 1974. *Relationships of Student Characteristics and Experience with Attitude and Value Changes in a Program of Study Abroad*, unpublished PhD thesis, University of Colorado.

Marion, P. 1980."'Relationships of Student Characteristics and Experiences with Attitude Changes in a Program of Study Abroad." *Journal of College Student Personnel* 21(1), pp. 58–64.

Marshall Commission. 2007. *Marshall Scholarships*, downloaded from http://www.marshallscholarship.org on 11/11/07.

Marshall Foundation. 2009a. *History 1953–1957*, downloaded from http://www.marshallscholarship.org/about/history/1953-1957 on 16/3/09.

Marshall Foundation. 2009b. *Mission Statement*, downloaded from http://www.marshallscholarship.org/about/missionstatement on 16/3/09.

Marshall Foundation. 2013. *Candidate Evaluation Criteria,* downloaded from http://www.marshallscholarship.org/applications/criteria on 4/5/2013.

Matross, R., R. Paige, and G. Hendricks. 1982. "American Student Attitudes Toward Foreign Students Before and During an International Crisis." *Journal of College Student Personnel* 23 (1), pp. 58–65.

McColl, E., A. Jacoby, L. Thomas, J. Soutter, C. Bamford, N. Steen, R. Thomas, E. Harvey, A. Garratt, and J. Bond. 2001. "Design and Use of Questionnaires." *Health Technology Assessment* 5 (31), downloaded from http://www.journalslibrary.nihr.ac.uk/__data/assets/pdf_file/0006/64833/FullReport-hta5310.pdf on 27/6/13.

McConnell, D. 2000. *Importing Diversity.* Berkeley: University of California.

McMurry, R. 1972[1945]. *The Cultural Approach.* London: Kennikat.

Melissen, J. 2005. *The New Public Diplomacy.* Basingstoke: Palgrave.

Messer and Wolter. 2007. "Are Student Exchange Programmes Worth It? *Higher Education* 54, pp. 647–63.

Miliband, D. 2008. *Hansard Written Ministerial Statements 13/3/08 FCO Scholarships and Fellowships C23WS,* downloaded from http://www.publications.parliament.uk/pa/cm200708/cmhansrd/cm080313/wmstext/80313m0001.htm#08031365000102 on 17/8/10.

Mitchell, J. 1986. *International Cultural Relations.* London: Allen and Unwin.

Montgomery, C. 2010. *Understanding the International Student Experience.* Basingstoke: Palgrave Macmillan.

Morris, R. 1960. *The Two-Way Mirror.* Minneapolis: Minnesota University Press.

Murphy-Lejeune, E. 2002. *Student Mobility and Narrative in Europe.* London: Routledge.

NCIV—The National Council for International Visitors. 2000. *A Salute to Citizen Diplomacy,* downloaded from http://www.worldlearning.org/wlid/docs/nciv_salute.pdf on 14/8/07.

NCIV. 2006. *The Power of Citizen Diplomacy,* downloaded from http://www.rifc.org/The%20Power%20of%20Citizen%20Diplomacyric.ppt on 12/11/07.

Neave, G. 1991. "On Programmes, Universities and Jacobins." *Higher Education Policy* 4 (4), pp. 37–41.

Ninkovich, F. 1981. *The Diplomacy of Ideas.* Cambridge: Cambridge University Press.

Ninkovich, F. 1996. *US Information Policy and Cultural Diplomacy.* New York: Foreign Policy Association.

Nye, J. 1990. *Bound to Lead.* New York: Basic Books.

Nye, J. 2004. *Soft Power and the Struggle Against Terrorism,* downloaded from http://www.project-syndicate.org/commentary/nye8 on 14/8/07.

Nye, J. 2005. *Soft Power.* New York: Public Affairs.

Oxford English Dictionary. 1989. "bijou, *a.*" in the *Oxford English Dictionary,* 2nd Edition. Oxford: Oxford.

Paige, R. 2002. *International Education Week Statement,* downloaded from http://exchanges.state.gov/iew2002/statements/paige.htm on 7/11/06.

Pallant, J. 2003. *The SPSS Survival Manual.* Maidenhead: Open University.

Papatsiba, V. 2005. "Political and Individual Rationales of Student Mobility." *European Journal of Education* 40 (2), pp. 173–188.
Perraton, H. 2009. *Learning Abroad*. Newcastle: Cambridge Scholars Press.
Petit, I. 2007. "Mimicking History." *World Political Science Review* 3 (1), pp. 1–25.
Pew Research Centre. 2008. *Global Economic Gloom—China and India Notable Exceptions*, downloaded from http://www.pewglobal.org/2008/06/12/global-economic-gloom-china-and-india-notable-exceptions/ on 13/6/13.
Potter, E. 2002. *Canada and the New Public Diplomacy*, downloaded from http://www.clingendael.nl/publications/2002/20020700_cli_paper_dip_issue81.pdf on21/1/07.
Potter. E. 2009. *Branding Canada*. Montreal/Kingston: McGill-Queen's University Press.
Random House Dictionary. 1966. "bijou, *a*." in the *Random House Dictionary of the English Language*. New York: Random House.
Reynolds, N. 2007. "Ross Perot Sells 13th century Magna Carta." *Daily Telegraph*, 12 November, downloaded from http://www.telegraph.co.uk/news/uknews/1564126/Ross-Perot-sells-13th-century-Magna-Carta.html on 25/3/09.
Richmond, Y. 2003. *Cultural Exchange and the Cold War*. University Park: Pennsylvania State University Press.
Riordan, S. 2002. *The New Diplomacy*. Cambridge: Polity.
Rogers, E. 1995. *Diffusion of Innovations*. New York: Free Press.
Rose, R. 1991. "What Is Lesson Drawing? *Journal of Public Policy* 11 (1), pp. 3–30.
Ross, C. 2003. "Public Diplomacy Comes of Age." In Lennon, A. (ed.) *The Battle for Hearts and Minds*. Cambridge, MA: MIT.
Salter, C., and A. Teger. 1975. "Changes in Attitudes Toward Other Nations as a Function of the Type of International Contact." *Sociometry* 38 (2), pp. 213–222.
Saunders, F. 2000. *Who Paid the Piper?* London: Granta.
Schoch, L., and J. Baumgartner. 2005. *The Economic Benefits of International Education to the United States for the 2004–5 Academic Year*, downloaded from http://www.nafsa.org/_/File/_/eis2005/usa.pdf on 11/11/07.
Scott, F. 1956. *American Experience of Swedish Students*. Minneapolis: University of Minnesota Press.
Scott-Smith, G. 2003. "Her Rather Ambitious Washington Program." *Contemporary British History* 17 (4), pp. 65–86.
Scott-Smith, G. 2005. "Mending the 'Unhinged Alliance' in the 1970s." *Diplomacy and Statecraft* 16, pp. 749–78.
Scott-Smith, G. 2006. "Searching for the Successor Generation." *British Journal of Politics and International Relations* 8 (2), pp. 214–37.
Scott-Smith, G. 2008. "Mapping the Undefinable: Some Thoughts on the Relevance of Exchange Programs within International Relations Theory." *Annals of the American Academy of Political and Social Science* 616.
Scott-Smith, G. 2011. "Mutual Interests? *Journal of Transatlantic Studies* 9 (4), pp. 326–41.

Sell, D. 1983. "Research on US Students who participate in Foreign Study Experiences." *International Journal of Intercultural Relations* 7, pp. 131–47.
Selltiz, C., and S. Cook. 1962. "Factors Influencing the Attitude of Foreign Students Toward the Host Country." *Journal of Social Issues* 18, pp. 19–20.
Selltiz, C., J. Christ, J. Havel, and S. Cook. 1963. *Attitudes and Social Relations of Foreign Students in the United States*. Minneapolis: University of Minnesota Press.
Sigalas, E. 2008. *Cross-border People Mobility and EU Legitimacy*. Unpublished PhD thesis, University of Reading.
Sigalas, E. 2010a. "Cross-Border Mobility and European Identity." *European Union Politics* 11 (2), pp. 241–65.
Sigalas, E. 2010b. "The Role of Personal Benefits in Support for the EU." *West European Politics* 33 (6), pp. 1341–61.
Simon, H. 1957. *Administrative Behaviour* (Second Edition). New York: Free Press.
Snow, N. 1992. *Fulbright Scholars as Cultural Mediators*. Unpublished PhD dissertation, American University.
Snow, N. 2006. *Propaganda vs. Public Diplomacy*. Interview with Nancy Snow broadcast on *Worldview*, Chicago Public Radio, 27/11/06.
Snow, N. 2009. *Valuing Exchange of Person in Public Diplomacy*. In Snow, N., and P. Taylor (eds.) *The Routledge Handbook of Public Diplomacy*. Abingdon: Routledge, pp. 233–47.
Socrates Erasmus Council. 2006. *2004/5 UK Erasmus Outgoing and Incoming Study Periods by Host Country and UK Country*, downloaded from http://www.erasmus.ac.uk/statistics/stats_ab_04_05/table_1_2.xls on 1/2/07.
Sprokkereef, A. 1995."Developments in European Community Education Policy." In J. Lodge, (ed.) *The European Community and the challenge of the future*. London: Pinter, pp. 340–347.
State Department. 2004. *International Education Week 2004*, downloaded from http://exchanges.state.gov/iew/promotional/brochure.pdf on 28/7/07.
State Department. 2006. *Completed Evaluations*, downloaded from http://exchanges.state.gov/education/evaluations/completed.htm on 1/12/06.
State Department. 2013. *International Visitor Leadership Program*, downloaded from http://eca.state.gov/ivlp/about-ivlp on 2/5/13.
Stephan, W. 1985. "Intergroup Relations." In G. Lindzey and E. Aronson, (eds.) *Handbook of Social Psychology Volume 3*, pp. 599–658.
Teichler, U. 2004. "The Changing Debate on Internationalisation of Higher Education." *Higher Education* 48 (1), pp. 5–26.
Teichler, U., and F. Maiworm. 1997. *The Erasmus Experience*. Luxembourg: OOPEC.
Thomas, L. 1997. "Retrospective Power Analysis." *Conservation Biology* 11 (1), pp. 276–80.
Useem, J., and R. Useem. 1967. *Western-educated Man in India*. New York: Dryden.
US-UK Fulbright Commission. 2005. *General Selection Criteria*, downloaded from http://www.fulbright.co.uk/awards/uk/postgrad/index.html on 12/11/07.

US-UK Fulbright Commission. 2008. *History*, downloaded from http://www.fulbright.co.uk/about-fulbright/history on 10/2/10.

Vickers, P., and B. Bekhradnia. 2007. *The Economic Costs and Benefits of International Students*, downloaded from http://www.hepi.ac.uk/downloads/32Economiceffectsofinternationalstudents.pdf on 10/11/07.

Wiers-Jenssen, J. 2008. "Does Higher Education Attained Abroad Lead to International Jobs?" *Journal of Studies in International Education* 12 (2), pp. 101–30.

Williams, P. (ed.). 1981. *The Overseas Student Question*. London: Heineman.

Wilson, A. 1993. "A Cross-national Perspective on Re-entry of High School Exchange Students." *International Journal of Intercultural Relations* 17 (4), pp. 465–92.

Wilson, I. 2011. "What Should We Expect of 'Erasmus Generations'?" *Journal of Common Market Studies* 49 (5), pp. 1113–40

Woods, R. 1995. *Fulbright: A Biography*. Cambridge: Cambridge University Press.

World Values Survey. 1999. *Online Data Analysis*, performed using http://www.worldvaluessurvey.org, variable F104 on 21/4/08.

Wright, J. 2000. "Anglo-French Relations, 1958–1998." In Sharp, and G. Stone, *Anglo-French Relations in the Twentieth Century*. London: Routledge, pp. 324–343.

Yun, S. 2005. *Towards Theory-Building for Comparative Public Diplomacy from the Perspectives of Public Relations and International Relations*. Unpublished PhD thesis, University of Maryland.

Ziegler, P. 2008. *Legacy*. New Haven: Yale University Press.

Index

Alliance Francaise, 9
Alumni tracking (see also elite-multiplier model), 32–3, 52–3, 175–91
Analysis of Variance, 83–6
Anderson, K. M., 24, 26
Association of Commonwealth Universities (ACU), 23, 28
Attrition, in survey response, 80–2

Balance Theory, 144–5, 155
Bijou program, 37
British Council, 14, 16, 26, 35–8, 163, 176
British Council Fellowships, 28, 35
Bureaucratic success, 21

Canada, government of, 14, 31
Career trajectories, 20, 32, 69, 124, 153, 163–4, 173, 178–91
Chevening Scholarships and Fellowships (formerly FCOSAS), 2, 16, 33–7
Cold War, 31, 47, 52
Commonwealth, 30–3, 184–5, 187
  Proposed Development Bank, 31
  Secretariat, 31–2
Commonwealth Scholarship and Fellowship Program, 28, 30–4, 177–80
Contact hypothesis, 48–50, 153–4
CROUS (French pastoral agency), 38
Cultural diplomacy (see public diplomacy), 2
Cultural relations (see public diplomacy), 2, 14, 47
Curle, J. N. O., 24, 26

De Klerk, F. W., 50
DfID (UK Government Department), 31, 179
Diefenbaker, J, 31
Diplomats
  Professional, 3–4, 14, 17, 23–8, 36–9, 43, 164, 182–3
  Students in ambassadorial role, 14, 27–8

Education model, 12, 38–42, 69, 115–29, 181, 185–91, 199–201
Elite networking model, 12, 69, 180–3, 197–8
Elite-multiplier model, 3, 6–7, 13–4, 17, 36, 163, 175–6, 197–201
English Speaking Union, 25
Entente Cordiale Scholarships, 37–45
Erasmus Program, 16, 53, 55–6, 65–72,
  Impact on students, 89–174
Erasmus Students' Network (aka European Students' Network), 53
Eurobarometer, 69, 88, 90, 109
European Citizenship, 69, 71
  Adonnino Report, 69
European integration, theories of, 66, 70
  Neofunctionalism, 66–8
  Intergovernmentalism, 66–7
  "Supranational," 66–71
European Social Survey, 72, 88
European Union, 65–71, 106–11, 137, 161–4
Exchanges (including pseudo-exchanges), 9–11

228 INDEX

Foreign and Commonwealth Office (UK), 2, 16, 23–47, 181, 183
Foreign and Commonwealth Office Scholarship and Award Scheme (FCOSAS) (see Chevening)
France, government of, 37–8, 41
Fulbright Program (scholarships), 2, 13–4, 17, 28, 115, 137

Gatekeepers, 72, 79
German Academic Exchange Service (DAAD), 60–4, 203
Goethe Institute, 9, 14
Gravier vs. City of Liège, 67–8

Ho Chi Minh, 50

Indoctrination (see propaganda)
Intercultural Education (journal), 51
International Visitor Leadership Program, 17

Japan English Teaching Program, 14
Japan Foundation, 14
Journal of Research in International Education, 51
Journal of International Students, 51

Language, 114, 156, 158, 163
"Leaven" for public opinion, 26

Magna Carta, 24–5, 31–3, 42
Makins, Roger, 23–5, 206
Mallaby, Christopher, 38–41
Marginal costs and benefits, 43–5
Marshall Aid, 23–6
Marshall Scholarships, 23–30, 33–4, 62
  Endowment proposal, 26–7
  Foreign Office grant, 26–8
  Proposal to fund teachers, 26
  Statutory creation, 26–7, 33–4
Methodology, 48–57, 60–1, 75–9, 84–6, 152, 175–7

Multiplier effects, 6, 11, 90, 115, 140, 163, 176, 189–91, 194
Differential multiplication, 48, 190–1, 196

Natural experiment, 48
  Mobility as, 48–9, 71
  Treatment group, 51, 55, 72, 87
  Control group, 5–6, 51, 55, 73–5

Objective drift, 29, 37, 42–6, 196–7
Opinion-leader model, 3–5, 11–6, 21–2, 26–9, 33, 36–7
Overseas Research Students Awards Scheme, 28

Policy dynamics, 19–46, 66–71, 196–7
Policy entrepreneurs, 70–1
Policy learning, 199–200
Private funding (philanthropy, sponsorship), 1, 26, 37–9, 41–5
Propaganda, 3, 26–7, 41, 188
Public diplomacy, 2, 22, 27, 36, 45, 193–4, 200

Rhodes Scholarships, 24–6
Russell, M. S., 24, 26

Sarkozy, Nicolas, 50
Selection criteria, 6, 12, 24, 16–8, 28, 36–7, 40, 59, 62, 140, 182, 200–1
Signaling (see also symbolic value), 3, 11, 24–5, 30, 32, 39, 42–4, 193, 196
Sleeper effects, 175, 182
Soft power, 3, 12, 15–6, 137, 194, 200
Soldiers, 9, 49
State Department (US), 2, 3, 17
Statistical power, 83–6
Student experiences, background to, 139–50, 152–72
  Social status, 48, 50, 141, 153–4
  Maturity, 63–4, 141
  Prior experience, 155–6

Contact with host nationals, 63,
  148–50, 158–60, 195
Friendships, 142–8, 172, 195
  Modeling, 141–50
Studies in Higher Education (journal), 51
Symbolic value (see also signaling), 3,
  24–6, 29–30, 31–4, 193–6
Sympathy, 3, 5, 14–5, 41, 194, 197

Friends of a country, 2, 3, 13, 15, 28,
  33, 34, 194,

U-curve, 56–7, 61, 78

W-curve (see U-curve)
World Values Survey, 88, 94–6
Wrench, Evelyn, 24–5

GPSR Compliance

The European Union's (EU) General Product Safety Regulation (GPSR) is a set of rules that requires consumer products to be safe and our obligations to ensure this.

If you have any concerns about our products, you can contact us on

ProductSafety@springernature.com

In case Publisher is established outside the EU, the EU authorized representative is:

Springer Nature Customer Service Center GmbH
Europaplatz 3
69115 Heidelberg, Germany

www.ingramcontent.com/pod-product-compliance
Lightning Source LLC
LaVergne TN
LVHW051913060526
838200LV00004B/120